Cades Cove

A Southern Appalachian Community

Durwood Dunn

Cades Cove

THE LIFE AND DEATH OF

A Southern Appalachian Community

1818–1937

THE UNIVERSITY OF TENNESSEE PRESS

Copyright © 1988 by The University of Tennessee Press / Knoxville.
All Rights Reserved. Manufactured in the United States of America.

Cloth: 1st printing, 1988; 2nd printing, 1989.
Paper: 1st printing, 1988; 2nd printing, 1988; 3rd printing, 1989;
         4th printing, 1989; 5th printing, 1992; 6th printing, 1995;
         7th printing, 1997; 8th printing, 2000; 9th printing, 2002;
         10th printing, 2005; 11th printing, 2007; 12th printing, 2010.

Frontispiece: John Cable's Mill, 1934, from the Oliver Family Collection.

The paper in this book meets the requirements of American National Standards
Institute / National Information Standards Organization specification Z39.48-
1992 (Permanence of Paper). It contains 30 percent post-consumer waste and is
certified by the Forest Stewardship Council.

Library of Congress Cataloging in Publication Data

Dunn, Durwood, 1943–
        Cades Cove: the life and death of a southern
        Appalachian community, 1818–1937.

        Bibliography: p.
        Includes index.
        1. Cades Cove (Tenn.)—History. 2. Cades Cove
(Tenn.)—Economic conditions. 3. Cades Cove (Tenn.)—
Social conditions. I. Title.
F444.C26D86   1988   976.8'885 87–18212

ISBN 10: 0–87049–559–3 (pbk.: alk. paper)
ISBN 13: 978-0-87049-559-5

Dedicated to
the First and the Last
John Oliver
Who Lived In Cades Cove

Contents

Illustrations

Preface

Although the mountain people and culture of Southern Appalachia were not identified or seriously examined as a separate entity from mainstream America until the 1880s, in the intervening years they have become the subject of both enduring stereotypes and literary, if not scholarly, debate. Before 1880, only three humorists — Augustus Baldwin Longstreet, George Washington Harris, and Harden E. Taliaferro — had considered the Southern mountaineer noteworthy or distinct enough to caricature. With the advent of local colorists such as Mary Noailles Murfree, however, the entire mountain culture was depicted in fictional works that brought national recognition to the area.

Murfree, who visited Cades Cove, painted a sympathetic — if unrealistic and highly romanticized — portrait of the mountain people. By the late 1880s, however, a rival group, motivated by both genuine reformist impulses and a naturalistic reaction to the saccharine excesses of the local colorists, began a systematic literary counterattack. These "Mountain Muckrakers," obsessed with the degradation and misfortune of the mountain people, depicted them as living lives of stark brutality and desperation, an existence particularly characterized by excessive cruelty to women and children. Yet another group of writers at the turn of the century idealized the Southern mountaineer as the last vestige of "pure" Anglo-Saxon Americans living an existence far superior to their fellow Americans in a nation beset by the complications of burgeoning industrialization, urbanization, and an influx of "un-American" foreign immigrants.

The nadir of Southern Appalachian stereotypes occurred in 1913 with the publication of *Our Southern Highlanders* by Horace Kephart. Kephart also visited Cades Cove, but completely distorted and misrepresented mountain life and customs. Possibly his major thesis was that among Southern mountaineers, no sense of community or leadership existed. Addressing Kephart's representation of mountain life is a major objective of this present study.

Confronted with such a bewildering plethora of stereotypes, few scholars have made any effort to analyze the conglomerate area we call Southern Appalachia. Three seminal works, however, have recently made significant, if not revolutionary, progress in attacking and refuting these stereotypes. Henry D. Shapiro's 1978 *Appalachia On Our Mind: The Southern Mountains and Mountaineers in the American Consciousness, 1870-1920*, Gordon B. McKinney's 1978 *Southern Mountain Republicans, 1865-1900: Politics and the Appalachian Community*, and Ronald D Eller's 1982 *Miners, Millhands, and Mountaineers: Industrialization of the Appalachian South, 1880-1930* are all ground-breaking studies which force us to critically re-examine Southern Appalachia.

The present study of Cades Cove, a small mountain community in the heart of the Great Smoky Mountains, was undertaken to examine a specific geographical entity as it grew and developed throughout the nineteenth and twentieth centuries. The advantages of such a study in considering basic questions about the larger region are obvious. Was Cades Cove a "neo-frontier," a frontier area which had simply never developed further, or a frontier which had retrogressed due to particular geographical or environmental factors?

How did the cove develop in relation to the region and state? Was it always backward, or had its comparative position in 1840, for example, been much closer to the mainstream of the Westward Movement than after the Civil War? When and how did its citizens develop a separate culture, and what were the distinguishing characteristics of that culture? In all these questions, the key problem throughout this study has been the origin, degree, and nature of change—how and when Cades Cove deviated from regional and national norms of development—and the causes of this change.

The goal of this book—to analyze carefully the development of a single community in Southern Appalachia—imposes critical limitations on forming broader generalizations about the region as a whole, however. Key features in the cove's development, notably the high fertility of its soil from the days of earliest settlement, determined that the community would develop quite differently from other less fortunate areas of the larger region. Actually, the uniqueness of these individual mountain communities, often situated only a few miles across high mountains from each other, yet quite distinctive in their culture and economy, demonstrates the dangers of making any broader generalization about Southern Appalachia or the mountain people. With these limitations clearly in mind, the present study should nevertheless serve as a useful testing ground for larger hypotheses long held by regional scholars.

The main source of primary materials for this book is the Oliver family collection, which the writer inherited. The first permanent white family to settle in the cove, the Olivers kept extensive records of the community's history in the form of diaries, church records, unpublished sketches and histories, and miscellaneous memorabilia — Civil War passes, store receipts, tax records, deeds, and other quasi-legal transactions — which made this study possible. In addition to these written sources, many of the folkways and traditions of the nineteenth-century community have been preserved orally, and have been carefully utilized throughout this book both as cited sources and as a constant monitor for written records. Through interviews with former residents, attitudes and personal reactions of the cove people to various crises are thus illuminated by the folk memory to a degree impossible to obtain from written records alone.

Regarding the heavy use of Oliver family records, an inevitable question or critique must be: to what extent did the Olivers form an elite, or how representative were they of the average cove farming yeomanry throughout the nineteenth and early twentieth centuries? The answer lies in the type of leadership that the family exercised; their influence was primarily moral and depended on the voluntary respect or esteem they commanded from their neighbors of equal or greater property. They were certainly never wealthy themselves, and their social position was comparable to any other "respectable" family in an essentially egalitarian society that judged both individuals and families on the basis of their behavior — public and private — rather than on the amount or type of their material possessions. In this sense, the Olivers were certainly "representative" of the average cove farmer — representative in a way such entrepreneurs as Daniel D. Foute could never be.

Other primary source material from outside observers which corroborates the conclusions drawn from the Oliver records include Dr. Abraham Jobe's Memoirs and the record of Lt. Charles G. Davis, a Union soldier escaping Confederate prisons who was assisted by the cove people during the Civil War. Particularly useful in delineating economic and demographic changes were the manuscript census returns from the cove between 1830 and 1900. The work of genealogists and local historians, notably the excellent work of Inez Burns on Blount County, has illuminated the cove's development within the larger region and assisted the writer in placing many otherwise loose ends in a meaningful context. Blount County records — deeds, wills, and circuit court minutes — have been invaluable for both the nineteenth and the twentieth centuries. Finally, in the twentieth century, local newspapers, particularly the *Maryville Times,* have chronicled many events on a daily basis which otherwise would have been lost.

The writer is indebted to the wise counsel and encouragement of the late Stanley J. Folmsbee, dean of historians of Tennessee. To the late Professor Norbert Riedl, gratitude is due for exposing me to the broader questions and opportunities of the German *Volkskunde,* a branch of cultural anthropology especially suitable to the scholarly analysis of East Tennesse's folk culture. Professor LeRoy P. Graf, my mentor, deserves special commendation for his continuing patience and friendship. I am indebted to the National Endowment for the Humanities for a Fellowship for Independent Study and Research, and to the Pew Memorial Trust for funding a sabbatical which made completion of this work possible. Marylin Bell Hughes of the Tennessee State Library and Archives has been unfailingly courteous and helpful. Finally, much gratitude is due to my long-suffering friends and colleagues at Tennessee Wesleyan College!

1

Settlement and Early History

In the winter of 1818-1819, Lucretia Oliver fervently wished she had never heard of this place called Cades Cove. From the moment of their arrival in the fall of 1818, everything had gone wrong. Joshua Jobe, their neighbor from Carter County in the northeast corner of Tennessee, had persuaded her husband, John Oliver, to make the move. But Jobe had gone back to Carter County, leaving the Oliver family alone in this howling wilderness. And wilderness it was, Lucretia grimly assured herself, since there were no cleared fields and much of the lower end of the cove was covered by a pestilential swamp. She couldn't decide whom to blame most, her husband John for believing he was moving to a land of milk and honey, or Joshua Jobe for all his fine promises.

Nobody had told her about the Indians, for instance. Everytime the wood popped or crackled in the fireplace of their crude log shelter, Lucretia involuntarily startled, and clutched their baby daughter, Polly. John assured her these cove Cherokees were friendly Indians, like the Cherokees who had fought side by side with him at Horseshoe Bend against the Creeks. He had actually seen one such Cherokee, Junuluska, swim under water at the bend of the Tallapoosa river and cut loose the Creek canoes, thus preventing their escape.[1]

Yet John had also related how in his company one sentinel after another had been murdered before the battle until all the soldiers were afraid to volunteer for night watch. Finally one brave man had agreed, promising to sound the alarm if he saw anything move. On guard that night, he became suspicious of a wild hog which kept moving closer and closer. Firing at the hog, he discovered a Creek warrior in disguise, wrapped up in a hog skin.[2]

So every wild animal Lucretia saw thereafter seemed to be an Indian in disguise. And even the more settled area of Carter County from where they came was in 1818 still barely out of the frontier stage of development. The hostility of the Cherokees toward the Watauga settlement during the Revolutionary War was within living memory of her friends and neighbors there. The intervening years had been filled with tales of Indian atrocities against isolated pioneer families. Practically everyone had friends or relatives who had thus suffered, and the more spectacular attacks, such as the Kirk family massacre, had reached legendary proportions through constant retelling on the Tennessee frontier.[3]

John Oliver shared his wife's forebodings, yet he was determined to remain here. Born in 1793 in Carter County, he had never been able to afford any land of his own, since most of the fertile areas had already been claimed. No trace of his parents or any other close relatives remains in the Carter County records, and John would later recall only the grinding poverty of these early years. A collier by trade, he had dreamed of owning his own farm since childhood. Shy and unassuming, he drifted along in his trade, working for other people, until the War of 1812 erupted.[4]

Caught up in the wave of patriotic fervor sweeping the Western country, he had enlisted at Knoxville on January 5, 1814, in Captain Adam Winsell's Company, Colonel Ewen Allison's Regiment, East Tennessee Militia.[5] It was not the war itself, however, so much as his encounter with General Andrew Jackson which transformed the quiet young soldier, with his sandy hair and deep blue eyes, into an intrepid Indian fighter. He had never before seen such a man as Jackson — completely fearless. Fifty years later he could still envision General Jackson riding up and down the line, exhorting his troops, refusing to take cover, unwilling to ask his men to undertake any dangerous assignment in which he himself would not willingly participate.

John returned from the war in 1814 with an exaggerated sense of the importance of the battle of Horseshoe Bend and a bad case of hero worship for Jackson. Like his idol, Oliver was now determined never to be afraid of anything or anyone again. If Jackson's army of raw frontiersmen could defeat the whole Creek Nation in such a short time, anything was possible! He needed only determine what he wanted, attack it as fearlessly as he had gone over the rampart at Horseshoe Bend (even after the man ahead of him was shot and fell back dead), and he was certain to succeed.[6]

His first battle on returning home was winning Lucretia's hand. Orphaned at an early age, Lucretia Frazier was "bound," in the terminology of the day, to a local family for her support and upbringing. Whether she inherited her vivacity and temper from her English parents or learned these traits from her foster family is unclear, but her characteristic outspokenness became apparent early in their courtship. When John went off to war, she became engaged to two other men. She was determined, as she later told her grandchildren, to have a husband whether he returned or not.

Having finally persuaded Lucretia to marry him in April 1814, John next set about to realize his lifelong dream of owning his own farm. He had continued working as a collier until after their first child, Polly, was born on July 18, 1817, in Carter County. At this point his friend and fellow soldier Joshua Jobe had told him about a fertile valley in the Great Smokies which was still uninhabited. Jobe had learned about the cove from his wife's family, the Tiptons.[7]

A Revolutionary soldier at the age of fifteen, William Tipton was engaged in that most American of all occupations—land speculation.[8] It was eminently respectable—George Washington and Andrew Jackson were two famous speculators—and usually extremely profitable. Land speculation also seemed to serve the national interest by rapidly populating newly opened areas with white settlers, who in turn formed a buffer zone between the Indians and the older settled regions. The system seemed to work to everyone's advantage, although the distinction between personal gain and the public's welfare often became blurred. But regardless of how large or promising a tract of land, it remained relatively worthless until settlers could be persuaded to move there. They attracted other settlers, and the land doubled and tripled in value with each successive wave of homesteaders.

Accordingly, the Tiptons and Joshua Jobe had persuaded the Olivers to move to Cades Cove in return for enough supplies for the trip and enough money for his own farm, once the title to the land was cleared.

And it would only be for a short period; in a year or so a group of neighbors from Carter County would join them. In the meantime their survival would convince other more timorous settlers that the cove was at last safe. Yet in spite of all these arguments, John and Lucretia had realized they were gambling with their lives.[9]

Consequently, it was a collective effort, as was so often the case on the American frontier, that led to the settlement of Cades Cove, but with one important difference. The entire plan rested on the willingness of one individual, John Oliver, to take his family alone into this isolated wilderness to determine whether permanent white settlement was possible there. John was consciously attempting to improve his social as well as economic status, because if the experiment succeeded, his comparative position in the new community would be much higher than his propertyless existence in Carter County. In terms of motivation, the effect of Jacksonian ideology on him cannot be overemphasized. Both the theoretical right to a new and better life, and the psychic energy necessary to achieve it, were clearly defined by his understanding of Jacksonian egalitarianism.[10]

Yet the loneliness and isolation of the cove must have chilled even the stoutest hearts as John and Lucretia descended the ancient Indian trail across Rich Mountain with their baby daughter in the early fall of 1818. The exact date of their arrival is not known, but Joshua Jobe did accompany them on the initial trip. The cove lay before them in primordial splendor; there were no cleared fields or roads and no other white inhabitants.[11] The descending Indian trail across Rich Mountain occasionally opens up on a wide prospect of the cove below, so that one entering by that route cannot fail to be aware of the terrain below. At such points they could clearly see that the cove was completely enclosed by high mountains and was covered by dense forest broken only by the swampy area in the lower end. Occasional glimpses of the Cherokees still living there only added to their uneasiness. But John and Lucretia were determined to remain, even after Jobe departed.

After spending their first night in an abandoned Indian hut, the Olivers had decided to settle in the upper end of the cove because the lower end was swampy, an environment they believed unhealthy and associated with pestilence. Near the base of the mountain, where they would be partially protected from the bitter mountain winds, John built his first crude homestead.[12] A later cabin, built in the early 1820s, is still standing today. A pile of stones some twenty-five feet north of the present building marks the chimney of the original 1818 structure. Fifty-five yards from the cabin is the spring which probably determined the selection of this particular site. Lying in a creekbed, it is best located when the stream dries up in the summer, leaving only a small trickle of cold water from the spring itself. The fact that this spring is apparent only in the dry season is corroborative evidence that the Olivers arrived in the early part of autumn.

In this autumn of 1818 most of the surrounding areas in Blount County had long been settled. The closest neighboring cove, Tuckaleechee, had been settled in 1797 by Peter Snider, a trader of German descent, although he had had to leave and come back again after a friendly chief warned him that the other Indians were hostile.[13]

Not that white men had failed to recognize the potential value of the cove long before 1818; as early as 1794 a North Carolina grant for 5,000 acres "in a place called Cades Cove on the south side of the French Broad and Holston rivers and west of Big Pigeon" had been issued to Hugh Dunlap. In 1809 Dunlap was reissued the grant from the new state of Tennessee because the earlier grant had been lost from the secretary's office in North Carolina.[14] The fact that this second grant was subject to previous occupant-entries and school reservations indicates other settlers had claimed land in the cove during the interim.

From land grants and allusions to Cades Cove in wills and other records it is evident that many speculators were attracted to the area during the first decade of the nineteenth century. In 1809 John Smith and William Crowson petitioned the state legislature for entry rights in the cove based on earlier North Carolina land grants. These grants were confirmed in 1820 when Aaron Crowson, son of William, petitioned the Tennessee legislature claiming that his father and a Mr. James Ross had both possessed "the Right of Occupancy and preemption to a Tract of land in Cades Cove on the waters of the Tennessee on the 6th day of February 1796." The first Tennessee grant, based on these older claims of the Crowsons, was issued to William ("Fighting Billy") Tipton on March 23, 1821, for 640 acres in Cades Cove.[15]

The Indians were evidently the main obstacle to permanent settlement. Isolated and completely surrounded by high mountains, an Indian-infested cove seemed, despite all its other attractions, too threatening to potential settlers. Little is known about Chief Kade, for whom the cove was named.[16] Peter Snider had learned enough Cherokee to trade with him from Tuckaleechee Cove, but the Olivers would later remember this chief only because of his name. Old Abraham of Chilhowee, on the other hand, was already legendary for his attacks against the Wataugans at the close of the Revolution. He gave his name, ironically, to the peaceful stream, Abrams Creek, which flows through the middle of the cove.[17]

The Indian name for Cades Cove, or at least for a settlement there on Cove Creek, was Tsiyahi, or otter place (from Tsiyû, otter, and yĭ, locative). In his memoirs Lieutenant Henry Timberlake, an earlier explorer, had mentioned seeing many "brooks well stored with fish, otters, and beavers," in the general vicinity of Cades Cove in 1762. But the Olivers did not mention otters in their written records or oral traditions; it is probable that these animals had been hunted to extinction before 1800. This important Cherokee place-name was discovered by the pioneer American ethnologist, James Mooney, during the last decade of the nineteenth century. Mooney's primary sources were the remnant Cherokees living on the Qualla Reservation in western North Carolina and elderly emigrants in Oklahoma who had left this area over half a century earlier.[18] Thus what scant knowledge we have of prewhite Cherokee life or civilization in the cove is not transmitted through the people who displaced them.

Yet Tsiyahi must have had some significance to the Cherokee political entity before 1800, if for no other reason than the strategic location of the cove in relation to some of the more important Indian trails of the region. One such route extended from the west prong of Little Pigeon River up the waters of Walden Creek, and entered Wear Valley by following Cove Creek several miles through a narrow gorge of cascades. This route eventually reached Little River in Tuckaleechee Cove, where several trails led to Cades Cove, ten miles over a high range of mountains. Writing in 1823, historian John Haywood stated that a Virginia trader, Mr. Vaughan, used this route as early as 1740 to reach the Cherokee Nation, and that it "was an old path when he first saw it."[19]

Another major route to Cades Cove was the Tuckaleechee and Southeastern Trail, which separated from the Great Indian Warpath where it crossed the French Broad River. This trail passed near present-day Sevierville to the Tuckaleechee villages on Little River, and from there went in a southeasterly direction through Indian Gap to the lower Cherokee settlements in South Carolina. A short route from the Valley towns to the Overhill towns of the Cherokees passed through Egwanulti Gap (corrupted by white pronunciation to the present Ekanetelee) and skirted the lower end of Cades Cove on its way to the Little Tennessee River. This latter trail leading into Cades Cove through Ekanetelee Gap was probably the most important route for later white settlers, particularly for those from the Pennsylvania-German settlements in Rowan County, North Carolina.[20]

The proximity to Cades Cove of all these major trails which connected the Valley Cherokee in South Carolina with their Overhill relatives indicates that Tsiyahi must have had some spatial significance to the Cherokee polity. Possibly it was no more than a hunting camp, but its strategic location near major arteries of commerce and communication within the Cherokee Nation could well have justified a larger permanent settlement. As the Cherokees withdrew steadily from the pressures of continuing white encroachments in upper East Tennessee following their defeat in the Revolutionary War, these same routes and trails first led white explorers and later permanent settlers into Cades Cove and surrounding areas.

Tsiyahi was still an active settlement when the Olivers arrived there in 1818. And both John and Lucretia had reason to fear the Indians because they had settled in the cove illegally, even according to the white man's law. Not until the Treaty of Calhoun in 1819 was the area legally open to white settlement. Of course the Olivers were typical of Americans throughout the frontier in not letting the legal niceties of treaties made at the national level cramp their style.[21] But more to the point, the Cherokees in Cades Cove were similarly unimpressed by a remote agreement which invalidated their right to the land. And the Cherokees living in such remote regions were certainly not in sympathy with their more civilized brethren who negotiated with Washington on their behalf. Possession, not treaty rights, was the only valid condition of ownership commonly accepted by both whites and Indians living in such isolated places.

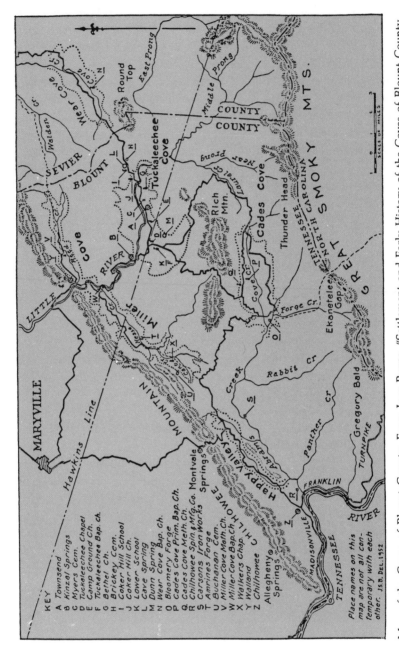

KEY
A Townsend
B Kinzel Springs
C Myers Cem.
D Tuckaleechee Chapel
E Camp Ground Ch.
F Tuckaleechee Bap. ch.
G Bethel Ch.
H Brickey Cem.
I Coker Hill School
J Coker Hill Ch.
K Lower School
L Cave Spring
M Dunn Spring
N Wear Cove Bap. ch.
O Bloomery Forge
P Cades Cove Prim. Bap. Ch.
Q Cades Cove Meth. Ch.
R Chilhowee Spin. & Mfg. Co. Montvale
S Carsons Iron Works   Springs
T Amrines Forge
U Buchanan Cem.
V Miller Cove Meth. Ch.
W Miller Cove Bap. Ch.
X Walkers Chap.
Y Walland
Z Chilhowee
   Alleghenya
   Springs

Place names on this
map are not all con-
temporary with each
other. JS.B. Del. 1952

Map of the Coves of Blount County. From Inez Burns, "Settlement and Early History of the Coves of Blount County, Tennessee," East Tennessee Historical Society *Publications*, no. 24 (1952), 48–49.

In the middle of their anxiety over the Indians during the winter of 1818-1819, the Olivers soon discovered their real enemy was starvation. A collier in Carter County, John had little previous experience in farming or hunting. They had failed to bring adequate supplies, and arriving in the fall meant it was too late to plant any crops. Jobe had returned home; their nearest white neighbors were miles away over the mountains in Tuckaleechee Cove. Heavy snows made it difficult for John to find game sufficient to keep them alive. Lucretia honestly thought they would starve to death.[22]

How ironic, Lucretia would later recall, that at this critical point none other than the Indians she had so feared would save them. Realizing the plight of the Oliver family, the Cherokees generously brought them dried pumpkin which kept them alive until spring. No one ever knew why they did it. Probably one forlorn family of whites seemed no real threat to the cove Cherokees at that time. Later, when large numbers of settlers moved into the cove, these same Indians would abruptly become hostile.[23]

Neither John nor Lucretia could recall names of individual Indians in later years. In spite of the fact these Cherokees had saved their lives, they would continue to refer to and conceptualize them as a collective entity: the Indians. The one exception, Chief Kade, made no particular impression, and nothing remains to give any clue about his personality or individual characteristics. Even Lucretia, who usually held strong opinions about everyone she met, would later be extremely vague in describing their first neighbors to her grandchildren.

When Jobe returned to the cove with a herd of cattle in the spring of 1819, he found the Olivers worn but alive. The indomitable Lucretia immediately took him to task, telling him how they had almost starved to death and blaming him for bringing them to such a desolate location in the first place. But Jobe escaped further tongue-lashing by promising to give her two fine milk cows from a herd his brother was bringing later. Now the only remaining problem was whether the cove soil was fertile enough to justify extensive farming.[24]

The Olivers won this gamble too; they had settled in a virtual garden spot. Secluded within the western part of the Great Smoky Mountains, which lie in eastern Tennessee and western North Carolina, Cades Cove and its environs form a segment of the much larger Appalachian

Highlands, that long belt of mountain ranges extending through the Southeastern states from Virginia to Georgia. Created as a fenestral, or window, by the overthrust of Unicoi rocks of Lower Cambrian age with Knox dolomite of Canadian age at such a low angle that the hanging wall has been worn through, exposing the foot wall, the cove is surprisingly flat in contrast to the rough mountainous topography on all sides. Two neighboring coves, Wear's and Tuckaleechee, are often grouped with Cades Cove by geologists for the sake of comparison, but neither can match the relative evenness of the floor of Cades Cove, with an average elevation of 1,750 feet, or compete with its almost complete enclosure by the surrounding mountains, the highest of which rise 2,000 feet above the cove.[25]

The great fertility of the soil is due to the cove's limestone base, which initially allowed its development as a fenestral through differential erosion. Limestone is soluble and poorly resistant to erosion, particularly in an area of heavy rainfall. Eighteen streams and branches enter the cove, all of which eventually contribute to Abrams Creek, which flows out the west side over tough blue slates of the Ocoee Series one mile west of the cove at Abrams Falls. These slates, which are very resistant, check the eroding power of the creek and allow the development of a temporary base level of erosion in the cove. Although the streams are intermittent, the alluvial material on the floor of the cove absorbs most of the excess water. Thus, according to one geologist, "the ground retains moisture and is excellent for farming in even the driest years."[26]

The sufferings and privations of their first winter in Cades Cove were never forgotten by the Oliver family, but the fertility of the cove soil soon amply repaid them for their sacrifices. Lucretia made the first soap they had had since leaving Carter County out of butter made possible by her new cows, with lye made from wood ashes. John cleared the first fields of timber by himself, using his horse to pull up the stumps.[27] Trees too large to be cut had to be girdled. In this process used throughout the American frontier, the farmer cut a girdle or circle around the tree deep into the cambium layer; the tree eventually died and could then be burned to clear the land.

Wheat grew particularly well on the newly cleared fields in the cove uplands, but John also grew corn, rye, oats, and vegetables in abundance. The pumpkins which had saved their lives during the previous winter grew so abundantly that John later asserted he could "walk over the fields on them without ever touching ground." The Olivers followed the Indian example of keeping their cattle along Abrams Creek, where they grazed on rich grasses during the summer and found forage and protection among the canebrakes during the winter. The completion of a log barn with two pens and a threshing floor between them provided space to store much of their first ample harvest. Finally, John dug a well sixty-four feet deep, and walled it up with smooth stones which he gathered from the fields.[28]

This well, dug in the summer of 1819 when their second child, Martha, was born, was destined never to run dry in over a hundred years of continuous use, and would later represent the deep roots which the Olivers had sunk into the fertile cove soil. But it gives an erroneous sense of permanence which simply did not exist in the 1820s. Life remained very tentative on the frontier, and no better example of this situation exists than the fact that John did not bother to obtain legal title to his land until as late as 1826, when he bought fifty-five acres from Isaac Hart for one hundred dollars in cash.[29] Even by 1830 most of the inhabitants living in Cades Cove according to the census had not formally registered their deeds at the county courthouse, and many families failed to do so until after the Civil War.[30] In this sense, traces of the frontier mentality remained in the cove long after people living in other areas of Blount County insisted on strict legality in matters of land ownership and title.

The success of the Oliver family in surviving during the years between 1818 and 1821 paved the way for the development of Cades Cove as a community. In 1821 Joshua Jobe settled there, along with numerous relatives and friends from Carter County. The exact number of families making this initial migration is hard to determine, since many of them moved on to other areas before the 1830 census, and the extant deeds are inconclusive. But an excellent picture of life in the cove during the 1820s has been left by Jobe's son, Abraham Jobe, who in later years became a prominent East Tennessee physician and attended Andrew Johnson on the latter's deathbed. Dr. Jobe distinctly remembered

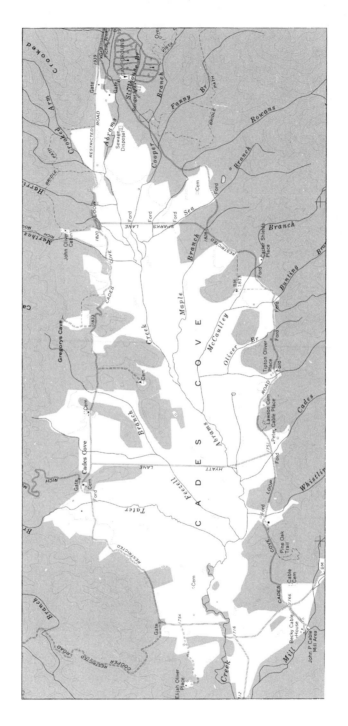

Cades Cove Quadrangle, from U.S. Department of the Interior, Geological Survey Map.

moving with his family to the cove in 1821, when he was only four years old, "on account of the fertility of the soil, and the superior advantages in raising stock."[31]

With the advent of many new white settlers to the cove in 1821, the posture of the Indians suddenly changed. They had tolerated and even assisted the lone Oliver family, but this sudden influx of whites threatened their possession of the land itself, and they became abruptly hostile. Evidently they abandoned Tsiyahi because Dr. Jobe recalled them "lingering in small bands, in the mountain fastnesses" surrounding the cove. He gave a graphic account of how these Indians murdered his uncle:

> All went well for a while. Indians could be seen only occasionally prowling around; but would soon leave, and get back into the deep mountain gorges. Game being very plentiful, my uncle was out hunting one day and had wandered farther than usual into the mountains, and did not return that night, and when search was made for him next day he was found in a deserted Indian camp, on his knees leaning against the side of the camp, where he had been murdered by the Indians. They had cut off one of his fingers and fled.[32]

The Cherokee "threat," as the Indians were now regarded, was ended in 1838 when the last of the cove's first citizens were removed for the "trail of tears" march to Oklahoma Territory. It is both sad and ironic that John Oliver was among the local militia charged with the final roundup of these remaining Indians.

With the exception of his uncle's murder, Dr. Jobe left an idyllic picture of his childhood in the cove during the 1820s. The land was so fertile it produced "abundant crops of everything that could be raised in that climate." Corn was the principal crop, although it sold for only 6¼ cents a bushel because there were as yet no roads to outside markets. Fruit was imported from Tuckaleechee Cove until the settlers had enough time to plant their own orchards. Game, particularly bear and deer, was plentiful, and there was a great abundance of smaller animals such as squirrels.

When not roaming through the woods with his pet bear or exploring nearby caves, Dr. Jobe attended school. Although discipline was rigorous in these "old field schools," students advanced rapidly under the tutelage of Butler Tipton, William Davis, and Arindatis Martin. It is surprising that the early settlers thought of education for their children during these grueling years of carving out homes in the wilderness. Actually, Jobe would maintain seventy-five years later, education in the cove in 1825 was "more commonsense and reasonable," and "better adapted to the wants of the people than the curriculum of studies generally taught now in the higher schools."[33]

Jobe's father, Joshua, set an important precedent for the community when he single-handedly defeated the cove's first bully, Jacob Tipton. Jacob was the son of William ("Fighting Billy") Tipton, who owned much of the cove during the 1820s. "Fighting Billy" sold much of his cove land to numerous relatives, beginning with 426 acres in 1821 to Joshua Jobe. The following year he sold another 426 acres to Isaac Tipton of Carter County; in 1824, 107 acres to Jacob Tipton, his son the bully; in 1825, 80 acres to his daughter, Martha Hart; in 1827, 103 acres to James Henry; and in 1830, 640 acres to Thomas Tipton. Even after all these sales, the extent of William Tipton's holdings in the cove is revealed in his will of 1848, in which he left 1,256 acres known as the "Iron Works tract," the "Potato Patch" of 500 acres, and a survey of unnamed acreage on Rich Gap.[34]

Such wealth evidently made his son Jacob extremely domineering and overbearing, a posture which ran counter to Joshua Jobe's egalitarian principles. Dr. Jobe describes a vicious fight over a farm dispute between Jacob Tipton and Jobe's father in vivid terms:

> They had been talking but a few moments until I saw Tipton grab Father by the throat, to choke him. Father was whittling a little stick with his pocket knife at the time, and he dropped his stick and cut Jake's throat from ear to ear, cutting *to* the jugular; but fortunately not cutting the vein.
>
> My father was of medium size, spare made and always feeble. Jake was in his prime, hale and hearty—the "Bully" of the Cove, and weighing 200 pounds or over. He immediately threw Father down, and jumped on him, and would have given him an unmerciful beating, in the presence of the six ruffian accomplices, and they never attempted to prevent him. But my brave Mother, having no friend to represent her, ran out and gathered a club and dealt him two or three blows; and he jumped up and kicked at her. By this time Father ran up with a rock in his hand and as Jake came at him hit him about the stomach, and he fell like a beef shot; but rose at once, vomiting.

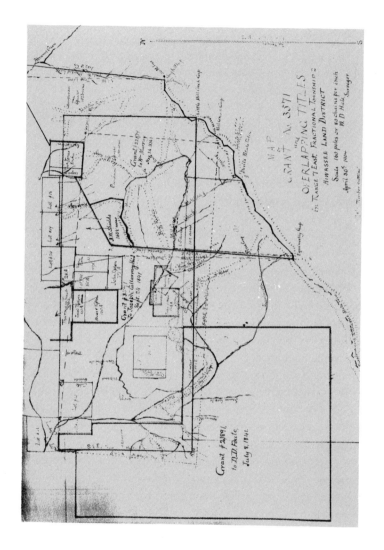

Map of overlapping titles in 1904 lawsuit involving many cove farmers. Blount County Chancery Court Minutes, Book 5, p. 623.

But nothing daunted, he was as brave as Sullivan and ready for a third round. As he came at Father this time he had a large flat rock, which he had to throw with both hands. Father dodged his head to one side, or it would have split his head open. By this time Father had gotten a large lump of clay, that had fallen out of the kitchen chimney, it was nearly as hard as a brick-bat, and as his antagonist came at him, he hit him in the mouth, as he was cursing and threatening what he would do with the carcass of Father, even out daring Goliah, when he was about to encounter David.

The dreadful lick so well aimed knocked out five teeth and split his upper lip to his nose, and mashed both his upper and lower gums in a frightful manner. He lay covered with blood from his throat and mouth for a few seconds, but still wanted to renew combat.[35]

By this time, Jobe had gotten his gun, and the fight ended. After Tipton recovered from his "severe injuries," he made overtures of peace to Jobe. Meeting at a neighbor's house half way between their homes, the two men finally settled their differences after Jacob admitted his fault and promised "ever afterwards to live in friendship." But the lesson was as firmly imprinted on the new community as it was on young Jobe's mind. From that time on, neither Tipton nor other men of great wealth and influence who lived in the cove were treated other than as equals by the small farmers there.

In addition to the Olivers, Tiptons, and Jobes, three other individuals merit particular attention for their early contributions to building the new community. Richard and William Davis, brothers, were instrumental along with the Olivers in obtaining an independent Cades Cove Baptist Church, established as an arm of the Wear's Cove Church on June 16, 1827. Richard served a moderator and William as clerk from 1827 until 1839, when both brothers moved to Walker County, Georgia. The establishment of this first church in Cades Cove represented to the cove people their single most important accomplishment in building the new community. Following a pattern very characteristic of frontier education in Tennessee, William Davis also served as one of the first school teachers.[36]

The other individual who deserves particular attention in the early history of the cove was Peter Cable. Born in Pennsylvania on December 20, 1792, he bought land in Cades Cove as early as 1825. Uncle Peter and Aunt Catherine, as he and his wife were affectionately called, "were leaders in church and community life and were honored and highly respected by both old and young." They were of Pennsylvania-Dutch stock, which probably accounts for Peter's leadership in technological skills and his widely acclaimed innovative genius. It was he who carefully designed and supervised the elaborate system of dikes, sluices, and log booms placed across the creeks, whereby the lower end of the cove was drained and transformed from an unusable swamp into the cove's richest farmland. Both public and private buildings in the cove bore evidence of his building craft, and many of the farm tools he invented were still in use at the close of the century.[37]

In 1830, Joshua Jobe moved to Georgia, attracted by the prospect of the Cherokee lands in the process of being vacated. Most of the Tiptons left during the 1830s, along with many families who had been part of the 1821 Carter County migration into the cove. Despite the cove's relative isolation, its population increased or diminished with the many internal shifts of population in the United States. The attraction of the Cherokee lands in Georgia during the 1830s, and later, the opening up of new territories in the West caused periodic fluctuations as older settlers left and new immigrants entered the cove. In this sense, the cove became a way station, even during the genesis of its community life during the 1820s, for the larger Westward Movement.[38]

These rapid shifts in population would enrich Cades Cove by the very diversity of new peoples arriving there. But the families who chose to make the cove their permanent home from the beginning actually built the community. They were the ones who built the schools, churches, mills, and roads, and who are buried in the quiet cemeteries that are one of the few visible signs of their presence still remaining in the cove today. John Oliver and Peter Cable, who remained best friends throughout their lives, contributed more to the spiritual than to the material development of the cove, however. They gave the ideological base for developing a permanent sense of community, a complex system of ideas and values which would determine the quality of life in Cades Cove throughout the nineteenth century.

This range of attitudes and ideas were implicit, often intangible, and always difficult to document or measure, but any study of the cove which does not take them into account makes a fundamental error in assuming that the community's character was predominantly deter-

Cades Cove Tour Map

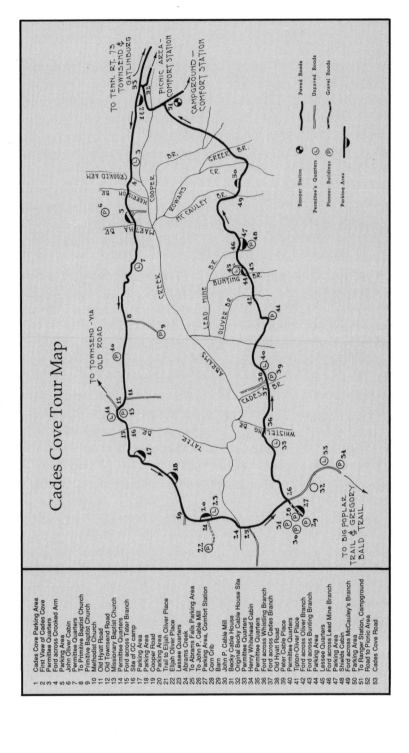

1   Cades Cove Parking Area
2   First View of Cades Cove
3   Permittee Quarters
4   Ford across Crooked Arm
5   Parking Area
6   John Oliver Cabin
7   Permittee Quarters
8   To Primitive Baptist Church
9   Primitive Baptist Church
10   Methodist Church
11   Old Hyatt Road
12   Old Townsend Road
13   Missionary Baptist Church
14   Permittee Quarters
15   Ford across Tater Branch
16   Site of CC camp
17   Parking Area
18   Parking Area
19   Cooper Road
20   Parking Area
21   Trail to Elijah Oliver Place
22   Elijah Oliver Place
23   Lessee Quarters
24   Abrams Creek
25   To Abrams Falls Parking Area
26   To John P. Cable Mill
27   Parking Area, Comfort Station
28   Corn Crib
29   Barn
30   John P. Cable Mill
31   Becky Cable House
32   Original Becky Cable House Site
33   Permittee Quarters
34   Henry Whitehead Cabin
35   Permittee Quarters
36   Ford across Whistling Branch
37   Ford across Cades Branch
38   Old Hyatt Road
39   Peter Cable Place
40   Permittee Quarters
41   Tipton-Oliver Place
42   Ford across Oliver Branch
43   Ford across Bunting Branch
44   Parking Area
45   Lessee Quarters
46   Ford across Lead Mine Branch
47   Parking Area
48   Shields Cabin
49   Ford across McCauley's Branch
50   Parking Area
51   To Ranger Station, Campground
52   Road to Picnic Area
53   Cades Cove Road

mined by its geography or economic structure. These ideas and values of its early settlers provided the cove with an ideological guide which remained pervasive despite the influx of new settlers with diverse backgrounds. The early years of sharing food and shelter with needy neighbors would leave a lasting sense of belonging to a larger family and persistent patterns of community service and cooperation which survived into the next century. Joshua Jobe's defeat of Jacob Tipton reinforced an egalitarian attitude among the cove's small farmers. None of the succeeding large landowners and entrepreneurs would ever attempt to dominate or lord it over their neighbors through sheer arrogance. Politically, the importance of Jackson's egalitarian ideology to John Oliver, and through him to the larger community, would have momentous significance at the outbreak of the Civil War.[39]

Certainly, however, a fundamental love of the land played a primary role in the formation of the new community. This intense attachment to their fertile soil is nowhere explicitly recorded by the small farmers of Cades Cove, who in any event would generally be inarticulate about basic assumptions which they regarded as common knowledge. But evidence of such devotion is clearly demonstrated by the fact that they carefully named, as they would their children, each tiny subdivision, each field or small rising, within the cove. The creeks were named early: Anthony, Forge, Mill, Rowan's, and Abrams were the main ones. In addition, scores of smaller tributaries were named, of which Cades, Sea, Tater, Wildcat, and Whistling are but a few. The important fact here is that even the smallest topographical features, significant trees and insignificant springs, were named with equally careful attention.

These place-names appear early in the land deeds, where they are frequently mentioned to mark boundaries.[40] But they represented an invisible map, a vast, detailed descriptive knowledge of Cades Cove with which all the inhabitants of the community were familiar, but which no outsider could begin to master until after long years of residence. Once named, such smaller geographic areas assumed an identity of their own, quite independent from the original owner, who might long since have died or moved out of the cove. An excellent example of this practice is the Hyatt Lane, a main route across the cove. The Hyatt family, for whom it was named, moved to Missouri during the 1840s, but their name continued to be used into the twentieth century.[41]

These smaller places almost assumed the personalities of people; with the passage of time, each entity might develop a history of its own, describing the human events which had transpired at that particular location fifty years ago.

So the land gradually blended with the people who settled it into one functional unity, and this unity represented in the best sense a community. Binding the people together was this pool of shared knowledge, an internal, invisible map with all its accompanying folklore, which they could recite as well as their family genealogy and which they shared with no outsider. Such intimate knowledge and familiarity with the land also preserved the sense of community by providing Cades Cove with an unchanging constant when the great migrations, into and out of the cove, began in the early 1830s. And it gave the first settlers a clear advantage, because such knowledge, and through such knowledge, full participation in the community's conscious life, could be acquired and perfected by cove residents only through the passage of time.[42]

The settlement period had scarcely ended in 1827 when the cove was introduced to the industrial age with the construction on Forge Creek of the Cades Cove Bloomery Forge, built and operated by Daniel D. Foute, the cove's single most important entrepreneur during the nineteenth century.[43] According to tradition, the noise which resounded throughout the cove from the first blow of the huge forge hammer proved to be too much for the wolves. Unable to cope with this sound, the frightened animals left that day, and were never seen or heard in Cades Cove again. To John and Lucretia Oliver, the departure of these wolves represented the welcome knowledge that a dangerous and often threatening symbol of their wilderness experience had finally ended. But to the remnant Cherokee Indians still living in the cove, the wolf (wá'ya) was revered as a hunter and watchdog; ordinary Cherokees would never kill a wolf if they could possibly avoid it.[44]

To these remaining Cherokees, then, the departure of the wolves foreshadowed a time in the immediate future when they, too, would be banished forever from their homes in the cove. Although many of these Cherokees worked for a time in Foute's forge, there was actually no place for them in the new order;[45] in the very genesis of the new community were implanted the seeds of their destruction. How the Cherokees living there regarded their fate is undiscoverable, but it is certainly reasonable to assume that they loved their fertile cove land no less than did the people who displaced them. Yet they were unquestionably trapped in an impossible situation; regardless of their behavior, whether they kept the lone Oliver family from starvation in the winter of 1818–1819, or murdered Joshua Jobe's brother in an abandoned Indian camp several years later, their fate seemed as inexorably fixed, or predetermined, as that of their fellow hunters, the wolves.

For the pioneering white families, however, the decade of the 1820s had brought prosperity and a sense of permanence to their newly established community as they cleared fields, planted orchards, drained swamps, and established schools and churches. They were still an island of settled land within the surrounding wilderness of the Great Smoky Mountains, and the larger problems of finding routes out of the cove for their marketable crops were yet unsolved. But families such as the Olivers looked forward to the future growth of the cove in 1830, confident that no problem would ever again arise which threatened their survival as had starvation in the bleak winter of 1818–1819. Nor would they ever again face such difficulties alone; the growing security of the community within the cove seemed to counterbalance any possible danger from the surrounding mountains outside.

2

The Impact of the Wilderness

Recalling his appointment to the Maryville circuit sixty-four years earlier, Isaac P. Martin, a Methodist minister in the Holston Conference for over half a century, gave the following account of his first visit to Cades Cove in 1890:

> The sun was high in the heavens when I passed the crest of the mountain and began the descent toward Cade's Cove. My first glimpse of the Cove was through openings in the forest, but presently I came to a cliff from which I could see almost the entire cove which nestles there among the crests of the great mountains. I had never seen anything quite so beautiful. Thunderhead Mountain, standing 5530 feet, rose to the southeast, rising nearly 3000 feet above the level of Cade's Cove.
>
> On the shoulder of Thunderhead nestled Spence Field, forever attesting man's desire to dwell on the lofty heights. A little further away to the southwest was Gregory's Bald with its parklike trees and its meadows in the sunlight. To the north was Rich Mountain, which I had just crossed; with Abram's Creek rising in the northeast and running obliquely northwest to spill its waters at the picturesque Abram's Falls, Cade's Cove is the dream of the Smoky Mountains.[1]

Martin's description of Cades Cove is significant not because of its uniqueness; few visitors during the nineteenth century failed to comment favorably, often using superlatives, on the natural beauty of the cove and its environs. It did not require the skill of Mary Noailles Murfree or Sidney Lanier, both of whom used Cades Cove as the background for many of their writings, to awaken the ordinary person's sensibilities to the extraordinary beauty of the cove. Even Parson Brownlow, the vituperative editor of the *Knoxville Whig*, whose sharp gaze seldom failed to uncover the most minute flaw in human or natural phenomena, had only praise for the cove and its surrounding mountains.[2]

Martin's description of Cades Cove is significant because it indicates the primacy and permanence of the wilderness setting of the cove in 1890, three years before Frederick Jackson Turner lamented the passing of the frontier experience for the rest of the nation. Cades Cove in this respect was an anomaly. Other sections in the United States, once settled, soon lost the flavor of their original wilderness environment as farms were surrounded by more cleared lands in the forward progression of the Westward Movement. Yet however intensely cultivated the fertile basin of the cove might become, the surrounding mountains and vast stretches of wilderness areas remained a constant factor, an ever-present element, in the lives of the cove people throughout the nineteenth and much of the twentieth century.

The inseparability of the physical wilderness and the geographic area of Cades Cove and the continuing interaction of their lives in the densely settled cove with the wilderness outside do not necessarily mean that the attitudes of the cove people toward their environment did not change or alter during the course of the century. An examination of the records of the people actually living in the cove, who were full participants in its community life, can provide answers to the important questions of their attitudes toward and the functional value of the wilderness. Later visitors and writers, seeing the natural setting of Cades Cove, often made quite erroneous assumptions about the importance of the wilderness in the lives of the natives.

One might assume, for example, that the wilderness impeded the development of an organized society and retarded agricultural practices and the development of a market economy in the cove. A recent student of an area with many similarities in West Virginia concluded that the very means which the pioneers were able to devise in order to survive in an inhospitable mountain region added to the geographic isolation of the area and eventually created a base of arrested development which left the entire area far behind the rest of the state and nation.[3]

On first observation this same situation might have occurred in Cades Cove because the cove suffered a serious retrogression after the Civil

War and had become increasingly the stereotyped static society of Southern Appalachia by the end of the century. Yet the whole situation was very different in the cove. First, the rich soil of the cove basin, unlike the poorer soil in West Virginia, allowed farmers to produce an abundance of marketable crops. Economic decline came not because their land could no longer produce, but because the market demand seriously declined after the Civil War, due to the generally depressed economy of East Tennessee and the larger region. Second, the constant influx of new settlers into Cades Cove, often from distant places, abruptly stopped after 1860.[4]

Thus the general economic decline after the Civil War was due to political and external factors and not to the isolation of the cove or the effect of the wilderness on the lives of the cove people. During the 1840s and 1850s, new roads and frequent commerce with the market centers of East Tennessee, as well as many new immigrants, had made the cove a prosperous and progressive agricultural community. Its decline after the Civil War was relative to the general decline of the entire region; the 1880 census, for example, illustrated the fact that the sixteenth civil district of Blount County (Cades Cove) was no less, and often more prosperous, than other more accessible areas of the county, although the entire county and region were still below prewar levels.[5]

Given a spatial definition of wilderness, what were the physical characteristics of this surrounding area of forests and mountains which today comprise the Great Smoky Mountains National Park? This southern section of the Unaka Chain is characterized by an amazing variety of flora and fauna, a variety due in part to wisps of fog and low-hanging clouds which make these mountains the nation's region of highest precipitation outside the Pacific Northwest. From the Fraser fir, or "balsam," which accounts for the bulk of forests in mountains over 6,000 feet, to the cove hardwood forests, the variety and size of more than one hundred native trees in the area gives this region a botanical variety unmatched elsewhere in the United States.[6]

From this array of natural bounty would come great economic benefit to the inhabitants of Cades Cove. One tree, the chestnut, which is now extinct, played an important role in the ecological system affecting both wildlife, domesticated animals, and human residents of the area. "The big tree of the Great Smokies forests," with some specimens achieving trunk diameters of nine to ten feet, the chestnut was regarded as the best hardwood tree in America because "its lumber was straight grained, easily worked, exceptionally durable, and of the highest quality."[7] The nuts were sweet and palatable, and formed a staple and highly desirable part of the average pioneer's diet. They were also a very marketable by-product, and each fall children in the cove collected chestnuts to sell in the larger urban markets of East Tennessee, usually Maryville or Knoxville.

A parasitic fungus, first discovered in New York in 1904, rapidly spread throughout the forests of the eastern United States, and during the 1920s and 1930s, killed most of the chestnut trees in the Great Smoky Mountains. Needless to say, the extinction of this fine tree seriously diminished many species of wildlife. Chestnuts also furnished mast for domestic hogs which grazed in the woods. The extinction of the chestnut and the consequent diminution of animals such as the black bear, which depended on it for food, help explain some basic ecological changes between the wilderness environment of nineteenth- and twentieth-century Cades Cove.[8]

A survey of the Southern Appalachian forests in 1905 revealed the following proportion of trees in the Cades Cove district: chestnut, 30 percent; chestnut oak, 20 percent; hemlock, 12 percent; sugar maple, 6 percent; red gum, 4 percent; black birch, 4 percent; black oak, 6 percent; and others, 6 percent. The percentage of chestnut (30 percent) in the Cades Cove district was considerably higher than regional averages (20 percent) in the Little Tennessee River basin. So at the end of the century the chestnut was clearly the most important tree in Cades Cove quantitatively, and its distribution was much greater there than in the larger region.[9]

A seemingly endless supply of trees from the surrounding mountains supplied the cove people with wood for houses, fence rails, and a great variety of household implements and agricultural tools. This form of the wilderness, the trees, had a very conditioning effect on the domestic economy of the cove, since some division of labor — i.e., coffin maker, cabinet maker, etc.— was very early necessary to utilize this basic commodity. It also bound together the ties of community — a large undertaking such as building a house or barn invariably required a collective effort. And socially, the abundance of and free access to wood had a leveling effect, since the poorest family had only to gather it in order to have a fuel supply equal to that of its richest neighbor.[10]

Another practical function of the wilderness was to supply an abundance of many types of game. Here, as with the forests, it is important to bear in mind that in the mountains surrounding Cades Cove, game remained constant as a food source throughout the century and did not, as was so often the case in other areas, become scarce or thinned out with the influx of new settlers. One reason for this situation was that the surrounding mountains and wilderness areas were never actually settled, or only very sparsely so in remote regions.[11]

As a food source, by far the most important game was deer. William Howell Oliver recalled in his Sketches that his father, Elijah, son of the first John Oliver, was an excellent hunter who could average three to six deer in a good day. Killing deer involved minimal waste, inasmuch as the meat was salted and could be preserved for fairly long periods of time. Elijah Oliver often refused to kill smaller game because deer was such an excellent quarry, and firing one's rifle at a squirrel might scare the more valuable deer away.[12] Venison remained abundant throughout most of the century and was always a favorite diet of the cove people.

In the beginning of settlement, hunting was a practical necessity, since game supplied an important part of the total food supply. As farms began to produce an abundance of various types of crops, however, killing game became less a necessity than a leisure pastime, or sport, for the men of the cove. Hunting became a ritual, usually solitary; most cove men preferred to hunt alone to escape, if only temporarily, from the intensive effort required in farming and from any personal or domestic crisis. Thus through this ritual the wilderness became a type of psychic safety valve for the men of the community.[13]

Hunting was a complicated activity. It required not only an accurate knowledge of the geography of the mountains, but the ability to determine weather conditions, to track game, and to build simple traps if one should run out of ammunition. In the process, or course of this ritual, an individual hunter frequently developed an intense fondness for his gun, illustrated by the fact that favorite guns were frequently given names such as "Old Bean," or "Old Betsy," and the cove men could often identify various guns by the sound of their discharge. The esteem in which individual guns were held by cove hunters is demonstrated by the fact that many of these flintlocks survived with reputations intact into the twentieth century. An example was "Old Betsy," the gun of George Powell. This Baxter Bean gun was "a splendid example of the Old Smoky flintlock."[14]

The transmission of this knowledge of how to survive in the wilderness formed an important part of the folk or informal education passed from father to son. Manual skills such as how to build fires or traps, skin wild animals, and use firearms tended to be male prerogatives with only rare exceptions. It occasionally represented the rites of passage from adolescence to adulthood but was usually a gradual and cumulative learning process begun in early childhood. The individual experience of going alone into the mountains provided a strong if inarticulate bond between father, son, and grandson. The transmission of such skills also provided a continuing guarantee that in any emergency a son alone in the wilderness would not be at a loss in knowing how to survive, protect, and feed himself.[15]

Skill in hunting was also due to the skill of the individual gunmaker in the cove throughout the century. Mason argued that "the very fact that the Southern mountain frontier gunsmith and marksman could manufacture, at his crude forge, with its scanty, homemade equipment, a short-range firearm of comparatively unvarying accuracy and hard-hitting qualities, is extraordinary, and no feat to rival it is found anywhere in history. It seems all the more remarkable when one is thoroughly conversant with the circumstances of his environment and his lack of scientific tools." The flintlock rifle gradually gave way to the "store-bought" barrel and rough-cast mountings for which the gunmaker paid twelve dollars. Later the more modern percussion cap-lock became widely used in the cove. "When the store-bought gun could be purchased in rough-cast form more readily by the mountain gunmakers, guncraftsmen sprang up like grasshoppers in every mountain cove and cabin, and the oldtime armorer, who proudly placed his nameplate in silver in the barrel of his brain-child, stored his headblock and screw-guide away forever. His trade was gone, but not his reputation, for he had forged a republic at his backwoods anvil."[16]

Thus hunting, first a necessity during the settlement period, gradually in the three decades after 1830 became a ritual carefully transmitted to the younger sons of Cades Cove. Because of this transmission, most of the cove people were able to survive the devastation of the Civil War. In the geographical center of a Confederate South, East Tennessee remained staunchly Union in sympathy, an isolated island in hostile Rebel territory on all sides. The Confederates, regarding East Tennesseans as traitors, unleashed guerrilla warfare against the civilian population. Periodic raids by North Carolinians, often little better than marauding outlaws, stripped the cove people time and again of their cumulated supplies of food, as well as their livestock and seed corn.[17]

These North Carolina raiders, who had easy access to the cove through Ekanetelee and other gaps, were not unaware of the various types of food the natives raised, nor of where such supplies were usually stored around their homesteads. Because these raiders lived in an environment very similar to that of Cades Cove, it required the greatest ingenuity on the part of the cove people to hide any of their food or livestock. Moreover, frequent prewar commerce with North Carolina meant that many of these raiders knew specific geographic details about the cove and its environs. It was not unusual for them to take food, often the last bite, from the table and strip the cove inhabitants of their best clothes and shoes or boots. Thus during the darkest days of the Civil War, when all food supplies and domestic animals had been stolen, the wilderness once again provided subsistence for the people of Cades Cove, as it had during the early years of settlement.[18]

During these war years, Elijah Oliver supplied his family with food by trapping many types of smaller animals, since powder for his gun was often difficult to obtain. William Howell, his son, recalled that his father made a very simple type of trap, which they called a "fall," whereby squirrels were baited into a small pit with a few grains of corn. After deer, squirrels and rabbits were probably the most important food source with an occasional wild turkey, if the hunter was particularly skillful and lucky. Bears were often hunted for sport because they provided something of a challenge, and many cove people prized bear meat. Various by-products from the bear, notably grease or oil, were thought to be efficacious for a wide variety of maladies.[19]

The disadvantage of an abundance of game was the corresponding plentitude of predatory animals. Opossums, foxes, and weasels posed a constant threat to chickens, ducks, and other domestic fowl in the cove. Bears slaughtered cattle on the open range and often made forages into the cove for hogs and sheep. Every fall, raids would be expected from the bears, lured into the cultivated areas by ripening corn. Often farmers would lie camouflaged in the fields during the harvest season to protect their corn crop against these marauders.[20]

Wolves, although they disappeared from the cove at an early date, continued to be a problem to various animals grazing in the mountains. They were always much more numerous on the North Carolina side of the Great Smokies because that wilderness area was less densely populated. Nevertheless, cove hunters ranged these mountains in search of wolves until the Civil War. The state of Tennessee had declared a bounty on them in 1812, and by the 1830s, three dollars per scalp was the going payment. Scalps were presented to the county court, whereupon the clerk of the court issued a voucher collectable from the state treasurer. Robert Burchfield, John Jones, and James M. Shields of Cades Cove were paid for a total of seven scalps between 1834 and 1840.[21] During the Civil War, the wolves greatly increased because fewer men were available to hunt them. After the war, the herders banded together in a concentrated effort to thin out the wolf population and succeeded in exterminating them in all but the most remote areas of the Great Smoky Mountains.

The wilderness also provided a wide variety of plants, or herbs, highly valued by the cove people for their medicinal properties. Using such published references as *Gunn's Domestic Medicine,* as well as their own family recipes, most households in the cove practiced some form of folk or home remedy for various diseases. Because the herbs were available to anyone, as well as the knowledge of how to use them, no single person, or "medicine man," evolved in the cove to monopolize such cures. And since doctors, such as were available, were usually located in distant towns like Maryville or Knoxville and were often prohibitively expensive, the use of herbal medicines served a valuable social end.[22]

The North American variety of ginseng, *Panax quinquefolium,* grew abundantly in the Great Smoky Mountains and in an economy starved for specie furnished a money crop greater than the chestnut. Ginseng had early played an important role in the American trade with China, where the roots of the plant had long been valued as a cure for many

ills and infirmities, and was in great demand because of the popular belief there that it was an aphrodisiac.[23]

André Michaux described in 1802 the abundance of the plant in the
mountains of Tennessee and Kentucky, and the method of preparation
for sale:

> It grows in the declivities of mountains, in fresh and constantly shaded
> spots, where the soil is richest. A man can scarcely draw in one day more
> than eight or nine pounds of fresh roots, which are always less than an inch
> in diameter, even after fifteen years of growth, if the number of impressions
> may be relied on that may be observed on the upper part of the neck of
> the root, and which are produced by the stalks that annually succeed. The
> form of the root is generally elliptic; and when it is bifurcated, which is not
> often, one of the divisions is much thicker and longer than the other. The
> seeds, which are of a striking red colour, and attached together, come to
> maturity between the 15th September and the 1st October.
>
> .   .   .   .
>
> In the United States . . . they begin to collect it in spring, and stop at the
> commencement of winter. Its root, which is then soft and watery, grows
> wrinkled by desiccation, but afterwards becomes extremely hard, and at
> length loses a third of its bulk, and nearly half of its weight.[24]

These same methods of recognizing the plant and preparing the
roots for sale were used by the cove people. Dr. Gunn stated in 1830
that ginseng "is found in great plenty among the hills and mountains
of Tennessee, and brought into Knoxville daily for sale." The price paid
to collectors varied. In 1802, Michaux said that merchants in Philadelphia paid six or seven dollars per pound. Dr. Gunn later indicated that
an occasional glut of the market brought the price down. The average
price per pound of ginseng rose steadily throughout the nineteenth century from 42¢ in 1822; 71¢ in 1841; 84¢ in 1861; $1.04 in 1871; $1.65
in 1881; $3.39 in 1891; $5.38 in 1901. So ginseng was one of the very
few products whose value continued to rise in the post-Civil War period when prices for other cove products were so depressed. Market
prices do not, of course, furnish any indication of what the individual
collectors were paid. But the fact that the cove people continued to
gather ginseng throughout the century, and considered it a "money"
crop, indicates that the price they received seemed well worth the effort.[25]

The wiser ginseng collectors replanted the bright red seeds when they dug up the roots in order to insure another year's crop. Although many cove people engaged in "sangin,'' or gathering ginseng roots to sell in Knoxville, there is no evidence that they ever used the herb in any home remedy or were even cognizant of its reputed properties. They seem to have agreed completely with Dr. Gunn's conclusion that it was nothing more than "a pleasant bitter, and a gentle stimulant for strengthening the stomach." In the revised 1860 edition of *Domestic Medicine*, Dr. Gunn had changed his mind. Here he stated that ginseng was "useful in nervous debility, weak digestion and feeble appetite, as a stomachic and restorative. It is considered a very valuable medicine for children; and has been recommended in asthma, palsy and nervous affections generally."[26]

Another wilderness product was the various animal furs, which also commanded excellent cash prices throughout the nineteenth century. Mink and muskrats along Abrams Creek were trapped, as were foxes, opossums, and raccoons in the mountains. Although deer were abundant, there is no evidence that deerskins were ever exported in great numbers from the cove. Very few instances are recorded of trapping as being the single occupation of any individual in the cove. Rather it was a widely practiced pastime to gain extra cash, engaged in by most of the cove farmers during the winter months after their crops had been harvested. Trap lines were laid in the usual fashion, and revenues from these furs remained a steady, if not excessive, source of income. Even after the Civil War, when regional markets were depressed, the demand for furs remained constant because the system was supplying an international market.[27]

In the mountains surrounding Cades Cove are a number of open areas which grow excellent grasses and are known as balds because no trees grow on them. Spence Field, located on the state-line ridge, and domelike Gregory Bald, which rises 3,000 feet above the cove in the southwest, are the two major balds, although there are a number of smaller ones, such as Parson's, immediately accessible through the cove. Very early in their history the cove people used these grassy uplands to graze their cattle during the summer months. Cattle, sheep, horses, and hogs could graze in these highlands throughout the summer months, leaving the cove land available for growing whatever crops were necessary.[28]

The origin of these balds has long been something of a scientific mystery. The records of Cades Cove indicate clearly that these balds were not "natural." John W. Oliver stated that James Spence burned trees and cleared the Spence Field in the 1830s. Other sources from Cades Cove indicate the presence of large stumps earlier in the century, an indication of a prior forest cover. Yet the presence of some of these balds is recorded in Cherokee legend before white settlement. The most recent scientific study of the balds indicates that the forest cover is rapidly returning. The rapidity of the invasion rate by various trees might indicate that the balds were never natural, as the cove residents maintained, and were kept cleared by fires and heavy grazing. Or the return of trees could be due to a warming of the climate. So there remains much conflicting evidence; no single theory explains the origins of the balds satisfactorily.[29]

These uplands proved to be such excellent grazing areas that many farmers in the neighboring counties of East Tennessee early began to herd their cattle and bring them here, usually through Cades Cove, during the summer months. One such Knox countian, Samuel McCammon, left a diary of his grazing activities between 1846 and 1854. In the middle of April with his herd he "set out for the top of the mountain"; in August he returned to the mountains, collected his cattle, and herded them home. This was the usual practice throughout much of the nineteenth century: the farmer could either sell his cattle to a buyer already in the mountains, or bring them back to one of the larger market centers of East Tennessee, usually Knoxville, and sell them there.

The routine problems of herding are succinctly outlined in McCammon's diary. Occasionally, cattle were lost, despite the fact that they were carefully "belled" before leaving Knox County. Usually he decided on the various herders according to whether he thought that their ranges were good. Snow killed some of his cattle in April 1847. In 1848, there was trouble about a new North Carolina law, so he took his cattle up the Little Tennessee River. The most frequent problem was the difficulty in rounding up their cattle in August, since some of the herd often became quite wild in the mountains.[30]

Either way, the people of Cades Cove prospered from these various transactions. First, owners of the mountain land usually charged some rent, however nominal, per head of cattle for the use of these meadows. Second, a herder was often employed from among the cove people to keep watch over the animals while they grazed during the summer months. Ace Sparks, a resident of the cove, recalled that his father, Nath, grazed as many as 700 head of cattle on Spence Field during the 1890s. In addition to fees spent on the cattle, farmers from other areas, such as McCammon indicated in his diary, had to pay for lodging and feed for their horses en route.[31] So the wilderness provided the people of Cades Cove with an excellent, accessible range to graze their own cattle and also with paying customers who used these highlands to graze cattle on a commercial basis.

Any enumeration of the practical functions of the wilderness to the cove people would be incomplete without mentioning the protection which the surrounding areas afforded during the Civil War. But the wilderness in this capacity was something of a mixed blessing. The surrounding mountains gave the cove people many excellent hiding places to keep their horses and more valuable farm animals if they received advanced warning, and during the worst years of the war, the cove men themselves frequently hid out in the mountains to avoid impressment into the Southern armies. But the easy access to Cades Cove from Ekanetelee Gap and other trails to North Carolina made some surprise guerrilla warfare inevitable, and often such attacks could be launched from the surrounding mountains without any prior warning. Also, the very location of Cades Cove in the heart of the Great Smoky Mountains made aid or assistance from other units of the Blount County home guard difficult to obtain.[32]

Although any exhaustive enumeration of the practical functions and uses of the wilderness surrounding the cove is impossible, certain definite themes emerge from the brief survey thus far. It is evident that the wilderness through its various products provided the cove people with a steady supplement to their income in addition to the livelihood they gained from farming. This seemingly inexhaustible abundance conditioned the inhabitants to patterns of waste and excessive consumption in the use of these wilderness products, although they might be quite frugal with their cultivated crops.[33] Without any effort at conservation, did they not incur the risk, sooner or later, of running out of some or all of these products, as happened so often to settlers in other sections after the passing of the frontier era?

The answer to this question of conservation, and to more basic questions about the ecology of the land, is supplied by the geography of Cades Cove. Situated as a virtual island of cultivated land in the middle of the mountains, the cove proper reached its peak population of 671 people in 1850, a level which had declined by 1860 and was not reached again during the nineteenth century. Thus, despite their excessive consumption, the limited quantity of arable land prevented the native population from rising above a fixed level. Game remained abundant because the wilderness surrounding the cove was large enough to resupply whatever was taken out without upsetting the ecological balance.[34]

In view of the many products and benefits from the wilderness, it seems evident that their mountain environment must have determined, to a great extent, the life style of the cove people. A careful chronological examination of their development, however, reveals that this was not true. The best illustrations of the primacy of external influences on their life style is to be found in their architecture. Although many cabins have been preserved by the Great Smoky Mountains National Park, other buildings more indicative of chronological developments were destroyed. All frame houses, for instance, were eliminated because the park wished to preserve only structures reflecting "pioneer" style.[35]

A careful comparison of both design and construction of these extant cabins with similar structures in other areas reveals no deviation from standard American building norms. In his comprehensive study of Southern mountain cabins, Henry Glassie defines a cabin as "a one room house not over one and one-half stories high." He identifies two basic types of cabins: the square and the rectangular. Both the John Oliver cabin and the Peter Cable cabin, the two oldest structures in the cove, built in the 1820s, clearly fall within Glassie's specifications in terms of height, type of roof, placement of chimneys and doors, construction, chimneys, fenestration, underpinning, and construction of walls, additions, and porches. Other later structures, such as the Carter Shields and LeQuire cabins, built in the 1830s and 1840s, likewise fall within these specifications as square cabins.[36]

The point of this comparison is that such standard forms were indicative of the larger American culture. These patterns almost approached

Above, John Oliver Cabin. *Below,* Peter Cable Cabin.

Carter Shields Cabin

standardization as they moved down the eastern seaboard, into the Piedmont, and westward. Nothing in the cove environment altered or disconnected any of these building patterns: not the wilderness but the broader culture, from which the cove people came, dominated how and and in what shape they built their homes. Glassie emphasizes the influence of Pennsylvania Germans in various construction techniques. In Cades Cove, Peter Cable, of Pennsylvania-Dutch extraction, was the acknowledged authority in all types of construction.[37]

The only architectural surprise in Cades Cove is Elijah Oliver's cabin, an interesting specimen of the formative dog trot house. Built in 1866, it had the prerequisite "two units of roughly equal size separated by an open 'hall,' or 'trot,' or 'passage,' with a chimney on each gable end." One division is higher than the other, giving the structure a split-level appearance. Both units were constructed at the same time, and both divisions, or pens, were functional units of the house. The dog trot house, common in other sections of the country, is only rarely found

Elijah Oliver Cabin

in the Southern mountains, according to Glassie.[38] The presence of this type of cabin in Cades Cove is further evidence that even the exceptions in building patterns were derived not from any indigenous inspiration due to the wilderness, but from the larger culture.

Although all frame houses were destroyed by the National Park Service in the late 1930s, there is ample evidence to indicate that such construction was common by the 1850s. An 1857 survey of Blount County indicates that two saw mills were located in Cades Cove. Daniel D. Foute, an early owner of Montvale Springs, moved to the cove in 1849 and built a frame house widely admired for its fine construction and landscaping. After the Civil War, many of the cove people returned to the simpler type of log construction because of its cheapness and utility. By the 1880s, however, as some degree of prosperity returned, frame houses were once again evident. Both the Henry Whitehead house and the Oliver-Tipton house, built in the 1880s, furnish clear evidence of transitional styles. Often owners of substantial log houses chose to weatherboard their homes in order to modernize them.[39] The two periods, or cycles, of building frame houses, from 1849 to 1860, and from the 1880s to the end of the century, again furnish clear evidence that

Above, Henry Whitehead House. *Below*, Oliver-Tipton House

the type of architecture found in the cove was a function of the relative prosperity of an agricultural-based economy, not of the surrounding wilderness.

There are other indications that during relatively prosperous times, the inhabitants chose to buy a wide variety of manufactured household and farm implements to replace the cruder homemade tools of an earlier period. While the typical farmer might wear homespun during working days, most of them could afford at least one suit of store-bought clothes for Sunday. Side by side with kitchen utensils made of wood, one might find an occasional set of imported china. Although purchases of the latter sort could usually be made only in Knoxville, there is no indication that cove farmers did not share an interest in purchasing a wide variety of manufactured goods in common with their counterparts in the rest of the country, provided there was ready cash. It is interesting to note, as corroborative evidence, that during the worst part of the Civil War, Elijah Oliver made frequent trips and brought back many purchases from Knoxville merchants. Receipts were from P.H. Cardwell (Dry Goods, Boots, Shoes, Hats, Caps, Stationery, Notions, etc.); Crooker & Bunnell's Funnel Clothes Washers (a rather frivolous and somewhat extravagant item for the sober Elijah to be buying!); Tedford & Lowe, Dispensing Druggists, Maryville; and a receipt for Dr. R.V. Pierce's *The People's Common Sense Medical Adviser.*[40]

The picture that emerges from an examination of the cove's domestic economy is one of wide diversity. Basic pioneer skills, such as spinning flax for thread from which homespun was woven, were in general use throughout the century. According to John W. Oliver, "each family grew flax from which to make articles of clothing and other household goods such as hand towels, bed spreads, etc. The coarse short part of the flax was used to weave hunting shirts, and if worn next to your body was irritating to the skin."[41] But these skills did not automatically exclude a desire for other manufactured products. The cove people seemed to be able to manage a careful exploitation of the surrounding wilderness and still keep abreast, during prosperous times, of more finished products available in the larger market areas such as Knoxville. This dichotomy makes any rigid characterization of their life style extremely difficult. And in analyzing their relationship to the wilderness, the continuous intercourse with larger regional markets makes the cove people appear rather more than less like their contemporaries in other parts of the country.

Attitudes toward the wilderness also varied greatly from one period to another, and among different groups during the same period of time. Dr. Jobe reflected the initial fear of the wilderness as a hiding place for hostile Indians and wolves, but even this attitude is obviously traceable from earlier experience and associations. He identified the Cherokees "who had been such a terror to the settlement in the Watauga Valley," and clearly transposed earlier difficulties with other Indians in East Tennessee to the new locale.[42] Since his uncle was killed by the Cherokees living in the cove, Dr. Jobe's fears were not unfounded. But the important point is that this whole range of fear and suspicion, linking the Indians to the wilderness as a sinister environment, was part of the cultural attitudes which he and other early settlers brought with them.

Once the threat of Indians was removed and the wolf population diminished, the wilderness lost much of its menacing quality to the cove inhabitants. Most were pragmatic about any possible dangers encountered while in the mountains, and from this attitude came a pragmatic view of the wilderness in general. It was true that various accidents, even death, awaited the careless hunter or unwary traveler. But such occurrences were invariably attributed to the individual's own neglect. For every danger, there was a preventive measure; if one's fire went out, or if one ran out of food or supplies, there were many alternative measures one could take to repair the loss. Because these various survival techniques were discussed and elaborated on at length by the cove people in their daily conversations, it was improbable that anyone could not have heard, at some time or another, the necessary details of how to survive in the wilderness.[43]

Although women generally were not expected to go alone into the mountains, or to possess any hunting skills, in various periods of the cove's history they were often required by circumstances to do so. The lore, or body of folk knowledge on how to survive in the wilderness, was a common topic of conversation at night around the fireplace. Consequently the women were regularly exposed to these details, and were usually not at a loss when required to confront the wilderness alone.

Such occurrences were rare, most happening during the Civil War, when a majority of the younger men were away.[44]

After the initial settlement period, the inhabitants did not conceptualize the wilderness as being dangerous; they therefore showed little fear of the surrounding mountains. Analyzing their attitudes is particularly difficult from manuscript sources: oral history provides far more insight into a people's values, since any group is normally reluctant to write down attitudes which they consider common knowledge. Corroboration of this lack of fear of the wilderness in Cades Cove is furnished by the fact that there are no tales of supernatural phenomena occurring in the mountains surrounding the cove. This is not to say that the cove folklore was not rich in supernatural stories; but all these ghost, or "hant," tales were associated with places in the cove proper; none occurred in the surrounding mountains.[45]

Occasionally various animals caused some fear. In the mountains, the scream of a panther could momentarily frighten anyone. Many tales relating to panthers, which were feared and thought to be aggressive by some of the cove people, have been handed down. Generally, however, wild animals were valued for practical reasons, since hunting them provided sport, food, and perhaps furs for sale. The cove people often allowed their children to make pets out of wild animals. The almost nonchalant attitude toward such pets and their easy relationship with such wild animals is reflected in the nostalgic recollection of Dr. Jobe:

> We had a pet bear for several years, he was very large, tame and gentle. He would get loose once in a while, but we could always catch him and tie him again. I remember he got loose one night, and came in at a window to where a younger brother and I were sleeping. It scared us badly, but as soon as he drank a churn-full of buttermilk, he went out at the window, and was roaming around about the barn at daylight. I have heard people say a bear could not be hurt by bees stinging them, but its a mistake. I remember one Sunday, while all were at Church, except a few of us little children, our bees swarmed, and settled on the body of the tree above where bruin was tied. He kept looking up at the big knot of bees, as though he would like to know what they were, so after a while he went up the tree, on a tour of inspection. He looked at them for a while, then he wiped them off with his nose; and the bees began to sting him, and he began to "holler,"

and rip and tare. He broke his collar at last and away he went to the woods, but returned in a few hours. They stung him on his breast and paws, but mostly about his nose and eyes.[46]

Some individuals preferred to live alone in the surrounding mountains and to keep contact with the densely populated cove at a minimum. Probably the earliest example of such an individual was James Spence, who moved from Virginia to the White Oak Cove, immediately adjoining Cades Cove, in the late 1820s. In 1830, he and his wife, Caroline Law, built a cabin on the top of the mountain at a place which now bears their name: the Spence Field. Both loved the wilderness and moved to the Spence Field early each spring and stayed until late in the fall. There they herded cattle and grew such vegetables and crops as the high altitude would permit. This type of nomadic life was difficult for Caroline. A few days before the birth of their son Robert in 1840, she walked alone ten miles to their home in the White Oak Cove in order to be near neighbors who could assist her. Other than such emergencies as childbirth and the approach of winter, however, nothing could induce them to leave their mountain.[47]

The Spences were willing to spend at least part of each year in the cove, but Wilson, or Wils Burchfield was not. Arriving with his wife, Elizabeth Baker, shortly before the Civil War, Wils chose to settle in what later became known as the Chestnut Flats, an area at the southwest end of Cades Cove. "A lover of sports and of the wilds of the forests and mountains, a greater hunter and frontiersman," Wils "loved to get as far away from civilization as possible." Among his most prized possessions was a flintlock rifle which he named "Old Bean" after its manufacturer, Baxter Bean of the Bean family, noted gunsmiths in the nineteenth century. Wils built his cabin just under Gregory Bald in the heart of the Great Smokies to escape any contact with the cove people. Hating and avoiding contact with any form of institutional life — churches, schools, etc.— he cleared his land and grew crops, and hunted wild game to support his large family in complete isolation from the social and political mainstream of the cove proper.[48]

The most famous man in the cove history, Russell Gregory, also loved the wilderness solitude. Moving to Cades Cove from Yancey County, North Carolina, in 1835 with his wife, Elizabeth Hill, he settled on a farm in the middle of the cove. Shortly after his arrival he entered several thousand acres of mountain land both in Tennessee and North Carolina, including Gregory Bald, which derived its name from him. On this bald he built a cylindrically shaped stone house with large windows, or "port holes," as he called them. On moonlit nights he concealed himself in this structure and poked his rifle, "Old Long Tom," through one of the windows to shoot deer which came near to lick salt.

As a rancher, Gregory came in contact with a large number of stockmen and became widely known. He was famous for his method of calling cattle. Using a large blowing horn, he summoned them to the top of Gregory Bald from miles around in order to salt them. The sight and sounds of hundreds of cattle converging on him with their bells jingling remained for many years one of the cove's most memorable spectacles.[49]

No one loved the wilderness more than Russell Gregory, or spent as much time alone in the Great Smoky Mountains. He even built his house in the cove facing Gregory Bald, so that he had a full view of his mountain during the winter months when he could not be there. Yet his love of the wilderness did not make Russell hate civilization, as it did Wils Burchfield. In many respects, Gregory personified the qualities most admired by cove people during the nineteenth century. He had a deep sense of responsibility, not only to his immediate family, but to the larger community and nation. Completely involved in all aspects of community life, he became a leader in church and a full participant in the political, social, and educational life of Cades Cove. This sense of responsibility was complemented by an even temper and calm disposition. Frequently he was called on to settle local disputes; his decision was seldom challenged or questioned.[50]

Spence, Burchfield, and Gregory were men of widely differing interests and attitudes, but each preferred to spend most of his time in the solitude of the mountains surrounding the cove. Yet the very complexity of these men's personalities makes it difficult to measure the impact of the wilderness on the larger number of men and women who chose to make Cades Cove their permanent home during the nineteenth century. Often former cove residents in their correspondence reflected regret at leaving the cove; almost always, however, economic opportunities were described as being better in their new homes in the West. Fragments remain which indicate cove residents often remained there at a conscious financial loss. A letter in 1854 from Isaac Hart in Athens, Tennessee, to his nephew, Colonel J.W. Hampton Tipton in the cove, illustrates this situation:

> Now if you will leave the Coves you can do well but if you lay out your money for land in the Coves, Goodby Hampton. You had better come down and look here, for land is advancing every day . . . .
>
> We made 100 bu. of fine wheat. We do not have to labor under the same difficulties as you do. We have thrashers here that can thrash from 100 to 200 bu. a day. You have to flail after the old dugout, go to the thicket, cut a pole and lay on all day. At night fan out 5 or 6 bu. with a sheet. Then you go 15 or 20 miles to get flour fit to eat.
>
> I'll say to Catherine to push you off. Here she need not spin anymore cotton for she can make more thread in three months raising chickens than she can spin in 12 months.
>
> But I don't think you will come. Your attachment is so strong for them mountains that it will be hard for you to part with that grand scenery.[51]

Yet basically the wilderness was important to the cove people primarily for economic reasons. The surrounding mountains provided them with both food and shelter, with marketable products, and with a safe retreat during the Civil War. Although some individuals preferred living alone there, the wilderness did not determine the pattern of their development or shape the life style of the majority of the cove people in any appreciable degree. Their basic beliefs — political, social, and religious — stemmed from the mainstream of nineteenth-century American culture, and proved surprisingly resilient to the many obstacles which later occurred. Like a mountain stream temporarily diverted into a quiet isolated pool, this basic cultural orientation never completely lost its identity, and could later rejoin the mainstream with little real difficulty. And like their contemporaries in other parts of the United States, the quality and style of their lives were largely determined by the market economy.

Gregory Bald from Cades Cove, 1934. Charles S. Dunn in foreground.
Oliver Family Collection.

Above left, John W. Oliver's farm in 1929, with large barn and silo. The family home is in the background. The broad flat meadows in the center of the cove had particularly fertile soil. *Below left,* George Tipton's barn near the center of the cove in the late 1920s. *Right,* Elijah Oliver homestead in 1934. *Oliver Family Collection.*

House and office of Dr. Thomas McGill, who moved to the cove in 1902 and practiced medicine several years before going to California. A rather surprising number of medical doctors lived in Cades Cove throughout its history; the earliest was Dr. Joseph Sherriell in 1840.

Above, smaller barn and silo on what was known as the Fisher place, owned by John W. Oliver. *Below,* the apex of John W. Oliver's devotion to scientific farming came in 1920 with the building of this modern barn and silo. The barn was forty by seventy-two feet, resting on a concrete foundation. The silo was twelve feet in diameter, thirty feet high above the ground and ten feet deep below ground level. *Oliver Family Collection.*

Henry Whitehead house with Mrs. John W. Oliver and Mrs. R.D. Burchfield standing before their father's house. Log homes frequently had frame additions added in later years. *Oliver Family Collection.*

The original John Oliver cabin and garden in the late 1920s.

Above left, Uncle Noah Burchfield standing before his barn in the late 1920s. Note log construction on the lower part of the barn; many such original log structures were later covered with planks for additional insulation. *Below left,* "Old home of George W. and Aunt Ann Powell in Chestnut Flats, a suburb of Cades Cove. Its history can never be written" (John W. Oliver's inscription on the back of the photograph). *Oliver Family Collection. Right,* Witt Shields house, 1936, built in 1900. *National Park Service.* Copied by A. Randolph Shields.

Left, William Howell Oliver's home and farm, late 1920s, including crib, woodshed, smokehouse, shop, and the storehouse where he once operated a country store for several years. *Above right,* Dave Sparks home, 1936. *National Park Service.* Copied by A. Randolph Shields. *Below right,* Uncle Noah and Aunt Sarah Burchfield in front of their home, late 1920s. *Oliver Family Collection.*

Above left, front view of John W. Oliver's home in the late 1920s. *Below left,* rear view of the Oliver home. *Right,* cattle grazing in Cades Cove, late 1920s. Cattle were kept in the cove during the winter months and grazed in the surrounding mountains during the summer. *Oliver Family Collection.*

Left, John W. Oliver's one-hundred-foot bee shed, which included a platform made of pine two-by-fours, suspended about eighteen inches from the ground by heavy galvanized wire anchored to the rafters along the entire front side of the shed. The purpose of this suspended platform, whose foundation posts were anchored in concrete, was to prevent ants from reaching the hives. *Right,* John Burchfield mowing hay in meadow for John W. Oliver, late 1920s. Oliver's home, granary, and barn in background. *Oliver Family Collection.*

Mrs. John W. Oliver with herd of Black Angus cattle at the lower end of the new barn, 1920s. Oliver imported the first purebred Black Angus into the cove. *Oliver Family Collection.*

3
The Market Economy

Geography was an important, but not a determining factor, in shaping the communal response of the cove people to their wilderness environment. In the development of a market economy, however, the effect of physiography on the trade routes of East Tennessee was the single most important factor. The economic life of Cades Cove must be analyzed within the context of larger regional, state, and national market patterns. At the same time that the cove men were struggling to get a passable road through the mountains to Knoxville, they shared an indirect, but nevertheless very important stake, in whether Knoxville achieved steamboat transportation, or later, railroads. Without this awareness of East Tennessee's century-long struggle, often unsuccessful, to obtain transportation facilities which would make her comparable to and competitive with other regions, the economic development of Cades Cove makes little sense.[1]

The high crest line of the Unaka Mountains, ranging from altitudes between 4,000 to 6,650 feet above sea level, formed a great barrier between East Tennessee and North Carolina. If Cades Cove had been located on the eastern, or North Carolina, side of these mountains, her economic development would have been quite different. Western North Carolina was mountainous in topography and never developed transportation facilities that permitted the growth of any commercial center comparable to Knoxville in East Tennessee. The few rivers which drained this mountain region, such as the Yadkin, Catawa, or French Broad, were "not navigable until they left the state." Inasmuch as road construction in the mountains was extremely difficult before dynamite and blasting powder came into use, the roads in the western portion of the state through most of the nineteenth century were "only a slight improvement over those of the colonial era." John Preston Arthur maintained that these western North Carolina roads were "frequently too steep even for the overtaxed oxen and horses of that time." The North Carolina coast, with its sand bars, frequent storms, and reputation as "the graveyard of the Atlantic," isolated the region from the seaways of the world and further retarded the commercial development of the entire state.[2]

So despite several Indian trails, such as the one through Ekanetelee Gap, Cades Cove never developed significant commercial ties with North Carolina, whose close proximity would under different circumstances have made that state the logical outlet for its marketable crops. It is interesting to note in this regard that when the eminent Knoxville physician and entrepreneur Dr. J.G.M. Ramsey first became interested in a direct railroad to the Atlantic seaboard in the 1820s, the projected terminus was Charleston or Savannah on a route which would completely bypass North Carolina.

Recent scholarship indicates much more commercial activity and road-building existed in western North Carolina than earlier historians had observed. But Ora Blackmun maintains that such changes brought about by improved trade arteries "did not reach back into the mountain coves and small isolated mountain valleys." In such remote communities in the westernmost part of the state, she notes, "nothing worthy of the name road entered."[3]

Cades Cove quite naturally fell within the sphere of the largest commercial center of upper East Tennessee at Knoxville, some forty miles northwest. Knoxville was situated four and one-half miles west of the junction where the Holston and French Broad Rivers formed the Tennessee River. The Valley of East Tennessee lies within a greater trough extending southwestward from New York to central Alabama. This Great Valley, as the larger trough is called, is bounded on the southeast by the Appalachian Mountains and on the northwest by the Appalachian Plateau. It has always served as an enormous internal highway; even later railroads followed the natural topography and have paralleled older routes. The Tennessee Valley, as a segment of this larger trade route, determined that East Tennessee would always be "bound more closely to eastern Pennsylvania and New York or Georgia and Alabama than to North Carolina."[4]

It is much easier to discuss geography and natural trade routes than to attempt to characterize larger ideas and attitudes which motivate an area's search for markets. The booster spirit in Knoxville, however, reflected so clearly in such men as Dr. J.G.M. Ramsey, was contagious. Despite difficult odds and frequent failure, these men boosted their area and almost seemed at times to believe their own propaganda that Knoxville was destined to become the commercial center of the Southeast.[5] This exuberant attitude was characterized by an inextinguishable optimism and by a restless, searching, and often creative energy on the part of the men who possessed it.

Dr. Ramsey may not have been personally acquainted with Daniel D. Foute, but as entrepreneurs par excellence they were certainly spiritual brothers. Foute had great dreams for the agricultural, commercial, and industrial development of Cades Cove, and spent his energy and fortune in attempting to realize these dreams.[6] His ideas and projects made the cove during the formative years of its economic development very closely attuned to the commercial aspirations of Knoxville and the larger region. In this sense, the entrepreneurial spirit accounted for subtle but nevertheless extremely important differences between western North Carolina and eastern Tennessee. Geography alone did not determine the cove's commercial and later political alignment with the latter section.

During the 1820s, the economic life of Cades Cove centered around basic problems of clearing the land of trees and draining the extensive swamps in the lower end. Although patterns of land development in the pioneer stage tended to be uniform throughout the larger region, draining the lower end of the cove presented problems beyond the usual scope of the early settlers. Peter Cable solved this problem by directing the construction of a series of dikes and log booms placed across Abrams Creek and some of the smaller tributaries. This ingenious arrangement allowed the fertile soil to be trapped and distributed evenly on the low areas.[7]

Through Cable's plan, the lower end of the cove was thus drained and actually raised several feet in lower areas. As a consequence, the prime land in the cove, the farming area most desired for its fertility,

shifted from the upper, or northeast part of the cove, which was somewhat hilly in places, to the broad flat meadows of the middle and lower
end. This reclamation occurred in the late 1820s, and explains in part
why earlier settlers had chosen to locate their homesteads in the upper
end of the cove. Usually first comers seize the best land, but in this instance, the better farming areas were developed after the initial settlement period.[8]

Peter Cable's engineering skills were part of his wide-ranging building skills, and were customarily attributed by the cove people to his
Pennsylvania-Dutch origins. Yet Cable left a more important legacy
than his many farm inventions or building skills. As the incident cited
above illustrates, he was deeply concerned with improving, extending,
and conserving the arable central basin of Cades Cove. Obviously there
were many farmers throughout the century who employed the worst,
most wasteful practices in their farming. But for the majority of cove
farmers, Cable set the example, almost from the beginning, of careful,
consistently conservative farming methodology.[9]

Cable lived until 1866, and several generations of cove farmers benefited from his wisdom and experience. He was always anxious to assist
anyone who needed help, and this very approachability meant that his
numerous skills were widely distributed in the community along with
his basic attitudes toward conserving the land. Cable was also aided
in his philosophy of careful land use and conservation by the geographical limitations of the cove: there was only so much arable land, and
if it was not carefully used, some cove residents might be forced to
leave the community. So community ties were inextricably bound up
in the careful cultivation of a limited amount of land, in striking contrast to their wasteful consumption of products supplied by the surrounding wilderness. The net result of Cable's efforts was that the rich
soil of the cove basin remained productive at the end of the century
and was not depleted, as happened in so many other areas within the
larger region.[10]

During the formative years of the 1820s, a heavy dependence on
neighboring Tuckaleechee Cove is clearly discernable. Tuckaleechee
Cove was older and more established, having been settled in the late
1790s, and the geographic proximity of the two coves formed a natural

basis for close ties between the two communities. Although many of the initial cove settlers had come from Carter County, their ties with upper East Tennessee proved difficult to maintain and were soon dissolved. For example, between the presidential elections of 1832 and 1840, Carter County became overwhelmingly Whig in opposition to Jackson and his policies. Settlers such as John Oliver who had left the county before 1832 and settled in Cades Cove were unaffected by this "almost mass transformation of public opinion" and remained loyal to Jackson.[11]

Dr. Jobe mentioned in his autobiography that no fruit trees had been planted in the cove when his family arrived, and for several years the cove inhabitants had to get all their fruit from Uncle Billy Scott in Tuckaleechee Cove. Until 1873, the closest store was that of George Snider in the adjacent cove. All farm machinery or tools, as well as seed for a variety of crops, could be bought at Snider's store. His account book proves that the cove people were buying a wide variety of goods, e.g., clothes, shoes, cloth, and hats, which were not essential to their daily lives, since they presumably had the skills to make these items at home. The continuing purchase of nonessential items is a clear indication that the cove people remained oriented to the larger regional market economy, even in the difficult years just after the Civil War. Snider assisted the cove people in many other ways. He reduced his profit on goods sold to them because of the distance they traveled, and extended credit on a fairly liberal basis.[12] Snider's example is only one of many instances in which the established community helped Cades Cove in the struggling years of the 1820s. But those close economic ties foreshadowed a future time when the cove's political allegiances followed those of Tuckaleechee Cove, and the early economic connections, if not determinative, certainly would be a strong contributing factor.

Their early economic tutelage under Tuckaleechee Cove, however, did not mean that the people of Cades Cove would imitate their neighboring community in the important matter of land distribution. Possibly no other single index can be cited to document basic economic changes within the cove than the average number of acres per farm throughout the century. Unfortunately the only agricultural schedules which give these statistics are in the 1850, 1860, and 1880 censuses.

These records, however, correlated with deeds and with the population schedules of the same census, form a clear picture of basic changes in the pattern of land distribution.

Records from the deeds before 1850 are incomplete, but it is evident from the records which have survived that the average size of the cove's farms between 1820 and 1850 usually ranged from 150 to 300 acres.[13]

This impression excludes such large landholders as William Tipton and Daniel D. Foute, who will be considered separately. Part of the problem in analyzing the size of a typical farm before the first agricultural census in 1850 is that deeds make no distinction between improved and unimproved land, that is, between land actually being cultivated and land held for timber or pasture. Often entrepreneurs such as William Tipton sold tracts of their land or gave such tracts to their children in a gradual division of what were initially extremely large holdings.[14] Other cove farmers were adding tracts of land to their holdings during the prosperous 1840s and 1850s. From the extant records of such transactions, the impression is clear that farms in the cove before 1850 varied greatly in size, and the estimate of between 150 and 300 acres represents an average rather than a mean distribution. It is also clear that the number of land transactions was much greater in the formative years 1820-1860 than in the thirty-five years after the Civil War.

The agricultural schedule of the 1850 census reveals that over three-fourths of the cove inhabitants lived on farms of 100 acres or less of improved land. The acres of improved land are the only reliable guide to farm size, since they represent land under actual cultivation, and the unimproved land could well be forested land in the mountains outside the cove proper. The figures given below make no distinction between owners and tenants; land ownership will be analyzed separately. Excluding the extensive holdings of Daniel D. Foute, in 1850 one-third of the cove farmers lived on farms of from 1 to 25 acres of improved land; almost one-fifth lived on farms of from 26 to 50 acres; slightly over one-fourth lived on farms of from 51 to 100 acres; one-eighth lived on farms of from 100 to 150 acres; and one-eighteenth lived on farms of from 151 to 200 acres.[15]

By 1860, almost one-third of the cove farmers lived on farms of from 26 to 50 acres of improved land; slightly over one-half lived on farms of from 51 to 100 acres; one-tenth lived on farms of from 151 to 200 acres; and one-eighteenth lived on farms of from 201 to 300 acres. This substantial increase in the size of farms during the 1850s is possibly attributable in part to the great decline in the total population of the cove from 671 in 1850 to 296 in 1860 caused by a mass migration in the 1850s to the West. A more probable explanation is that the 1850s were prosperous years in terms of market commodities in East Tennessee, particularly for wheat, and this general prosperity evidently allowed cove farmers to increase their holdings, however modestly.[16]

No figures are extant from the 1870 agricultural census, but by 1880, it is evident that the Civil War had had a devastating effect on land distribution in the cove. According to the agricultural census of 1880, three-fifths of the cove farmers now lived on farms of from 1 to 25 acres; slightly over one-fifth lived on farms of from 26 to 50 acres; one-seventh lived on farms of from 51 to 100 acres; and 3.9 percent lived on farms of from 101 to 200 acres. The dramatic reduction in the size of cove farms is attributable to the economic devastation of the region following the Civil War. The extent of reduction is further emphasized by the fact that almost a third (32.9 percent) of the cove farms in 1880 contained only 10 acres or less of improved land.[17]

From these figures it is evident that land distribution in the cove was not correlated to the size of the population. In 1850, for instance, with a total population of 671, the average farm was 83.98 acres. In 1880, with a much smaller total population of 449, the average farm had dropped to 30.84 acres.[18] So the size of the average cove farm in any given year was determined not by the total population of the cove, but rather by the general economic conditions of the larger region. This conclusion reinforces the fact that the cove economy was market-oriented; a more self-sufficient community would not have experienced the rather drastic alteration of internal land distribution resulting from a regional depression in farm prices.

The price of land in the cove does not furnish a clear index to changing economic conditions throughout the century. During the 1820s, land varied in the initial grants from $1.00 to $5.83 per acre. Between 1830 and 1860, unimproved mountain land remained in the category of from $1.00 to $2.00 per acre, but the fertile land of the cove basin brought from $2.00 to $8.00 per acre, usually averaging between $4.00 and $5.00 per acre.[19]

Land prices are difficult to analyze due to a wide range of intervening variables which are illuminated only by a careful reading of all the extant deeds for cove land in the nineteenth century. Obviously there were differences in the land itself; some parts of the cove were more fertile than others, a situation confirmed by later geological studies. Ayres and Ashe pointed out in 1905 that there were spots in the cove of "so-called 'dead land,' where the soil seems to contain some ingredient unfavorable to plant growth. The areas of this sort are not large, however."[20] The condition of a particular farm also determined its value, as well as the number and type of "improvements," houses or barns, on the property. The only really valid generalization one can make is that land in the center of the cove always brought higher prices than did land on the periphery.

Time was another important variable in determining the price of land. Although there is really no discernible increase in land prices between 1830 and 1860, there is often a wide fluctuation in prices within any given decade. Economic depressions in the larger region obviously affected these prices. The pattern of emigration from the cove also played a role. Many cove residents sold out in the 1840s, to move to new lands being opened in the West, and the prices they received from such hurried sales were often far below par.[21] Large entrepreneurs, particularly Daniel D. Foute, had enough capital to buy such farms cheaply from residents emigrating to the West and hold these lands until prices increased.

If one examines Foute's numerous transactions carefully, however, there is no real evidence to indicate that in the majority of land sales he paid less than the standard rate for land in the three decades after 1830. Foute was interested in obtaining title to large holdings of mountain land for various speculative enterprises, but he also bought up large holdings of the fertile farming basin.[22] His active interest in the economic development of Cades Cove probably kept land prices up, but the community benefited from his numerous enterprises, such as building roads.

Foute's speculative ventures illuminate another important variable in the price of cove land: the shortage of specie, or cash, among the majority of cove farmers throughout the century. John Oliver said in later years that the best farm in the cove could be obtained for a milk cow in the 1820s. Specie remained scarce, however, and this scarcity kept land prices low throughout most of the century. An 1857 survey listed the total value of taxable personal property in the cove at $1,349. There is some evidence that during the Civil War land prices rose dramatically, but the explanation lies in the fact that Confederate money was used in such purchases.[23]

The real key to understanding the price of land lies in the elaborate kinship structure which developed in the cove, and in the growing sense of communal responsibility. Parents frequently deeded land to their children for a nominal fee or gratis. The common term in such deeds was "for love and affection," and this phrase appears in many transactions throughout the century. Responsible individuals often gave land for the construction of a church or other public buildings such as schools. Widows were often provided for by collective land contributions.[24]

Such transactions for charitable purposes are easily recognizable in the land deeds. More subtle exchanges involved land sales to one's kin of varying degrees of relatedness. In such transactions, the price was adjusted by the relationship of the donor and the degree of need on the part of the grantee. This transposition of the kinship structure onto land values, clearly reflected in the deeds, may seem supererogatory in strict economic terms, but it reinforces the conclusion that the cove economy was inextricably bound up in a value system which did not perceive land or commodity prices within the cove in absolute or fixed terms.[25] Land ownership usually conferred status on the individual farmer, but it was only one of many factors which determined comparative standing within the community.

On rare occasions, the community could act collectively to fix land prices. The auctioning of the extensive holdings of Foute after the Civil War was one such occasion. The community appeared *en masse* at this sale and refused to bid against one another, or to allow outsiders to bid on cove land. Consequently the land was sold for ridiculously low prices; 160 acres went for $10.00 to Dan B. Lawson, for instance, and the old Hyatt farm containing 80 acres was sold to J.C.N. Bogle for

$16.00. The really interesting part about these auctions, however, is the fact that not all the land went cheaply. Those able to pay were obliged to make a bid more comparable to the actual value of the land.[26] So the community, acting collectively, not only assured poorer cove farmers the right to bid in their land cheaply, but actually effected a gradation of land prices to fit the condition of the land and the comparative ability of the buyer to pay.

Postwar land prices remained depressed throughout the century, reflecting the larger regional depression. At the end of the century, according to Ayres and Ashe, "the best farm in the valley can be bought for $5.00 per acre," and fifty cents an acre was considered a good price for the mountain land surrounding the cove.[27] Even though units of land sold after the war contained fewer acres than did prewar farms, the price per acre was generally much lower. So given the complex variety of intervening variables, postwar land prices were not really any index to the general state of the economy, particularly in view of the increasing importance of the kinship structure.

If the Civil War drastically reduced the size and price of the average cove farm, it produced no such comparable reduction in land ownership. Actually, tenant farming was well established by 1860. According to the census of that year, 20 heads of household owned their farms, and 24 heads of household were tenants. So in 1860, 54.5 percent of the cove farmers were tenants, and only 45.5 percent owned their own land. The Civil War changed these figures only slightly. In 1870, 23 heads of household owned their own land, and 32 were tenants.[28] Thus the percentage of land owners had dropped from 45.5 percent in 1860 to 41.8 percent in 1870, and the percentage of tenants had risen from 54.5 percent to 58.2 percent. A drop of 3.7 percent in land ownership after the war is really not significant when compared to the much more drastic reduction between 1860 and 1880 in the size of cove farms.

In 1880, with a steady increase in population from 296 in 1860 to 382 in 1870 to 449 in 1880, the percentage of land owners had risen dramatically. In that year, 53 household heads owned their own land, and 23 remained tenants, an increase in number of owners from 41.8 percent in 1870 to 69.7 percent in 1880, a dramatic rise of 27.9 percent. Since regional farm prices actually declined during this period, an explanation other than the return of general prosperity must be found to account for the great reduction in tenant farming between 1870 and 1880. Part of the answer obviously lies in the drastic reduction of the size of cove farms, with almost one-third of these farms numbering ten acres or less by 1880. A more complete explanation may be found in the changing social structure of the cove population between 1850 and 1880. In 1850, there were 86 surnames in a total population of 671. By 1880, this number had dropped to 45 surnames for a total population of 449. The proportional drop in the number of surnames was 21.8 percent, and indicates that many more cove families were related to each other by 1880. Even this figure is misleading because through intermarriage most of the cove families were indirectly related in a kinship structure of varying degrees not reflected completely in the number of surnames alone.[29]

The fact that by 1880 most cove families were directly or indirectly related had tremendous implications for the economic life of the cove after the Civil War. This pattern of the extended family reinforced community ties and through close cooperation and assistance allowed the individual nuclear family to survive comfortably on a minimum amount of land. The drastic reduction between 1870 and 1880 in the proportion of cove farmers who were tenants is further explained by this expanding kinship structure. Few families would allow their relatives to remain tenants or to be without the basic necessities of life. Because of the high fertility of the soil and the assistance from their extended family, few cove families were unable to survive the general depression of agricultural prices on farms as small as ten acres or less in size.[30]

Obviously this self-sufficiency was communal, not individual, and did not obviate the continuing necessity of finding a marketable crop after the Civil War. Without some continuing demand for such products as the weak market provided after 1870, the larger family units would have faced economic ruin, and with them their many dependent relatives. So the small farmer had an indirect but nevertheless vital stake in the continuation of the market economy.[31] In selling his crops in Knoxville, the small farmer was also assured shared transportation with some of his wealthier relatives because of this close communal structure. Thus much if not most of their agricultural production continued to be marketed after the Civil War; the structure of transporting the goods, and the market demands might have been substantially altered, but the new effect was still a viable market economy.

The fact that the elaborate kinship structure controlled the economy of Cades Cove after the Civil War and did not allow, as so often happened in other sections of the South, the small farmer to fall completely into a pattern of subsistence farming is further documented by the close proximity in which many of these extended families lived. One notable example in the middle of the cove was actually named Myerstown because members of that family lived there so close to one another.[32] This geographic concentration of families added to the convenience of joint marketing ventures and other forms of collective economic cooperation. Adjacent relatives in poor circumstances might be a source of constant complaint on the part of wealthier members of a particular family, but it was equally true that such families were never allowed to starve.

The economic disadvantages of such an elaborate kinship structure were evident in the drastic reduction of new families entering the cove after the Civil War. There were other reasons, of course, for this decline in immigration, including the general postwar depression of the region. But it is also evident that after 1865 few new families, especially those with no relatives there, chose to come in and compete with the well-established kinship structure. This situation is in marked contrast to the numerous immigrants, often from foreign countries, who had entered the cove during the 1840s and 1850s.[33]

The economic decline after the Civil War determined the type as well as the extent of emigration from the cove. Prewar emigrants usually had considerably more holdings than did those leaving after 1865. During the prosperous prewar decades emigrants were in the mainstream of the Westward Movement, and often went to new lands opening up in Missouri or farther west. In contrast, postwar emigrants usually moved into neighboring communities seldom more than fifty miles away. The obvious conclusion is that postwar emigrants did not have the necessary funds, even when they sold out their holdings in the cove, to move very far.

According to John W. Oliver's mail route directory in 1904, families left Cades Cove for new homes in other parts of Tennessee, North

Carolina, Georgia, or Arkansas. These forwarding addresses clearly indicate that the pattern of emigration was still affected in the twentieth century by the poverty of the postwar decades. The development of an elaborate kinship structure might have also prevented many of these people from moving further away from the cove, but all evidence points to primarily economic limitations.[34]

The basic cereal market crops raised in the cove were corn, wheat, oats, and rye. Corn remained the most important single crop throughout the century, since it could be used for home consumption, sold directly in Knoxville, or fed to the livestock. In 1850, 33 out of 44 cove farmers in the census of that year grew corn. They produced 27,580 bushels, or 788 bushels per farmer growing corn. In 1860, all 20 farmers grew corn, producing 17,750 bushels, or 887.5 bushels per farmer. By 1880, 65 out of 76 farmers were producing 18,050 bushels, or only 277.69 bushels per farmer. Wheat, oats, and rye were grown to a lesser extent, and the pattern of production followed that of corn.[35]

Other crops produced in lesser but still marketable quantities included hay, clover seed, and other grass seed, and flax, used for home consumption as well as sold. Various garden products were sold, including peas, beans, and Irish and sweet potatoes. The cove proved to be excellent for the growth of various fruit trees, whose yield could be sold as produce or distilled into various brandies. Butter and eggs formed the staple product of exchange with the local store, but these items were also shipped to Knoxville in the fall along with other products. One family in the 1850 census reported making cheese, but the skill never became widespread in the cove, and no other census lists this product. Molasses, honey, and beeswax were produced in great quantities for sale in Knoxville. The value of forest products has been previously discussed, but it is interesting to note that by 1880, 1,411 cords of wood were produced, with the price of a cord averaging between 35 and 65 cents.[36]

Tobacco was also grown by many farmers for their own use and for sale. William Howell Oliver recalled how his father, Elijah, prepared his tobacco:

My father was a great tobacco user and would maneuver him a good patch so his tobacco would not fail. He would worm and succor it until it would get ripe. He always cut and hung his tobacco in the shade to cure, and when it was well cured he would hand it off in bunches and pack it down in large gums and pack old quilts or cloths around it so it would keep in case all winter. He then loved to set up of nights till eight, nine or ten o'clock and stem and twist tobacco . . . .

Pa had a tobacco prise a hole cut through a tree and a heavy log beam went through it. He would fill up a gum with twists and set it under his log prise and let it down on his tobacco, and then put a sled load of rocks on his beam and leave it until it be so hard when it would come out it would never get dry and crumley. This was the way he made his money. He would sell his tobacco made this way, all over the county and in N.C. He sold it at twenty-five cents per pound. He made so much of it that three twists would weigh a pound.[37]

The prewar livestock industry in the cove was larger and more prosperous than in surrounding East Tennessee counties, primarily because of the availability of extended grazing land in the mountains. In 1860 the average number of cattle per farm, for instance, was nearly four times greater in the cove than in other parts of the region. The grazing activities of most of the cove people and the accessibility of this large mountain range used by farmers throughout the area have already been discussed. It should be pointed out, however, that this section of East Tennessee was at the crossroads of an important cattle drive from the South and West before the war. According to Gray, many herders stopped in these fertile cove areas to fatten their cattle before taking them on to market in Knoxville. So the cove certainly benefited from the influx of herders from other areas of the state and larger region.[38]

From all indications, it is evident that although the cove witnessed a decline in overall population between 1850 and 1860 from 671 to 296 people, the general prosperity of the average cove farmer greatly increased during the decade. By 1880, however, the economy had declined drastically in every area, from livestock to basic cereal crops. To cite only one example, the number of horses per farm in 1850 was 2.9. That ratio had gone up to 6.1 horses per farm by 1860, but dropped drastically to 1.3 horses in 1880. All available evidence points to the great economic devastation caused by the Civil War.[39]

Unfortunately the 1870 agricultural schedule is missing from the census of that year. Other evidence, such as the deeds and legal transactions during this period, indicates that the drastic decline in the cove's economy did not suddenly occur after the war, but was rather a steady decline between the years 1865 and 1880. If this hypothesis is correct, the cove economy would be coordinated with the larger economy of East Tennessee, which followed a similar pattern.[40] In any event, the steady economic decline in the three decades after 1865 is the single most notable event in the economic history of nineteenth-century Cades Cove.

In spite of this drastic postwar decline, however, Cades Cove remained market-oriented. The total number of cattle and swine produced in 1880 compares favorably with the number being produced before the war. Cattle were certainly produced largely for market. In the fall of each year, many cove inhabitants slaughtered beef and shared it with their many neighbors and relatives. But at other times, because of the difficulty in preserving the meat, cattle were not widely used as a food supply by the inhabitants themselves. Pork was the universal meat of choice.[41]

There are numerous other examples in the 1880 census to indicate that the postwar economy still produced many items which by their very nature and quantity had to be marketed. No better illustration of this situation exists than the rapid increase in the production of sheep. By 1880, wool had become an important market product from the cove. In that year, 1,320 pounds of wool were produced, averaging 17.37 pounds per farm. In 1860 a total of 339 sheep were listed; by 1880, the total had risen to 698.[42] This increase in the number of sheep grown is directly correlated to the increase in the market demand; obviously the cove people had not increased their own use of either mutton or wool during the interval. That the cove economy could adjust, in the midst of such a great depression, to the changing market demands, is mute testimony to the continuing viability of the market economy.

Distilling became an important industry for some of the cove people who lived in the outlying regions, particularly in the area at the southwest end of the cove known as Chestnut Flats. Before the war, Julius Gregg owned a large distillery, processing apples and corn. After the war, George Powell "operated one of the most elaborate distilleries in Blount County" here, maintaining an orchard of several hundred fruit trees and manufacturing fine brandies. According to the *Maryville Index*, September 18, 1878, a revenuer raid at his place destroyed eleven tubs of beer and mash, four tubs of pomace, 130 gallons of "singlings," five bushels of meal, two bushels of rye, and two bushels of malt. Forty shots were exchanged in this encounter, but the "engineer of the mash mill" escaped unharmed. Powell's "apple wagon" was one of the most popular attractions when he came to market in Maryville during court week; "he always had choice quarters at the livery stable where he slept close to his wagon."[43]

The daily life of the average cove farmer in the nineteenth century seems from all accounts to have been one of unmitigated labor. The great fertility of the soil was always an incentive to raise a surplus of crops for the market. In addition, the impulse of their religious beliefs gave value to hard work as meritorious in itself. Most farmers spent the greater part of the day in such heavy tasks as plowing, planting, or harvesting crops, mending fences, or feeding the livestock. Even the late hours of the day were occupied in various smaller tasks, such as repairing harnesses or making shoes for the family. John W. Oliver recalled the family at work in the evening:

> Mother would card wool and spin it into yarns and weave it into cloth to clothe the family. The older children, both girls and boys, were taught to assist her in this work. I have quilled the thread for the shuttle many times while she wove it into cloth. Mother was never happier than when she was in the loom or turning the spinning wheel.
>
> At the same time, father would be busy making or mending shoes for the family. Some of the children would sometimes hold a rich pine torchlight to give more light in the house. The hot rosin would drop on our hands or toes and how we would jump! Sometimes we dropped the torch. If the torch began to get dim we would snub it on the dog irons to remove the burned coals, like snubing the ashes from a cigarette.[44]

Children were an important part of the labor force. They were trained at an early age to perform a wide variety of jobs so that the family could work together as a unit. Throughout the century, cove families were large. If married children did not move away, as was increasingly the case after the Civil War, the larger family formed an extended labor pool, to which grandchildren were eventually added. The number of children per family is difficult to determine accurately from the census records alone, since the infant mortality rate was high, and children married at an early age and established their own homes. Six to eight children per family was average; fifteen was considered large, but not unusual.[45]

Although tenant farming declined after the Civil War, some of the larger farmers continued the practice of hiring laborers for fixed periods to work on their farms. In 1880, when only eight out of seventy-six farmers hired others to work on their farms, the pay was extremely low, averaging between $2.00 and $3.00 for a week's work. Many cove farmers worked several weeks each year for these larger farmers in order to obtain extra cash before they sold their own crops in Knoxville. Not until the end of the century did sawmilling become a widespread source of additional income.[46]

For the average farmer who could not afford to hire labor during harvest or an emergency, the community responded collectively. John McCaulley outlined this collective response as he remembered it during the last decade of the nineteenth century:

> We looked after one another. If there was sickness in a family and a crop needed working, we'd all hear about it at church on Sunday.
>
> The next morning, on Monday morning, there'd be as many as 50 neighbors in that field and around that house doing up everything that had to be done.
>
> If somebody died, everybody left his own work and turned his attention to the dead person's family. There wouldn't be a single person working in those fields in the Cades Cove bottoms until the funeral was over.
>
> If a widow was left, she and her children were cared for. Everybody saw to it that they didn't want for a thing.
>
> The older folks were taken care of, too, when they couldn't work no more. Nobody went to the poorhouse.[47]

Many larger projects were undertaken through community effort. Barns were raised, houses built, and new fields were cleared by the community working together. Again the intense communal life of Cades Cove dominated the labor market, and no individual farmer ever had to face a particularly large task alone. In one sense, this system might have contributed to the low level of wages which the average farm laborer received, but in the long run it benefited everyone, since all were engaged primarily in farming.

The division of labor remained limited during the first three decades after 1818. There were individuals in the community whose skill at some particular task—cabinet-making, carpentry, coffin-making, or blacksmithing—created a demand for these specialized services. In the majority of cases, however, these men were basically farmers who practiced their trade as a sideline. Peter Cable's services were always in demand, for instance, as a carpenter or tool-maker, but he kept his farm as a basic source of income and listed his occupation in the census as a farmer.[48]

By 1850, the census recorded a variety of highly specialized trades in the cove, reflecting the growing wave of immigrants from widely divergent parts of the United States and Europe. There were five carpenters from Holland, three mechanics from England, a lawyer from Pennsylvania, a physician from New York, and a boatswain from North Carolina, in addition to the usual farmers, millers, and blacksmiths listed. By 1860, most of these people were gone, but one additional occupation was listed—that of bell-maker.[49]

The presence in 1850 of these men with specialized skills is something of a puzzle in an essentially agrarian society. The best explanation for their attraction to the cove is to be found in the extensive mining operations being undertaken there and in the surrounding mountains. Largely forgotten in the twentieth century, swarms of prospectors entered the area during the 1850s, were disappointed in their search for gold and other minerals, and moved on to other mining areas, leaving few records of their undertakings. One such mine was located on Rich Mountain between Cades Cove and Tuckaleechee Cove in a small valley inappropriately named Eldorado. Local historians have concentrated on describing the iron industry in this area, but it is evident from a letter written in 1847 by Dr. Isaac Anderson, founder of Maryville College, that other minerals—zinc, copper, tin, silver, and gold—were actively being sought.[50]

Mills were probably the single most important industry throughout the century because everyone needed to have grains, corn or wheat, ground to make bread. Dr. Jobe recalled that during the 1820s "it was two or three years before we had mills suitable to make flour; the only mills we had were little 'Tub mills' to crack corn. Father built a mill soon after we moved there, but it was seldom one saw wheat bread on any table there." In 1850 there were references to Foute's mill and Emert's mill, but in 1854 one writer complained that cove inhabitants still had to "go 15 or 20 miles to get flour fit to eat." An 1857 survey of Blount County listed two sawmills and two gristmills, valued at $450.00, in the cove.[51]

There is frequent mention of these small tub mills before 1840. Robert Shields moved from Georgia to the cove in 1835 and built a tub mill on Forge Creek two miles east of Chestnut Flats. Daniel D. Foute had built a similar structure on his farm during the early 1830s. These tub mills were evidently widely scattered throughout the cove before 1840, but they were too small to receive mention in any of the census statistics.[52]

During the 1840s, Frederick Shields, son of Robert, built the first overshot wheel structure which replaced the smaller turbine mills. This large structure housed "equipment for milling and bolting wheat flour . . . with one of the largest native stone rocks in the Smoky Mountains for grinding corn, as well as a sash saw for lumber production." The Shields Mill gave the community a much greater sense of self-sufficiency because it was no longer necessary to carry wheat to Tuckaleechee Cove to be ground. It also centralized milling, reducing the number of turbine mills in the cove. Shield's, and later Cable's, mill became a gathering place for the community.[53]

The largest mill was built by John P. Cable, a nephew of Peter, who moved to Cades Cove from Carter County in 1865 at the close of the war. He bought land and settled in the lower end of the cove near the junction of Forge and Mill Creeks. The rather elaborate nature and construction of the Cable Mill in 1868 is described by John W. Oliver:

> Soon after his arrival he began the development of water power by building a corn and wheat mill and also a saw mill. In order to get sufficient water power to pull all this machinery he dug a canal to run Forge Creek into Mill Creek just above his mill. This required quite a lot of labor because it all had to be done with pick and shovel. It also required building two dams, one on Forge Creek just below the Old Forge site to turn the water into the canal and another on Mill Creek where the canal emptied into Mill Creek. From this last dam he built a long rase or floom to carry the water to the

overshot wheel which pulled the machinery. So in time he completed his enterprise, lifted the floom gate, and turned on the water. The huge overshot wheel began to turn and his plant was set in motion. For many long years he did a thriving business. In addition to this he ran his farm and raised livestock.[54]

The first mercantile business in the cove was started in 1873 by Leason Gregg fron Johnson County, Tennessee, in a room in his dwelling house. Gregg later built a store on the Cable farm, the first store built in the cove. He bought the cove people's produce and sold them dry goods and staples, such as sugar, coffee, and salt. Once a week he took produce to Knoxville and returned with general merchandise. For most people it was an advantage to have the mill and store so close together because they could shop while their corn or wheat was being ground.[55]

Earlier, cove residents had relied upon George Snider's store in Tuckaleechee Cove as previously mentioned. During the 1840s, Daniel D. Foute at his hotel in Montvale Springs also operated a mercantile business which was patronized by the cove people. The fact that a permanent store came as late as 1873 indicates that the market economy was slowing down during the depression following the war. In earlier times farmers had made frequent trips to sell their goods in Maryville and Knoxville and had bought merchandise there, thereby making the construction of a general store in the cove largely unnecessary. In this sense, Gregg's first store in 1873 is one indication of the general retrogression of the cove economy after the war.[56]

The iron industry developed very early in Cades Cove, and references to "forge tracts" in deeds during the 1820s indicated that mineral interests had initially attracted the attention of several entrepreneurs. The first forge to begin operations in Blount County was the Cades Cove Bloomery Forge, built in 1827 by Daniel D. Foute. Earlier mining had been undertaken by William Tipton, who sold the site to Foute. The forge was located near the point where the millrace now leaves Forge Creek, and the ore was removed a mile northeast of this site. Coaling signs are still visible in the vicinity.[57]

The Cades Cove Bloomery Forge was only one of many such forges which sprang up in East Tennessee and western North Carolina during the 1820s and 1830s. The low grade ore and expense of burning charcoal for these forges made them unprofitable in the long run, and Foute's operation closed in 1847. The Foute forge was important to the cove's early economy for several reasons, however. It offered employment to many of the cove men during the years of its operation. Many farmers, under the direction of Peter Cable, made their own tools from the iron produced here. The forge was an incentive to Foute's road-building, since he needed reasonably cheap transportation to make the industry profitable. Finally the discovery of iron ore here convinced other entrepreneurs that more valuable minerals might be located in the cove or its environs.[58]

Transportation for the cove's market economy was provided by various entrepreneurs for a wide variety of reasons. Long before white settlement, the area was intertwined by numerous Indian trails which continued to be used by white settlers, particularly the Ekanetelee Gap route to North Carolina and the old Indian Grave Gap trail across Rich Mountain to Tuckaleechee Cove. Expanding these older trails into roads large enough to allow wagons to travel them was often a gradual process which required many decades.[59]

John Oliver remembered that the first wagon which crossed the Cades Cove Mountain was held by eight men with ropes on both sides. The old Laurel Creek road, which left the northeast end of the cove and went through Schoolhouse Gap into Dry Valley, was also a route which remained extremely difficult for wagon passage, requiring an extra team of horses to pull any load over the mountain. Another route which was gradually improved until it achieved the status of a road was the Rabbit Creek road, which left the extreme southwest end of the cove and had its terminus in Happy Valley.[60]

The Rabbit Creek road and the old Laurel Creek road were built without any aid from the county, and no exact date can be given to their construction, although both were in use before 1860. Neither was used for extensive commercial traffic, but both provided easy access to neighboring communities. At various times during the cove's history these roads fell into disrepair. The Rabbit Creek road was remembered as the major exit for North Carolina guerrillas herding stolen cattle and horses out of the cove.[61]

The most important road for commerce was built by Daniel D. Foute between Cades Cove and Maryville through Montvale Springs. Foute received permission to build this road, or turnpike, on January 25,

1852, from the Tennessee General Assembly. Later called the Cooper road, this route remained the main commercial egress to Knoxville and Maryville throughout the century. Foute was involved in numerous enterprises in the larger region, all of which would benefit by the construction of this road. The Cades Cove Bloomery Forge probably motivated its construction initially, although this industry had closed down by 1847. Foute envisioned other mining operations in the cove, however, which would require cheap transportation. This road also connected the resort hotel at Montvale Springs, which Foute operated between 1832 and 1850, to Cades Cove.[62]

Foute also built a road in 1852 from the cove out through Chestnut Flats in the southwest end to intersect Parson's Turnpike to North Carolina. This road aided farmers in taking corn to Julius Gregg's distillery in Chestnut Flats, but never became a major commercial artery into North Carolina. Road-building was extremely difficult in western North Carolina because of the terrain; the rivers were unnavigable, and little commercial development existed to lure cove farmers there over high mountains. In contrast, the Cooper road followed an easy grade forty miles to Knoxville, the major commercial center of upper East Tennessee throughout the century.[63]

Attempts to build roads across the Great Smoky Mountains were made for other than commercial reasons. One such venture was undertaken during the 1840s by Dr. Isaac Anderson. This route passed through Schoolhouse Gap out of Tuckaleechee Cove, and around Boat Mountain. According to his biographer, Dr. Anderson undertook this construction "with a view to increased means of carrying forward his project of educating young men for the ministry," since this route would open the back country to missionaries. The road was also intended to assist the Cherokees, who furnished the labor for its construction. Dr. Anderson paid the Cherokees working on his road in calico; each Indian received one yard of calico for a day's work. Only the Tennessee portion of this road was completed, "due to the energy with which Dr. A. pushed forward the work." This Anderson road, which approached the head of Cades Cove, was built "in the expectation that a road from the mouth of Chambers creek, below Bushnel, would be built over into the Hazel creek settlement, and thence up the Foster ridge and through the Haw gap to meet it." Unfortunately North Carolina failed to do its part, and the Anderson road was finally abandoned.[64]

With five roads out of the cove by 1860, including the Foute road to Knoxville and Maryville which gave the cove people easy access to regional markets for their crops and livestock, it is not surprising that the technological development of the cove, particularly in farm machinery, kept pace with the rest of Blount County. The boom period in obtaining modern farm equipment evidently occurred during the 1850s, although most farmers gradually recovered in the three decades after the Civil War and by 1890 were able to afford new equipment coming on the market. At mid-century, the total value of farm implements and machinery was listed as being $3,119, or $55.69 worth of equipment per farm. By 1860, the value of farm machinery had risen to $5,345, despite the drastic reduction in population, and the worth of equipment per farm averaged $267.25. Two decades later, the value of farm machinery had dropped to $2,306, averaging $30.34 worth of equipment per farm.[65]

Yet despite the drop in the value of farm machinery after the war, there were always many farmers who could afford the newest equipment. Again, the communal, or collective, nature of the cove economy determined that such equipment would be shared by a wide variety of poorer friends and relatives. An excellent example of this sort of sharing was the telephone station which Dan Lawson constructed during the 1890s. The wealthiest man in the cove at that time, he organized several of his neighbors to construct a phone line across the mountains to Maryville. Several homes had phones, and the phone at Lawson's store was available to everyone in the cove. Another excellent example of this collective activity was the graded road built in 1890 across Rich Mountain by volunteer labor from the cove and county funds.[66]

The cove's leading businessman, Daniel D. Foute, also served as clerk of the circuit court of Blount County from 1822 until 1836, and was in an excellent position to learn of any new land being offered for sale. He built the main road from Cades Cove to Maryville in the 1850s, and had opened the cove's first industry, his Bloomery Forge, in 1827. Engaged in a wide variety of business ventures and speculations, many of them connected with the cove, Foute was interested in the mineral wealth of the surrounding mountains, and in developing agriculture in the cove by introducing new fruit trees and experimental crops. His purchase of large tracts of land in the cove and surrounding mountains made him a preeminent land speculator both in Blount County and in the larger region.[67]

After Foute decided to build his home, "Paradise Lost," in the cove in 1849, this energetic and capable man apparently transferred his main interest to the community. The following year he sold his interests in the resort hotel at Montvale Springs and seemed to concentrate his efforts on buying up land in the cove and surrounding region until the Civil War. Although he remained a man of comparative sophistication and wide vision, Foute took an active interest in the community and was willing to help any of the cove people with a variety of civic problems. He served as justice of the peace and acted as legal adviser to the community. His adherence to the Confederate cause during the war ran counter to the political beliefs of most of the cove inhabitants. Yet even the bitterness ensuing from this conflict did not completely destroy the respect and esteem in which he was held by the community. It is important to point out that his death, resulting from being dragged by Federal troops from his sick-bed in the cove to Knoxville in 1865, was caused by his alienation from prominent East Tennessee Unionists, such as his former friend Parson Brownlow, not by any hostile act on the part of the people of Cades Cove.[68]

A leader of less importance was Dr. Calvin Post, a physician and mineralogist who came to the cove in 1846 from Elmira, New York. Dr. Post was crippled by an accident en route when the steamboat which he was aboard exploded on the Mississippi River, killing one of his brothers who was accompanying him. Recovering from this accident at the home of William Thompson in Maryville, he married one of the daughters of his host, Martha Wallace Thompson, in the autumn of 1846. Shortly thereafter, they moved to the cove, where Dr. Post established his home, "Laurel Springs." This home was "a kind of botanical garden," or "horticultural Eden," according to his granddaughter. It contained beautiful native trees and flowers, "acres in vegetable gardens and other acres in fruit trees," and was surrounded by "crystal-clear brooks and creeks."[69]

Although he was interested in a wide variety of scientific phenomena ranging from astronomy to geology, Dr. Post's primary interest in the cove was exploring and exploiting its mineral wealth. He represented New York mineral companies, and his correspondence is filled with pleas to get capital investment into the cove. His Notebook for 1849 reveals a knowledge of geology and mineralogy that is surprising for nineteenth-century America; whether he obtained his medical and scientific training in Holland, as his family believes, has not been verified. At any rate, Dr. Post was certainly the first scientist comprehensively to study and chart the geologic structure of the cove and its environs.[70]

From his numerous descriptions of hidden veins in the cove's geologic structure, it is apparent that Post believed that the area contained rich deposits of gold and silver. Earlier he had visited Dahlonega, Georgia, during the gold rush there, and was familiar with techniques for mining gold. He was interested, of course, in other minerals such as copper and iron, and his correspondence with his New York investors reveals a cost-analysis approach to mining in the cove. He argued, for instance, that even if gold or silver were not found, the cost of mining would be recovered by an abundance of less valuable minerals there. As a physician, he asserted that the vein waters from these mines "will in the healing art be much prized when proved and recommended by the scientific profession in dispepsical and liver diseases." "This much abused vein," he concluded, "will in time give great employment to laborers and wealth to the owners."[71]

He also theorized that the Balds were caused by "an immense vein of arsenical copper ore," which if traced would lead to "deposits of gold and copper."[72] Dr. Post never discovered gold in the cove, but his presence there until his death in 1873 furnished the inhabitants with an excellent physician.

The only individual who approached the status of an entrepreneur in the cove after the Civil War was Dan Lawson, who married the only daughter of Peter Cable, took over the Cable farm after the older man's death in 1866, and expanded it into one of the largest holdings in the cove. These holdings "extended from mountain top to mountain top, one-half mile wide, across the center of the valley." Although Lawson had a general store and operated the post office for many years, he never had the wealth, know-how, or vision significantly to expand the economy of the cove as Foute had done.[73]

One scholar has written that the years before the Civil War were the "Golden Age" of Tennessee agriculture, and that the next fifty years after the war were spent in trying to recover progress which had been made during the booming years of the 1840s and 1850s. The cove certainly followed this larger regional pattern in its economic growth, whether judged by the number of new settlers entering the area after 1865, the value of land and farm machinery, or the size of cove farms. In comparative terms, the average cove farmer closely fits the description of Blanche Henry Clark's yeoman farmer in East Tennessee between 1840 and 1860. If cove farmers could buy such a wide variety of goods from George Snider's store in Tuckaleechee Cove in the decade after the war, however, they still maintained their status as yeoman with a tenuous, yet still very viable, relationship to the regional market economy.[74]

Perhaps David M. Potter's thesis that economic abundance had a pervasive influence in shaping the American character applied directly to the nineteenth-century market economy of Cades Cove. The fertility of the cove soil which allowed such an economy to develop tied the people closely to regional markets, and through these markets, to the broad mainstreams of American political and social culture throughout the century. Without this prosperity, Cades Cove would have been no different in its development from patterns of poverty which characterized other sections of Southern Appalachia.

Entrepreneurs such as Daniel D. Foute and Dr. Calvin Post had great schemes for the cove's economic development before the Civil War, and their expectations and wide-ranging interests clearly identified them as a type of American businessman common in all sections of the country at mid-century. Even the economic devastation during the war and the depression afterward did not alter the cove's market orientation to the larger region. When this larger region began to show signs of recovery after 1900, the cove's economy would respond accordingly.

Cades Cove remained a small cog within the larger region's intricate patterns of trade, but this cog accurately reflected, during any given period, the condition of the larger machinery. How cove farmers imbibed political and social ideas as they sold their products in Knoxville and Maryville will be examined in later chapters. If larger regions in the country were influenced in their political thinking by conditions in the national market economy, however, it is logical to suppose that smaller areas such as the cove were similarly affected by current trends in such regional market places as Knoxville.

When cove farmers adjusted to the regional depression after the Civil War, they effected certain changes in the internal society and economy of the cove which were entirely indigenous. The geographic isolation combined with the regional depression and the developing kinship structure resulted in an intense communal life style which determined internal economic distribution of goods and labor. In this sense, the postwar economy of the cove reflected a basic dichotomy. Outwardly market-oriented, internally they made every effort to distribute all the necessary components of life to needy friends and relatives. Whether this sort of communal life style could have developed in a less fertile area is open to question. But the result was so far-reaching that any examination of the cove's economic life must be focused within this much larger, and far more significant, sense of community which dominated all aspects of the average cove farmer's life throughout the nineteenth century.

John Cable's mill, 1934. *Oliver Family Collection.*

Above, little house near Cable's mill, built for people to keep warm in while they were waiting for their corn to be ground (late 1920s). *Below,* "The remains of the old Frederick Shields corn mill which had stood for over 60 years before the park began its destruction" (John W. Oliver's inscription, early 1930s). *Oliver Family Collection*

A group of tourists staying at Oliver's Lodge in late 1920s, en route to camping trip in the mountains which Oliver regularly organized. *Oliver Family Collection.*

Oliver's Lodge Very Popular

Cades Cove—James Trent, Sr., Mayor of Knoxville with a large party of young people spent this week-end Feb 1, 2 at Oliver's Lodge in Cades Cove, although the roads were at their worst. The beautiful mountains all wrapped in their blanket of white and the comfortable and commodious cabin made it a most delightful affair.

Mrs. Oliver, proprietor of the Lodge, is predicting this to be the greatest year in the history of her lodge. Her place was visited last season by northern people, several of whom went back home and gave the Cove and Oliver's Lodge a write up in many of their magazines.

She is receiving many inquiries from northern neighbors, relative to accommodations this summer.

Maryville Times clipping.

Above, John W. Oliver delivering mail in the cove in the late 1920s. *Below,* John W. Oliver at the Cades Cove ballot box, late 1920s. *Oliver Family Collection.*

Above, students and teachers before the consolidated school in the 1920s. At the time of construction in 1915, the *Maryville Times* called this school building the most modern in Blount County. *Below,* baptism by Cades Cove Primitive Baptist Church, late 1920s. *Oliver Family Collection.*

State of Tennessee; the primitive Baptist Church
Blount County of christ in Cades Cove now in
Session Sendth greeting to her belove Sister in arans
Cove of the primitive order dear Sister in gospel Bonds
we wish you to Send us your ministerial aid to assist
us at a Sacrament meeting to commence on friday before
the third Saturday in November 1847
done by order of the Church the third saturday in august
1847

An 1847 request for a minister from the Cades Cove Primitive Baptist Church.
Frequent visits from ministers in other churches were common and were
usually accompanied by visits from the laity in other churches.

The primitive Baptist church
of christ in Caades Cove now
in session dus heare by certify that
our beloved Alexander White
is in full fellowship with us
and is hedrby dismissed from us
when joined to another church
of the same faith and order
Done in Church conference
December the 22nd 1888

Andrew Gregory Mo
Elijah Oliver Clerk

Church members in good standing were given letters when they left Cades
Cove. Similarly, new members moving into the cove could be accepted if they
brought church letters from the same denomination at their previous location.
Oliver Family Collection.

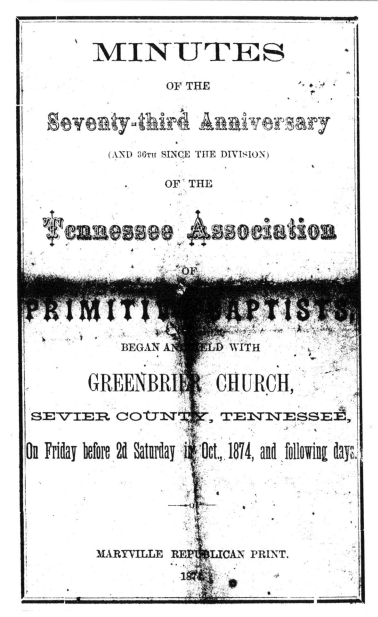

MINUTES

OF THE

Seventy-third Anniversary

(AND 36TH SINCE THE DIVISION)

OF THE

Tennessee Association

OF

PRIMITIVE BAPTISTS

BEGAN AND HELD WITH

GREENBRIER CHURCH,

SEVIER COUNTY, TENNESSEE,

On Friday before 2d Saturday in Oct., 1874, and following days.

MARYVILLE REPUBLICAN PRINT.

1874.

Printed minutes of the 1874 Tennessee Association of Primitive Baptists, meeting that year at Greenbrier Church in Sevier County, indicate the careful record kept of church activities. *Oliver Family Collection.*

Funeral at the Primitive Baptist Church, late 1920s. *Oliver Family Collection.*

4
Religion and the Churches

The dominant role of religion in the life of the average citizen of Cades Cove during the nineteenth century is evident from the large number of surviving documents and records relating to church activities. These records reveal an active and often absorbing inquiry throughout the century into religious questions which have a timeless quality about them. It is as though the problems, disputes, decisions, and organization of the church were being conducted in complete isolation from the many social and economic trends which characterized any given decade. Although the Civil War had a dramatic impact on the economic and social life of Cades Cove, this great conflict had only a temporary effect on the internal life of the church. Of much greater importance was the debate over missions during the late 1830s; the war was only a footnote, albeit an important one, in the totality of church history.

The Baptist church, its ideas and doctrine, represented a kind of "invisible government" monitoring the lives of cove dwellers almost from the beginning of the community. Yet the whole question of religion is surrounded with complicated and seemingly irreconcilable contradictions. Determined in principle to remain separated and completely distinct from the civil government, the church nevertheless became so inextricably bound up in deciding crucial questions involving the local autonomy and moral leadership in the community that it was embroiled in what became a political dispute during the Civil War and was forced on that account to end its meetings for the duration of the war.

After 1840, the Primitive Baptist church tried to isolate itself from the corrupting influences of the great changes in religious doctrine which were occurring among Baptists in other sections of the country. But the very act of trying to freeze their theology, to preserve the purity of their doctrine, caused them to confront other questions and debate issues in a dialectical process which led them almost against their will toward the formulation of new answers. This overriding impulse to keep their doctrinal purity led in turn to an amazing variety of smaller divisions and dissensions within the church toward the end of the century. Finally, although the church imposed its behavioral standards on most of the community, only a small part of the total cove population ever obtained membership.

Religion was introduced to the cove at an early date by the first settlers, John and Lucretia Oliver. Although neither of them had belonged to a church in Carter County, it is evident from the following passage from their grandson's sketches that both John and Lucretia were early exposed to some form of proselytism:

> After being married some few years, my Grandfather got under convictions for his sins and felt that he was not prepared to die and go unto Judgement. So he became wonderfully alarmed, day and night, he would get up of nights, and go out to pray. Granma said that one night he was out so much that she could not sleep and she thought he was going crazy. So she gets up and started to go around the house to look for him to tell him what she thought of such, and she said that as she went around the house, that she met him rejoicing in God his Savior, he told her that he had found the Lord and was happy, and that he wanted her to seek the Lord and be happy too and throwed his arms around her. She said that she fell to the ground and instead of telling him what she thought of such crazy spells, that she became crazy herself. She said that she never had any more rest untill she found the Lord herself. Thus they were both happy in the Lord. This was about the year 1819 or 20. It was not long after they came to this place, Cades Cove.[1]

In contrast to the indifference of many of their pioneer contemporaries to religion, the early efforts of the Olivers to obtain a religious organization in the cove are surprising, especially when one considers the many obstacles and greater problems involved in their initial settlement. Bishop Francis Asbury had earlier expressed the opinion that "it is as hard or harder for the people of the West to gain religion as any others," in view of the great difficulties and distractions of frontier life.[2] In this regard, the Olivers' success during the early 1820s in obtaining formal religious services in the cove placed a distinctive stamp on the community in its infancy.

Religion, as Asbury pessimistically pointed out, frequently seemed the antithesis of the usual style of frontier life in other areas of the Old Southwest. Small log cabins often housed families of ten or twelve, who lived in a tumbled filthy atmosphere. One writer argued that "scenes of bloodshed and partisan animosity" were common occurrences. Although Bishop Asbury saw these problems almost entirely from his own sectarian frame of reference, he was not blind to the practical effects of religion in preventing social disorder. Violence or bloodshed were anti-social acts committed not only against God, he concluded, but to the detriment of the entire community.[3]

In this sense the early development of religious institutions in the cove may have prevented a period of anti-social individualism which characterized the contemporary frontier development of other communities in the larger region. Writers other than Asbury had long observed a direct connection between the lawlessness of frontier life and the distance of these isolated communities from more settled regions of the country. Judged by these standards alone, the cove because of its relative isolation might well have produced frontiersmen such as those Asbury so vividly described as poor creatures "but one remove from savages themselves."[4]

Despite the practical benefits of religion to their community, the Olivers evidently labored in vain to obtain a church in the cove during the early 1820s. By the middle of the decade, however, they had succeeded in getting enough members to warrant holding services under the auspices of the Miller's Cove Baptist church in a neighboring community. The first reference to the cove in the Miller's Cove church records occurred on March 5, 1825:

> Brother Davis request the Church to visit in Church order in Cades Cove to receive members and the Church agree to go and set to wait on and appoint the Fourth Saterday of this Instant and appoint Brethern Augusteen Bowers, James Taylor, Wm. Blair, James Williams, Richard Williams, George

Snider, Wm. McKey, Isaac Russell and two of them to site on a Church with members thats is there and so Dismist to First Saterday in Aprile at Meeting House.[5]

"In church order" meant that the presbytery from Miller's Cove was authorized to conduct church business in the cove. Numerous references in the following months indicated the Cades Cove members wanted to expand their membership. "Received a letter from Cades Cove for us to appoint a Church meeting among them in order to receive members" is a reference on May 6, 1825, which aptly characterizes this exchange of correspondence. On June 11, 1825, Lucretia Oliver joined the church, which now called itself the "Church of Christ of Miller's Cove in Cades Cove."[6]

The colonizing process of the Miller's Cove Baptist church revealed a number of interesting features about the basic organization of these churches and their relationship to one another. No single principle characterized them more accurately than the idea of local autonomy. Each Baptist church insisted on complete independence and freedom of action, and no challenge caused greater anger and theological denunciation among them than the slightest questioning of their independence. Yet they moved with great deliberation toward authorizing any of their members to establish a separate church with the same freedoms, although the distance and geographic isolation of the Cades Cove group obviously justified such a move.

Finally satisfied with the orthodoxy of the Cades Cove group, or perhaps merely weary of their importunings, the Miller's Cove church recorded on November 3, 1826, that "the members belonging to this church who live in Cades Cove have petitioned for letters of dismission and it is granted." Although they remained on good terms with the Miller's Cove church, the Cades Cove group obtained their letters of dismission in order to establish themselves as a branch of the Wear's Cove Baptist church. No explanation is offered for the change, but in practice the Wear's Cove church proved to be more lenient in authorizing steps toward complete independence.[7]

The group that constituted the formal establishment of the "Cades Cove Arm of the Wear's Cove Church" on June 16, 1827, was small in number. Ten people, including Richard Davis, the pastor, and his brother

William, the clerk, were the charter members. In addition to John and Lucretia Oliver, the other members were James Oliver (a brother), James Johnson and his wife Emily, Christopher Winters, Edward James, and John Lacy. John Oliver purchased the church book for $1.50, and the first meeting on June 16, 1827, was duly recorded.[8]

Complete independence came on June 19, 1829, when the "Arm of the Wear's Cove Church in Cades Cove" finally became a separate entity, the Cades Cove Baptist church. A presbytery "called for came forward for the purpose of constituting a church in Cades Cove, viz., Brother Thomas Hill and Brother Augustine Bowers, and after the necessary examination they on the 20th instance pronounced them a Church." The presbytery from the Wear's Cove church evidently felt it was necessary to subject the Cades Cove members to the most rigorous examination before they finally conceded their orthodoxy.[9]

Although small in membership throughout the century, this oldest established church in Cades Cove continued to dominate the social and cultural mores of the community and, in a very real sense, to determine the fabric of the developing community. Other churches will be discussed later, but the internal life of the Baptist church is illuminating for many reasons. The important battles were all theological disputes, with the possible exception of the debate over the Civil War. A careful examination of these theological disputes, however, will answer basic questions about the source of their religious socialization, to what extent it was only isolated localism, or whether it reflected regional and national patterns.[10]

The Cades Cove church in 1829 was still very much in the mainstream of Baptist theology in Tennessee and the larger region. Essentially Calvinistic, they shared with other Baptists an abhorrence of infant baptism, and an insistence on complete separation of church and state. The basic tenets of their theology had long been established; they would have felt completely at home with the London Confession of Faith of 1644 or its American restatement in 1742 as the Philadelphia Confession of Faith which affirmed the Baptists' belief in the doctrine of particular election and the baptism by immersion of believers only.[11]

To recapitulate in minute detail the doctrines or theology of the Cades Cove church would be repetitious, since these beliefs have been carefully enumerated by other scholars.[12] There are certain basic ideas, however, which early shaped the development of the cove church and later determined its response to new movements within the church. These ideas were succinctly outlined by W.H. Oliver, pastor of the church from 1882 until his death in 1940:

> It is well known that Primitive Baptist believe the doctrine of Church succession that the church first organized by Christ has existed in all ages of the world to the present, and we claim to be in that succession, the oldest Baptist church in America was planted by Dr. John Clark before Roger Williams was baptized . . . . The new testament contains all that entered into the faith and practice of the apostelic churches. It is the only revealed record of Christian truth. It covers all they had. The church of the first century forms the standard and example for the church of all future ages. We Baptist claim that from the time of its organization on earth, it has stood distinct and visible untill the present time . . . . We believe that Jesus Christ himself instituted the Church, that it was perfect at the start, suitably adopted in its organization to every age of the world, to every locality of earth, to every state and condition of the world, to every state and condition of mankind, without any changes or alterations to suit the times, customs, situations, or localities. The old church of God has never tolerated any innovations of men.[13]

From this quotation it is evident that these Baptists believed their doctrines represented a revealed truth which was fixed for all time. Such an attitude logically made the church conservative because any later innovation would in this frame of reference be contrary to their basic doctrine of revealed truth. Yet it was to be admitted that men in their fallible state might occasionally mistake or misinterpret the truth.

In such circumstances, the only reliable guide was the Bible, the revealed word of God, and for this reason, they insisted on literally following the scriptures and ordering their church polity as closely as possible to scriptural injunctions. The phrase "thus saith the Lord" was a powerful expression among them, and they were prone to try everything by the scriptures. It logically followed that any institution or practice which was not specifically mentioned in the scriptures was an erroneous, temporal improvisation of man. Such innovations they were bound by the nature of their theology to denounce under the common opprobrium of "institutions of the day."[14]

Maintaining their doctrinal purity according to the scriptures was too great a task for any one individual. In the Cades Cove church, the functional unit organized for this purpose consisted of all the church members who obtained their standing through the long and difficult process of the conversion experience. Baptist churches are often termed democratic, but that concept has only limited application to the real mechanism of control, which was the group. Operating within a consensus mechanism, each new idea presented to the church had to be approved by the majority of the church members, that small number which constituted the visible saints.[15]

It is probably within this church consensus that the sense of community for the larger area of Cades Cove developed. The majority of church members had absolute control over all functions of the church; their pastor maintained his position not by appeals to new ideas or doctrines, but by seeming to confirm the old truths of what they already believed. The Cades Cove church was characteristic of other Baptist churches of their generation, inasmuch as they had a very acute knowledge of Baptist history and an awareness of their own role in its unfolding process. This awareness explains in part their intense sense of accountability, and their insistence that extraordinary caution be taken in preserving the church book, their written record of the church's earthly transactions.[16]

The local group knew, for instance, that much if not most of their former troubles and persecutions stemmed from efforts on the part of outside ecclesiastical or civil authorities to dominate or destroy their local autonomy. Even in the new world, Baptists had undergone bitter persecutions, particularly from the established Anglican Church in Virginia before the Revolution. This consciousness of past persecutions added a touch of paranoia to the church group in Cades Cove which lasted throughout the century. It made them more determined than ever to avoid any vestige of ecclesiastical form or hierarchal structure which threatened to wrestle control of their church from the local congregation.[17]

Under these circumstances, the role of their pastor quite naturally was severely limited and circumscribed. After the Revolutionary War, the fear developed in Virginia and other Southern states that an educated ministry would be conducive to building up a strong and aggressive ecclesiastical hierarchy. "When once our ministry becomes educated," Virginia Baptists argued, "we will become an ecclesiasticism like our persecutors, and lose the simplicity vouchsafed to the churches of Jesus Christ." No lesser a personage than Patrick Henry had argued against any hierarchy or delegation of powers which would remove control from the local church. "Down with anything," Henry argued and Baptists everywhere agreed, "which would tend to make us like our persecutors."[18]

According to this line of thought, paid or salaried preachers were an anathema to the early Baptists, because a salary represented both a tendency toward an ecclesiastical structure contrary to the early church practices and an unhealthy independence on the part of the pastor. Their preachers were "raised up" from among the congregation. A person thus compelled to preach was allowed to exercise his "gifts"; if the entire congregation approved these "gifts," he was then subjected to a rigid examination by a presbytery of other ministers which led ultimately to ordination.[19]

Ordination in itself was no guarantee that a preacher would continue in this role indefinitely. If he veered from the path of orthodoxy, or seemed weak and ineffectual as a preacher, the congregation could vote to deny the right to continue exercising his "gift" in the pulpit. The essential point throughout the entire process whereby an individual became minister is that at no stage did his status escape absolute control by the congregation. His continuance depended on a consensus of approval by the majority; if this approval ended, or was compromised, his usefulness among them was at an end.[20]

Although a minister was not paid a regular salary, church members felt constrained from time to time to contribute various articles to his support. But none of the ministers in the Cades Cove church throughout the century were able to manage without an outside occupation. In this regard, the life of the minister was particularly difficult. In addition to his regular church duties, which were never few or easy, he was obliged to work during the week. His behavior and performance were under the constant critical scrutiny of his entire congregation which placed little value on individual privacy. One of the cove ministers, William Brickey, succinctly stated the problem in the 1894 association minutes:

What shall the minister do? If he does not support his family the church does not want to hear him preach, if he neglect the churches they will suffer for the preaching of the word, if he neglect his family they will suffer for a temporal support, so the minister finds himself between two scorching fires. 'Woe is unto me if I preach not the gospel!' 'Woe is unto me if I provide not for my own family!' What shall the ministers do? What shall the churches do?[21]

Given the difficulty of their position, it is surprising that the tenure of the Cades Cove Baptist church's ministers lasted as long as it did. Richard Davis, chosen as the first pastor for the church at its initial meeting on June 16, 1827, had been a very active preacher in the Wear's Cove, Tuckaleechee Cove, and Miller's Cove Baptist churches from the first decade of the nineteenth century. He and his brother, William, who served as clerk, removed to Walker County, Georgia, in 1839 in the general migration to the newly opened lands of the Cherokee Nation.[22]

Other ministers in the Tennessee Association assisted the Cades Cove church in its early years but were never actually pastors there. The significance of their names lies in the fact that not one of these eleven men left the older church when the break among Baptists over missions occurred in 1838. The Cades Cove church was thus influenced in its formative years by the most orthodox clergymen in the old Tennessee Association, and this influence would determine to a large extent the conservative course of the church throughout the century.[23]

After an interim during which visiting preachers officiated, Johnson Adams became pastor in 1833, continuing in this capacity until he was removed from office August 16, 1845, for joining the Missionary Baptist church. Rumblings against Adams appeared as early as October 21, 1837, when he was accused of "deviating from the draft of doctrine he used to preach." The following day, Adams temporarily assuaged criticism by submitting a "summary of the principles of doctrine" which he adhered to in his preaching. Further deviations, however, led to his final dismissal, a step which the church appeared reluctantly and painfully forced to take.[24]

Various members of the church acted as moderator, or pastor, from 1845 until the Civil War, including John Chambers and John Oliver, both of whom were deacons. Ace Delosur and Humphrey Mount from

Stock Creek Primitive Baptist church were the moderators most frequently called during this period. Absalom Abbott was ordained minister May 17, 1856. After the war, Jackson B.J. Brickey was chosen pastor of the church on October 28, 1871, and continued in this capacity throughout the remainder of the century. Remembered by the church as the most able minister of the nineteenth century, he proved to be an excellent debator when defending his denomination's beliefs against the doctrines of other churches. W.H. Oliver was ordained minister on August 27, 1882, and served in this capacity until his death in 1940.[25]

The size of Oliver's presbytery — six men — underlined the growing trend in the years after 1870 toward a collective ministery, although this practice is nowhere explicitly stated. Ordained ministers had always been exchanged by churches within the association, and after 1880, the Cades Cove church had many preachers who officiated either at the home church or elsewhere. Elders William and Jackson B.J. Brickey, William H. Oliver, W.A. Gregory, John and James Abbott, Giles P. Dunn, John H. Brickey, and G.P. Adams served the Tennessee Association of Primitive Baptist during the last two decades of the century.[26]

Many church members aspired to preach but were unacceptable to the congregation. The old church book contains numerous examples of men who were "liberated to exercise their gifts in public," but who failed eventually to be ordained. Occasionally the church limited the area of this type of practice preaching to either the home church or a few neighboring churches. At any rate, the congregation kept close control over its ministers in each stage of their development. The trend toward a collective ministry at the end of the century was perhaps another unofficial measure to assure orthodoxy, since the rivalry which ensued among the ministers gave the congregation even greater power over the selection and continuance of their pastor. Even these preachers were only a small percentage of the total number of men who aspired to the ministry but were never approved by the congregation.[27] Power was given grudgingly, and a minister, even after achieving his position as one of the chosen few, could at any point be removed from the pulpit.

Although the pastor nominally held the most important position in the church organization, in reality the role of the church clerk was far more significant. The clerk was elected to his position, as was the pastor, by the entire congregation, but usually held his position for much longer periods of time. The clerk was entrusted with all the church correspondence—letters of dismission, requests for pastoral assistance, and communications regarding association meetings. Although ostensibly acting only to carry out the wishes of the congregation, most clerks in the Cades Cove church managed to place the stamp (however unconsciously) of their own personalities and viewpoints on this correspondence.[28]

By far his most important function was keeping the church book current. Every month a business meeting was conducted in which the pastor served as moderator and the clerk recorded all official business in this book—new members, exclusions, and occasionally a restatement of the church doctrine or articles of faith. Extraordinary significance was attached to this record. Only the most orthodox and faithful member could be entrusted with such a responsibility.[29]

There is a remarkable sense of historicity in the Primitive Baptist church book which makes it the single most important contemporary manuscript source for the nineteenth century. The various clerks seemed well aware of their relative position in the course of Baptist history, and the church book reflects this intense sense of accountability. Great pains were taken carefully to explain and justify every action of the church. In any dispute within the church, both sides immediately sought possession of this record, since it alone gave legitimacy.[30] Although they would have rejected the theological implications involved in any comparison, the church book in reality functioned as their ark of the covenant.

There were only three regularly appointed clerks during the nineteenth century. William Davis, brother of Richard, served as the first clerk from the organization of the church in 1827 until he removed to Walker County, Georgia, in 1839. During the next four years, various members acted as clerk pro tempore. On September 15, 1838, Peter Cable was appointed clerk and served until his death on January 27, 1866. Elijah Oliver, son of John and Lucretia, was appointed clerk on August 19, 1867, and served for thirty-seven years until his death on February 22, 1905.[31]

Meeting only once a month, usually on the fourth Saturday and following Sunday, the congregation collectively assumed responsibility for church discipline. The causes of expulsion from the church are numerous and reflect the heavy emphasis placed on pietistic living. Members might be excluded for nonattendance at the regular monthly meetings, for joining another denomination, or for failing to observe some form of the church rules of decorum. The church book was always explicit about the excommunicant's particular failure. Elizabeth Slaughter was charged with adultery and excluded on April 19, 1834; Butler Tipton was excluded on March 21, 1884, for "betting and shooting"; Rachel McCauley was excluded on the same day for failure to be baptised.[32]

These exclusions, and many others too numerous to cite, reveal a careful scrutiny kept on the community by the entire congregation. In the Baptist church every member assumed these duties and did not rely on church officials to keep an eye on the flock, as did the Methodists. There were, however, certain procedural guarantees against being falsely accused. Any member of the church might bring a particular charge against another member, or charges might be introduced against a member whose offense was exposed through "public clamor."[33]

The church then, according to scriptural injunctions, voted to send an elder or deacon to confront the offending member and request him to answer the charges before the entire congregation. The accused could either deny the charges (which was rarely successful) or acknowledge his fault and ask the church's forgiveness. While the congregation invariably voted to exclude anyone who ignored such notification, they were always indulgent in forgiving a repentant sinner who thus "made his acknowledgments." The most common sin was drinking; the Baptist remained strongly opposed to alcoholic consumption throughout the century.[34]

The total number of active members was never large in the Primitive Baptist church, although membership greatly increased in proportion to the total population after the Civil War and was always far greater than that of any other denomination in the cove. In 1881, for instance, there were 52 members out of a total population of 449.[35] The average size of the congregation between 1879 and 1900 was 84 members. These membership figures are meaningless, however, since they give no real indication of either the actual size of church attendance or the influence of the church throughout the community, and it is within the context of this larger consensus mechanism that the real significance and power of the Primitive Baptists must be understood.

This larger mechanism of the church's influence within the community is extremely complex and difficult to analyze because of the many apparent contradictions. Although difficult to obtain, church membership was open to anyone, and the congregation remained intentionally classless; political power or wealth could not gain influence over the basically proletarian group. Neither of the entrepreneurs, Daniel D. Foute or Dr. Calvin Post, ever joined the Baptists; they remained Presbyterian. As has been previously discussed, the structure and theology of the Baptists kept the power of any individual, even the pastor, in close check.[36]

The church nevertheless sought through moral persuasion to control the mores and attitudes of the community. The larger community acquiesced in this control because it came essentially from a broadly-based group consensus within the church, and was not dictated by one individual, or even by the Baptist sectarian theology, but rather by the attitudes and behavior of the entire congregation. It is a well-known fact that a small, highly motivated and organized group can effectively control a larger, disorganized group. As such, the Baptists had the added advantage of appealing to religious values and associations already held by the larger community, regardless of whether they were members of the church or even attended.[37]

The net result of the church structure was that the Primitive Baptists held far more power over the community than either the civil authorities, political parties, or the prominent entrepreneurs. Not that the church ever sought such political power; complete separation of church and state was one of the oldest Baptist tenets. But the potential power remained great throughout the century, and decisions about whether to use this power were made in almost complete independence from any extraneous interference. This potential political power and independence of action within the church are two key factors in understanding how the community reacted to various crises such as the Civil War.[38]

The Baptists constructed a meeting house in 1832 which was built of logs and "was very crude in construction." Up until that time, they had met in the school house or in private homes, occasionally holding services at night. In 1836 one of the cove's early leaders, William Tipton, deeded to "John Oliver and Peter Cable agents for the Baptist Church" a tract of land including "a half acre of land the place where the Baptist meeting house now stands" for "the use of publick worship forever." The Primitive Baptist church constructed a more modern building on this site in 1887 to replace the older log structure.[39]

The great Baptist division known as the Anti-mission Split occurred in East Tennessee between the years 1825 and 1845, reaching a climax in 1837–1838. The bitterness with which the issue was debated is clearly reflected in the "tongue-lashing evidences of white-hot feeling" in the 1830–1840 issues of the *Baptist,* a church periodical published in Nashville. Lawrence Edwards cites three basic reasons why some Baptists reacted so vigorously against organized missionary activity by the church: the uneducated condition of the masses of Baptists, the emphasis placed upon the hyper-Calvinistic view of the scriptures by an illiterate ministry, and the "activity of a very strange and powerful personality, Daniel Parker."[40]

The Cades Cove church is an excellent weathervane for analyzing the dispute at the local level and testing Edwards' hypotheses because the issue there was bitterly debated and led to an angry split or division among the congregation. On September 15, 1838, the church book records a growing debate among members over missions, the Baptist church convention, Sunday schools, and temperance societies, all of which were denounced by the conservative members as being "institutions of the day" without scriptural authorization.[41]

When the dispute appeared to be continuing unabated, the (then still undivided) Tennessee Association of United Baptist sent a committee to investigate the Cades Cove church. This committee filed the following report on May 11, 1839:

> Thus met the following brethren, to-wit: Elijah Rogers, Samuel ?, Andrew Kanatcher, Eli Roberts, and Wm. Billue, five members of the committee appointed by the Association to examine into the cause of the division in the church in Cade's Cove, and we find that the church is divided on the subject of Missions — a part of the church having made joining or fellowshiping those that have joined any of the benevolent institutions of the day, a test of fellowship — and the above named committee, after using all the ar-

guments we were master of to show the brethren that such a course was unscriptural, contrary to the advice of the Association, and common usages of the Baptist church — that it was taking away the privileges of their brethern unjustly — but they appeared unwilling to take any advice; therefore, we believe the thirteen members, and those of the other party that were willing to grant liberty of conscience, and not to lord it over their brethern by making any new test of fellowship, to be the Baptist Church in Cade's Cove upon constitutional principles, and advise the church to act friendly towards the opposing party and as soon as they see their error to receive them into fellowship, and treat them with brotherly kindness.[42]

Neighboring churches were drawn into the vortex, as the following extract from the Ellejoy Baptist church records of August 1839 shows:

John Thomas having written a false report of the proceedings of the committee sent to Cades Cove by the Association to the editor of the Primitive Baptist — this church says he has done them injustice & appoint Wm. Johnson Jr. & James Davis to go to Cades Cove to obtain the record relative to the exclusion of the members who the committee recognized as the church & petition Johnson Adams & David Cunningham to attend at our next meeting in October to give testimony in the above case.

October 4, 1839   Excluded John Thomas for falsely accusing the committee that was sent to Cades Cove to settle a difficulty.[43]

When the dust finally settled on the controversy, thirteen members, including the pastor, Johnson Adams, had been excluded. These thirteen promptly formed the Missionary Baptist church. The older church assumed the name "Primitive Baptist church" on May 15, 1841, and resumed their church business as usual. It is interesting to note in this regard that in Blount County only Tuckaleechee and Cades Cove had strong enough groups of the Old School faction to remain active without faltering after the 1838 division.[44]

In the Cades Cove split, Edwards' explanation about an illiterate ministry and laity causing the division begs the question, since there was relatively no difference between the literacy rate of either faction, or any real indication that one side was more progressive than the other. Many ministers and clerks of the older church had served as school teachers in the cove; they objected to any ecclesiastical training or religious instruction in the schools, but were in no way opposed to secular education. Both sides maintained a hyper-Calvinistic view of the scriptures. The Primitives saw the whole question of missions as an unwarranted innovation, and the entire structure of their theology, as previously discussed, militated against any deviation from scriptural injunctions.[45]

The real key to understanding the division, however, is not theological, but organizational. The major impetus of the church had always been to keep absolute power over their own affairs within the congregation. The entire panoply of new organizational structures, such as a mission board, or the Baptist church convention, they interpreted as a movement away from local autonomy toward a centralized ecclesiastical structure similar to their persecutors. In this interpretation, the important point is that they felt their power to control their own affairs being threatened by outside forces which from their theological and historical perspective seemed counter-revolutionary. Their opponents, not the Primitives, were the reactionaries.[46]

The ultimate test of their determination to maintain control over their own congregation came with the Civil War. Inscribed on the church book is their formal explanation, or apology, for not holding church services between 1862 and 1865:

> We the Primitive Baptist Church in Blount County, Cades Cove, do show to the publick the reason why we have not kept up our church meeting. It was on account of the rebelion and we was union people and the Rebels was too strong here in Cades Cove. Our preacher was abliged to leave sometimes but thank God we once more can meet tho it was from August 1862 until June 1865 that we did not meet but when we met the Church was in peace.[47]

The reasons why the Primitive Baptist church remained defiantly Union in their political allegiance are complex. The important point here is that the congregation again asserted their independence, and determined on a course oblivious to the strong outside pressures to yield to the Southern ideology (as other Southern churches did), or at least to remain neutral. Once the consensus was reached among the congregation, however, the ideas involved were too widely dispersed throughout the fabric of the entire community to be destroyed by clos-

ing the church, murdering its leaders (such as Russell Gregory), or forcing them to hide out in the surrounding mountains.[48]

The question of slavery prevented some churches in the border states
from joining the Confederacy, but there is no mention in the Cades
Cove church book of slaves or slavery at any point during the century.
There were no slaves in the cove listed in the 1850 or 1860 census, although some of the larger landowners, such as Daniel D. Foute, owned
slaves at other locations in Blount County. An 1857 survey of the county
listed only one slave, valued at $500, living in the cove. The commun-
ity was composed of many men, such as Robert Burchfield (who in-
cidentally belonged to the Missionary Baptist church), who had owned
slaves at their former residences in North Carolina. There is no clear
answer, however, to the question of the Primitive Baptists' role as the
dominant church in keeping slavery out of the cove. Neighboring communities in Blount County, particularly Tuckaleechee Cove, had numerous slave-owners.[49]

A more probable explanation for the church's strong pro-Union position lies in the basic ideology surrounding their concept of the church's
role in society. As has been previously discussed, the Primitive Baptists
conceived of the church and its doctrines as being fully enumerated in
the scriptures. Any innovation, or "institution of the day," they regarded
with great suspicion and hostility. This same entrenched conservatism
carried over into their political attitudes. The South, from their point
of view, was attempting to impose radically new interpretations on the
civil order, the old United States, which they had long regarded as
ideologically fixed or complete.[50]

John Oliver, a founding member of the church and one of its most
influential deacons, clearly represented this line of thought. The golden
age of Jacksonian egalitarianism was fixed in his mind as the optimum
political settlement by his participation in the War of 1812 at Horseshoe Bend, and he could only regard the Confederate cause with abhorrence after the long decades of his isolation in the cove from other
Southern political mainstreams. Other members of the congregation
such as Peter Cable agreed that secession was a dangerous and unjusti-
fied innovation in the political status quo.[51]

Whatever their reasons for assuming a pro-Union position, the congregation was galvanized into underground political activity by the

threat of outside force when North Carolina guerrillas closed the church. That action ended all their doubts. Church members might have been willing to assume a nonactive stance in the conflict, despite their pro-Union sympathies, but direct action set off an ideological chain reaction based on their earlier political and theological socialization.[52]

Long acutely aware of their numerous persecutions as a denomination in the past, some of the congregation had grown weary during the relatively prosperous and free years of the 1840s and 1850s of being constantly warned by jeremiads of former persecutions in Virginia and of the distinct possibility, according to scriptures, of God's chosen again being subjected to persecutions because of their faith. And now, in 1862, *mirable dictu,* that very set of circumstances seemed to have occurred, jarring them out of their complacency just as they had so often been forewarned![53] This apparent confirmation of what they had long believed gave them a moral unanimity to resist the invaders.

The congregation of the Primitive Baptist church thus formed the core of resistance to Rebel guerrillas. To their political differences was now added the conviction that their theology was under attack. In this sense, the North Carolinians made no greater mistake than to force the cove churches to close. In so doing, they triggered an ideological response which set strong motivational forces loose in the entire community. The whirlwind they reaped in terms of organized resistance from this wellspring of paranoia was out of all proportion to Cades Cove's usefulness to the Southern cause.[54]

Yet the war had only a temporary effect on the internal life of the church; no major doctrinal questions divided members over this conflict. They strongly resisted attempts by outside forces to disrupt their church meetings, but within the church all remained quiet. This anomaly of outer stress and inner calm was not observed by the majority of the congregation; doctrinal questions had always held the first rank in their priorities. An outward response, even armed resistance to North Carolina guerrillas, represented only a logical reaction which their theological socialization had for decades conditioned them to make. In this sense the Civil War represented a moral unanimity toward their persecutors and an inner suspension of doctrinal disputes which was seldom enjoyed in times of peace.[55]

The worst theological crisis in the nineteenth-century church occurred during the 1870s over the Two-Seed doctrine. This doctrine in simplest terms was an absolute or extreme form of predestination. All people were preordained according to whether they were of good or bad seed to salvation or damnation. The Cades Cove Primitive Baptists had always been Calvinistic; if only the elect could be saved, they had earlier argued, why send missionaries to point out the need for salvation? Yet in actual practice they had never been willing to concede the logical or extreme limits of predestination; there was always a flicker of free-will in their sermons (though they formally denounced Arminianism).[56]

Advocates of the Two-Seed doctrine thus confronted the Cades Cove church with a new interpretation of their theology based on tenets long held by the congregation. Confusion reigned for several years; no one appeared able effectively to combat this latest innovation, which seemed such a logical explication of their old beliefs. The majority finally reacted, however, and expelled all proponents of Two-Seedism. In so doing, they had taken an important theological step toward Arminianism, or free-will, quite involuntarily; attempting to prevent change in their theology, they were, in fact, compelled to make a subtle but very significant alteration in stepping back from the extreme end of Calvinistic predestination. The controversy flared up intermittently through the rest of the century, but the congregation remained adamantly opposed to Two-Seedism.[57]

A controversy of less importance erupted in the 1880s and 1890s over membership in secret orders or societies. The Cades Cove church debated the question of whether or not members of such secret societies ought to be excluded from church membership, and reached a consensus against them in conformity with most other Primitive Baptists in the larger region. Accordingly, on April 26, 1890, James Brown and Monroe Lequire were excluded for joining the Farmers' Alliance. No one else was excluded after 1890, however, and the controversy soon subsided.[58]

The Cades Cove church was the second largest in the Tennessee Association of Primitive Baptist, which dated its organization from 1802, but actually had formed a separate association in 1841 after the break over missions. Association meetings involved tallying membership lists from individual churches, numerous sermons, and affirming the articles of faith endorsed by the group. Queries on a wide variety of theological questions were received and answered, and an occasional circular letter was passed around which explained or clarified some point in doctrine. All these items were printed in the annual association minutes. The association was strictly congregational in organization; a member church could withdraw at any time, since decisions by the majority were in no way binding on the individual church. The right was reserved by the association, however, to exclude any church which deviated from doctrinal norms.[59]

Union meetings were held once a year, usually in the summer, when other association churches were invited to Cades Cove to share communion and the footwashing services. These meetings were conducted in strict austerity; no vanities in clothing or in church furnishings, which might indicate the pride and sinfulness of mankind, were permitted. The services were long; men and women were separated and sat on hard benches before a plain wooden pulpit and a crude table with a bucket of drinking water and a dipper. Unlike some other fundamentalist sects, the cove church frowned on any excessive emotional display during the sermon. In fact, a strict list of rules of decorum was drawn up to dictate the limits of acceptable behavior.[60]

In addition to their union and association meetings, the Primitives were on friendly terms with the Methodists in the cove, and frequently shared revivals with them. They never reconciled themselves to the Missionaries, however, and bitterly opposed any formal contact or communication with their former brethren. Within the larger community of Cades Cove they were active in innumerable charitable enterprises; if any church member reported an instance of need in the cove, the congregation responded quickly and generously. They did so primarily on an individual basis, however; like other Baptists, they believed that social concerns and welfare should be the business of the individual conscience, not of the collective organization of the church.[61]

In contrast to the Primitive Baptists, the Missionary Baptist church remained very small and inactive through most of the century. The band of thirteen which broke away from the older church in May 1839 was recognized by the Tennessee Association of Baptists as the legitimate church, but they did not gain widespread support within the community. The number of members remained fewer than twenty until the Civil War. There were long periods in which no regular services were held during the two decades before the conflict. The church closed from October 1862 until 1865 "on account of the awful horror of war," but there is no indication that its members were active in the conflict. From 1880 until 1889 no services were held. The year 1893, however, seems to have been a turning point; the church in that year held a successful revival led by Thomas Sexton, and gained twenty new members, raising the total membership to forty-two. In 1894, they were finally able to construct their own meeting house on Hyatt hill; up until this time, they had used the Methodist or Primitive Baptist church.[62]

Any sort of analysis of the Missionaries is impossible because of the paucity of their records. They continued to be hostile to the dominant Primitive Baptists, but never had the size throughout most of the century to make any significant impact within the larger community. Some of their members, such as Butler Tipton, had been excluded from the Primitive Baptist church for various offenses; whether these dissidents further altered either the theology or pietistic standards of the older church is not known. In general, their church decorum and practices seem to have imitated those of the Primitives.[63]

Methodists were active in the cove at a very early date. Dr. Jobe said that he could "distinctly remember hearing Rev. George Eakin preaching in Cades Cove" when he was only six or seven years old, which would place the date between 1823 and 1824. Eakin was one of the most prominent early Methodist circuit riders in East Tennessee; an Irishman, he was described by Dr. Jobe as "eccentric" but "a good man." The Methodist system of circuit riders and camp meetings, made famous by Bishop Asbury, was probably more responsible for bringing religion to frontier areas, such as the cove, than any other institution.[64]

In spite of their initial enthusiasm at such meetings, however, the Methodists were slower than the Baptists in organizing churches. In Cades Cove, the church did not build a meeting house until 1840, when a deed was given by James F. Deaver to Henry Seebow, Richard Kirby, Charles McGlothlin, and Francis Kirby, trustees for the Methodist Episcopal church in the cove. John W. Oliver gives the following description of this Methodist meeting house:

> The house was of a very crude nature built of logs notched down at the corners covered with hand-made shingles and weighted down with eight poles. The seats were made of split puncheons and set on round wooden legs without back rests, and were used for school and church. A furnace of stone and earth was built up in the center to build a fire and the smoke went up through the roof. As there were no sawmills in those early pioneer days the buildings were at first without floors. Later puncheon floors were put in. Puncheons were split and hewed slabs.[65]

From 1840 until 1878, there are virtually no records of the Methodist Episcopal church in the cove, although services continued to be held there regularly. During these years, the Methodists were on friendly terms with the Primitive Baptists, frequently sharing their meeting house and participating in joint revivals. Names of early nineteenth-century ministers have been lost; the Methodists never kept careful records of their transactions as did the Baptists. In the 1890s, prominent circuit ministers were I.P. Martin, C.A. Murphey, N.P. Swain, J.C. Bays, Bob Snyder, A.M. Hoyle, and C.T. Davis. Among the most devout and notable members of the church at the end of the century was William "Uncle Billie" Feezell, who welcomed every Methodist preacher into his home, as Isaac P. Martin recalls.[66]

Martin described the Cades Cove Methodist church as an "old pine-pole house," such as "Asbury and McKendree found all over Tennessee and Kentucky during the first quarter of the nineteenth century." The Methodists constructed a new frame house in 1902 which is still standing. Nevertheless, membership remained small throughout the century. Martin said that in 1891 the "Methodists of Cade's Cove were but a handful."[67]

The division or schism of 1844 within the Methodist church was reflected in Cades Cove by the construction in 1880 of a Northern Methodist church on the south side of the cove near the center. This church was donated by Dan Lawson, one of the wealthiest men in the community after the Civil War, but according to one scholar, it "never developed beyond a family affair." There is no real indication, moreover, that during the Civil War Cades Cove members of the Methodist

Episcopal Church, South, were more or less pro-Southern than the wider community; their church remained closed, as did the others, for the duration of the war.[68]

Although the Methodists and Missionary Baptists would enjoy tremendous growth in size and influence in the twentieth century, the nineteenth belonged to the Primitive Baptists. Leadership within the community came from the Primitives during every major crisis, including the Civil War; their power rested on a voluntary consensus of opinion in Cades Cove more potent than any government—county, state, or national. If the community acquiesced in the social and behavioral standards imposed by their denomination, the Primitives in turn made religion and church membership accessible to everyone; by the very nature of the group mechanism through which the church operated, there were no elites or individuals with excessive power. More than any other group, the Primitives fiercely defended the principle of local autonomy, of the right to make decisions affecting their lives without outside pressure or influence. They also formed, in their broader concern for the welfare of the entire cove, the largest single thread in the all-important fabric of community.

5
The Civil War

The Civil War was a major watershed in the cove's history, if judged solely from the enormous economic devastation apparent in the postwar agricultural census returns. Such statistical comparisons of the cove before and after the conflict, however, reveal a static and very incomplete picture of the four years that sharply changed the character of the cove people and their community. These changes can be fully comprehended only by examining the daily life of the average cove resident during the war. For him, loyalty to the Union meant years of excruciating hardships: devastation of his land and property, frequent starvation, and constant fear that he or his family might be murdered by Rebel guerrillas. The trials of the individual cove farmer increased yearly as the war progressed; for him the war experience was an intensely personal ordeal.

Another important theme is the testing of the fabric of community. Because of the divisive nature of the political conflict, all formal institutions were severely strained during the war. In the final analysis, an older sense of community reasserted itself, and the cove people acted collectively to defend themselves from the onslaught of guerrilla raids as they had earlier helped one another clear the wilderness. Because the new consensus which emerged from wartime experiences reflected attitudes and values quite different from those of the pre-1860 community, the transfer of responsibilities from traditional leaders like Daniel D. Foute to new leaders such as Russell Gregory assumed special significance.

Cades Cove's decision to remain loyal to the Union can only be comprehended within the broader context of conflicting regional patterns. Geography alone does not explain the community's Unionism, although it is true that the mountainous environs of the cove were not suited to the growth of cotton or any other staple crop associated with the slave economy of the lower South. Yet other mountainous areas in the South not bound to the cotton culture supported the Confederacy. Western North Carolina, an area contiguous to Cades Cove and similar in terrain, vigorously supported the Rebel cause with contributions of both men and material. Recent scholarship indicates that slavery, although proportionately smaller than in other areas of the South, was "fully entrenched and quite healthy in the North Carolina mountains." John Inscoe argues persuasively that enough wealthy and politically influential western North Carolinians had "sufficient vested interests in slavery to make it a predominant consideration" in the decision to leave the Union in 1861.[1]

Politically and ideologically, however, there were quite different crosscurrents in East Tennessee, particularly in Blount County. There cove farmers had been constantly exposed to the exhortations of numerous abolitionists, who in the decades before 1860 had made Maryville, the county seat of Blount, "a veritable fortress in the crusade against slavery." A local branch of the Manumission Society of Tennessee was active in Blount County as early as 1815. Before 1820, New Providence Church in Maryville had freed, educated, and ordained to the ministry two blacks, one of whom, the Reverend George M. Erskine, was later sent as a Presbyterian missionary to Liberia. The large Quaker element in the county also fervently opposed slavery, and, despite their conscientious opposition to war, many Blount Friends later demonstrated their deep convictions against the institution by fighting with the Union army. The Quakers were very active in promoting abolitionist literature throughout the area and in sending frequent antislavery memorials to the state legislature.[2]

During the 1830s, East Tennessee abolitionists openly agitated to establish a separate state out of their section in order to abolish slavery there. One such noted abolitionist, Ezekiel Birdseye, reported visiting in 1841 in Maryville with fellow abolitionists Robert Bagle and "Rev. Mr. Craig, a professor in the Maryville College." They informed Birdseye that "a meeting appointed at one of the churches to discuss the subject of abolition" was "well attended," and that no "disorder or disturbance took place." He found strong support among other Blount countians for future meetings and concluded that prospects there for the abolitionist cause "are very encouraging."[3]

Maryville College, founded in 1819 as the Southern and Western Theological Seminary by the Reverend Isaac Anderson, had long been a stronghold of abolitionism. Anderson nourished among his students the ideals of freedom, equality, and education for both blacks and Indians. One scholar there wrote in 1838 that "we take the liberty to uphold and defend our sentiments, whether it is agreeable or not to the slaveholder." He also mentioned "friends in the country around, among whom we have the privilege of distributing without fear a considerable number of pamphlets." Of the thirty students in the seminary preparing for the ministry, he concluded, twelve were abolitionists.[4]

Through his students at Maryville College, Dr. Anderson made a great ideological impact on other areas of East Tennessee. Some writers credit the section's decision to remain in the Union to his teachings and moral leadership. At any rate, he preached the abolitionist doctrine at camp meetings throughout the region, including numerous sermons in Cades Cove, where he had mining and mineral interests. He was also a close friend of Dr. Calvin Post, the New York physician who had moved to the cove in 1846. Both men shared a commitment to abolitionism and were indirectly related, since Anderson's only son had married the sister of Dr. Post's wife.[5]

If the cove people were not fully exposed to abolitionist propaganda in Maryville, where they attended court, paid their taxes, and sold their crops, they certainly were familiar with Dr. Post's convictions. Serving as the cove's only physician, this outspoken man found the time to write numerous antislavery tracts to government officials and to many Northern newspapers. Although no documentary proof exists to substantiate the claim, tradition holds that Dr. Post made Cades Cove a station of the "underground railroad" aiding runaway slaves escaping to the North.[6] The cove's geographic position and the fact that an underground railroad later operated in the community during the Civil War to aid Union soldiers escaping Southern prison camps lends logic, if not corroboration, to these assertions. From the tone of his correspondence, moreover, it seems unlikely that Dr. Post would have shrunk from the task, or that he would have hesitated to enlist his neighbors' aid in helping fugitive slaves.

Some indication of the effect of this abolitionist activity on Cades Cove lies in the fact that there is no record of any slaves living in the community in the 1850 or 1860 census. Men like Robert Burchfield who moved to the cove from other areas of the South sold their slaves before arrival. An 1857 survey of Blount County lists only one slave in the cove. Daniel D. Foute owned numerous slaves in other parts of the county and may have brought this slave to "Paradise Lost," his home in the cove. The absence of slaves from the cove was in marked contrast to surrounding areas, such as Tuckaleechee Cove, which contained numerous slaveowners. Other indications of the community's attitude toward slavery is found in the 1850 census, which lists a family of free blacks living there: Cooper and Ellen Clark and their four children. No family could have survived in such a close-knit, homogenous society without the tacit consent of the entire community.[7]

Within the context of decades of abolitionist agitation, it is not surprising that cove residents joined forces with others in the county who fervently opposed secession on the eve of the Civil War. Out of Blount County's total population of 13,270 in 1860, only 1,363 were slaves, while 196 were free Negroes. Clearly, neither the economy nor the social structure of the county was closely bound to the cotton culture; in that year, Blount produced only five bales of cotton in contrast to 106,341 bushels of wheat. Accordingly, in the presidential election of 1860, the county demonstrated its sympathy for the Union by casting a particularly heavy vote for John Bell, the candidate of the Constitutional Union party. In Maryville, Bell's campaign procession, some two miles in length and "headed by a wagon bearing a large bell," was met with "such ringing and shouting" as "had not been heard since 1840."[8]

By an overwhelming vote of 1,552 to 450, Blount County voted against withdrawal from the Union in Tennessee's secession-convention referendum of February 9, 1861. At this time, the majority of Tennesseans rejected secession 69,675 to 57,798. By summer, however, the tide had turned in favor of secession in Middle and West Tennessee. Yet on June 8, Blount countians again rejected secession by an even greater margin of 1,766 to 414. When East Tennessee counties assembled on

June 17 in Greeneville, Blount County sent such outspoken Unionists as John F. Henry and the Reverend W.T. Dowell to denounce the recent referendum as "unconstitutional and illegal, and therefore not binding upon us as loyal citizens." As Blount delegates joined other dissident eastern counties in petitioning the General Assembly for permission to "form and erect a separate state," a home guard was organized and meetings were held throughout the county to demonstrate the tremendous popular opposition to disunion.[9]

Aware of the area's strategic and economic importance, the Confederate authorities denied East Tennessee's right to secede from the rest of the state, and quickly moved in forces of from five to ten thousand soldiers to keep the section under control. Unpersuaded by a massive Rebel propaganda campaign which followed, Unionists adopted a program of obstructing the Confederate war effort and appealed directly to President Lincoln for military aid. "East Tennessee was now ablaze with excitement on account of the uprising and open rebellion of the Union men," who, according to one contemporary observer, "were flying to arms in squads of from fifty to five hundred." Infuriated by an abortive effort to burn key bridges in the region, Confederates finally dropped their conciliatory approach and instituted a series of harsh repressive measures to control the local population and to prevent loyalists from escaping to join the Union army.[10]

Despite President Lincoln's personal sympathy for the region, not until September 1863, when General Ambrose E. Burnside occupied Knoxville, were Federal forces again in control of East Tennessee. In the meantime, both sides used the mountainous region for bitter guerrilla warfare; "as a general thing," complained Confederate Secretary of War Judah P. Benjamin in 1861, "these bands of traitors would disband and flee to the mountains on the approach of an armed force of Confederates, therefore it was a difficult matter to do anything with them." Later, Rebel guerrillas used these same mountain strongholds to attack Federal forces. Even when Sherman came as far as Maryville to relieve Burnside on December 4, 1863, the surrounding areas such as Cades Cove were still disputed ground. Thus, regardless of which side was in control, the protracted guerrilla warfare continued unabated throughout the war, bringing havoc and desolation to the civilian population in this bloody no man's land.[11]

Confederate authorities justified the atrocities unleashed on the civilian population of East Tennessee "on the ground that these Union people were traitors, and contended that the sufferings which they were inflicting upon them were not cruelties, but righteous and well deserved punishments for their crimes as tories, traitors, and rebels against their own lawful government." Following this reasoning, the Rebels, according to one contemporary observer, argued that "Union citizens had forfeited all claims to their homes, that their possessions were no longer theirs, and therefore, that Confederates were justified in robbing Union families, plundering their farms, hunting them through the country like so many wild beasts, and shooting them upon the run like so many robbers and outlaws."[12]

Although Cades Cove suffered more devastation from such guerrilla warfare than any other section of Blount County, the majority of its citizens remained loyal to the Union throughout the war. Abolitionism, geography, and regional political patterns offer some explanation of the community's loyalism. The conservative theology of the Primitive Baptist church, which opposed changes in the religious status quo, transferred into attitudes of hostility toward any innovation in the existing political order. John Oliver, the first permanent white settler, had fought under Jackson at Horseshoe Bend, and nothing had occurred in the succeeding years to dim his memory of Jacksonian egalitarianism or to lessen his commitment to the old Republic. As a respected patriarch by 1860, he was not unheeded by the community in his outspoken opposition to disunion.[13]

Yet some of the younger men in the cove chose to join the Rebels. In the majority of these defections, relatives living in North Carolina or other parts of the South probably played a major role. Both the Olivers and Gregorys, for instance, had numerous relatives living in Yancey County, North Carolina, whom the younger cove men frequently visited. Such relatives in other parts of the South staunchly supported secession and the Southern cause, but did not break off correspondence with the cove loyalists. An excellent example of this continuity of family ties during the war is found in an extant letter from Mary Bird, Catoosa County, Georgia, to her cousin Jake in the cove. After making inquiry about all their pro-Union kin there, she concluded that "the Yankees may outnumber us and they may kill all our soldiers but never will get the Southern states."[14] Obviously some of this exuberant Rebel spirit infected visiting relatives from the cove, and partially explains why a minority of the younger men from Union families joined the Confederates.

The first blow to the community occurred early in the war, when many of the younger men left to volunteer in the Union army. Brothers tended to join together, and loyalties followed family patterns of allegiance as a general rule. There were agonizing exceptions; some sons of staunchly Union families, such as Charles Gregory and William Oliver, joined the Confederate army. The two squires, Daniel D. Foute and Curran Lemons, were Confederate sympathizers, and both their sons, Bose Foute and Lee Lemons, joined the Southern army. With the exception of Dr. Post, men such as the squires who had comparative wealth and some exposure to the outside world became Confederates; the mass of cove farmers of the middle or yeoman class remained loyal to the Union. The Oliver records list twenty-one Union soldiers from the cove, and twelve who joined the Confederates.[15] The majority of cove men, however, were unable to join Union forces and either hid out in the mountains or joined together in small bands to fight the Rebels. At any rate, by 1862 the community was depleted of most of its able-bodied men.

The absence of these men caused the collapse of the militia — the traditional defense force on which cove people had relied for protection since the earliest days of settlement. Organization of the county into militia companies for the purpose of taxation, elections, and local defense predated the establishment of civil districts in 1836. Every able-bodied man between the ages of twenty-one and fifty belonged to the militia, which as early as the 1820s was meeting for muster and drill on the south side of the cove. Last used to round up the remaining Cherokees in 1837–1838, the militia muster had evolved into a semi-holiday in the cove by 1860, with various shooting matches and other contests.[16] But it remained the only real form of collective defense for the community against outside attack. That defense had evaporated during the first year of the war, precisely at the time it was most needed.

Local justice was administered by two squires after 1836 when Cades Cove became the sixteenth civil district of Blount County. Most disputes involving quarrels, property division, petty violations and fines were handled within the community by their justices of peace; only rarely was it necessary to take a more serious offense to the circuit court in Maryville. These local magistrates were almost always men of some education and wealth, whose unquestioned integrity lent gravity to their judgments. The personal respect and esteem in which they were held by the cove people formed a secure consensus, or framework, of law and order within the community. This sense of security was shattered in 1861, however, when Daniel D. Foute and Curran Lemons, both of whom had served continuously as justices since the 1840s, gave their allegiance to the Confederacy.[17]

That their magistrates would join the Rebels and actively assist enemy guerrillas raiding the cove horrified the majority of residents who remained Unionists. It also meant that, for all practical purposes, their traditional form of local justice had collapsed because they identified the law with the personal integrity of their squires, and during the early years of the war no new officials could be elected. Nor was any redress possible from the county court at Maryville, where, even after Confederate occupation ended, Rebel forces continued their raids as late as the winter of 1863–1864. The old justice of the peace dockets reveal graphic evidence of this suspension of local justice in Cades Cove. Curran Lemons made his last entry on May 15, 1861; Foute's last entry in his docket was on February 7, 1862. Not until 1865 were entries resumed by newly elected justices Daniel B. Lawson and Nathan H. Sparks, both of whom were strong Unionists but far less literate than their predecessors.[18]

Foute was also serving the community as postmaster in 1861. Cades Cove had been established as a U.S. post office as early as June 28, 1833, and extant letters of the cove people testify to the importance and frequence of their correspondence with friends and relatives in other sections of the country. The war disturbed routine mail service, and Foute's Rebel allegiance discouraged attempts to send letters through normal channels, since intercepted correspondence might furnish information to Confederate authorities.[19] In an area of comparative isolation, discontinuance of postal services increased the cove people's sense of alienation and estrangement from the outside world, especially since newspapers were difficult to obtain in the war years.

Dr. Calvin Post, the only other prewar leader, acted as the official correspondent in the cove for Federal forces, certifying the loyalty of various individuals to Union authorities and writing passes for loyalists going through the Federal lines to Knoxville. Because of his outspoken loyalty to the Union and his prewar abolitionist campaigning, however, he was a particular target of the North Carolina guerrillas. Early in the war these raiders placed a price on his head, dead or alive, and forced him to go into hiding in the mountains. Not until 1865 was he able again to assume an active role in the community.[20] As a physician and scientist, moreover, Dr. Post was unprepared to provide the needed military leadership in forming a local defense organization.

In the spring of 1862, Confederate authorities "first attempted to disarm the people," according to a contemporary Blount countian, "and for this purpose sent troops through the country, taking up the hunting rifles wherever they could be found." Such rifles had long been a household necessity to cove families, particularly when guerrilla raids depleted other food supplies and forced them to subsist on game. North Carolina officials attempted to enforce the Confederate conscript laws in the same year, forcing the few remaining men in the cove to go into hiding. An elaborate scheme to construct a military road from Sevier County, Tennessee, to Jackson County, North Carolina, with forced Union labor also failed because the men in Cades Cove and surrounding areas had successfully evaded their persecutors by hiding out in the mountains.[21]

The greatest threat to the cove came in 1863 when North Carolina guerrillas began systematic attacks against the community. These "bushwhackers," as they were commonly called, were often outlaws who used the Confederate cause to justify their atrocities against the civilian population in the cove. "They would make raids into Tennessee for the purpose of robbing the people of their horses, cattle, and goods," reported one contemporary observer, "and would never fail to murder all the Union men they could find, and appropriate their property to their own use." On several occasions Governor Zebulon B. Vance denounced the excessive brutality of these raids from North Carolina, but the guerrillas were beyond the control of Confederate authorities in the rugged wilderness of the Great Smoky Mountains. Familiar from prewar commerce with both the terrain of the cove and the lifestyle of its people, these raiders struck without warning from the cover of surrounding mountains.[22]

Too distant from Maryville to receive any assistance from other Unionists, Cades Cove by 1863 reeled from a succession of these devastating guerrilla attacks. Murder became commonplace. In the prewar community, individual murders were remembered and recounted in great detail, such as the murder of Martin Wiseman by John Thurman in the early 1830s over an argument about an election, or the accidental shooting of Tom Frazier by William Davis, who mistook him for a deer. Now no one could keep count of the cove men who were ambushed by the bushwhackers, or who simply did not return from the mountains.[23] The vagueness of many such rumors was corroborated by the numerous examples of sudden deaths, ambushes, and traps which the cove people had witnessed themselves. A pervasive sense of helplessness only increased the terror and paralysis within the cove.

Typical of the hardships endured by the average citizens during this period are the experiences of Elijah Oliver's family. Early in the war, Elijah had moved his wife and four small children up on the Rich Mountain to escape guerrilla attacks. No place was immune, however, as Elijah's son, William Howell, later recalled in a poignant description of his family's ordeal:

> My father did not enlist in the Civil War. He would lay out and work in the fields of a day to make bread for his wife and children. He was a Union man in principle . . . .
>
> .   .   .   .
>
> Sometimes he would have to go down in the settlement and get a yoke of cattle to haul feed and firewood this was in time of war. On one occasion he went out after the cattle and the rebels caught him and kept him two weeks. This was one of the hardest trials my mother ever went through. They shot him in the hand before he surrendered. But after this he got away from them in the night and finally got back home. I can remember the shouts of my mother the night he come in.
>
> On another time we were grinding our cane on a wooden cane mill and boiling the juice in kettles in a furnace. In this way the people would make their molasses when all of a suden two armed rebels came up, they striped the horse and took him off with them, leaving our cane patch standing, and

us nearley on starvation. We never got the horse back. When we seen them comeing, my father ran off and hid thinking they would take him, but when they started with the horse and scarcely got out of sight my father came out and made for his gun. My mother caught around him telling him it would never do, that the whole army might come and kill us all, and so she constrained him to let them go, saying it would be better to lose the horse, than it would be to lose some or all of our lives.

At another time we lost every bite of bacon that we had, and it war times and none to sell, makeing it awful hard on the family of little children. Although I was small only from five to eight years old, I can remember hearing the cannons roar and when we would hear of the rebels comeing we would carry out the beding and Pa's gun and hide them in hollow logs until they would pass and be gone. I can remember Ma puting the best clothes on us that we had she said that they would not strip them off of us to take them.[24]

Food was the greatest problem. Not since the winter of their initial settlement in 1818–1819, when the Cherokees kept John and Lucretia alive with dried pumpkin, had the Oliver family been threatened with such famine. Guns were contraband, liable to be seized by the Rebels on any occasion, and ammunition was in short supply throughout the war. Elijah made frequent trips to Knoxville to purchase medicine for his family, as numerous extant passes and loyalty oaths indicate. He had little cash, however, since few marketable crops could be grown up on the Rich Mountain, and the produce from such subsistence farming as he was able to do was almost always stolen by the Rebels. Simple traps were used by the family to snare small animals such as squirrels and rabbits, but frequently the guerrillas stole such meager portions from their table before they could eat. This constant stealing and raiding made it almost impossible to accumulate more than a few days' food supply, so they subsisted daily on a hand-to-mouth basis, threatened constantly with starvation.[25]

Throughout East Tennessee, the situation was similar. Traversed by both armies which lived mainly off the countryside, the region was stripped of food by guerrilla outlaws and retreating Rebel soldiers after Burnside's occupation of Knoxville in the fall of 1863. The *Pennsylvania Relief Report*, commenting on the worsening condition of the people in the winter of 1863–1864, noted that even the thrifty Quaker settlement in Blount County, formerly one of the most prosperous communities in East Tennessee, now was forced to apply to the army for quartermaster rations. Brownlow's *Knoxville Whig and Rebel Ventilator* reported in March that Union people living outside the Federal lines were deliberately plundered of everything they had; even such items as blankets and shoes were forcibly stripped from their owners. Although the East Tennessee Relief Association was successful in obtaining food and clothing from the federal government and Northern philanthropic organizations, such assistance came too late materially to aid remote areas such as Cades Cove.[26]

In the spring of 1864, the few remaining old men in the cove organized to resist continuing guerrilla raids. In so doing, they revived an older sense of community among the cove people which enabled them to act collectively to defend themselves. Three reasons for this revival are apparent. First, the sheer desperation of their situation convinced many residents that some decisive action, regardless of the risks involved, was necessary if any of them hoped to survive the war. Burnside's long awaited occupation of Knoxville had not brought any relief from guerrilla raids. The remaining women and children could not continue indefinitely living at such a subsistence level, particularly since the approach of winter made game scarce and hunting more difficult. Any activity to acquire or store food in the daytime was observed by the raiders, who promptly stole every accumulation of supplies, including livestock and domestic animals. Although they were aware of frequent murders and other acts of retribution, most of the cove people were now willing to undertake some form of active resistance as the only possible alternative to slow starvation.[27]

Second, the guerrillas made a critical mistake in attacking the Primitive Baptist church, forcing it to close and the minister to flee for his life. Always fatalistic in their outlook, the congregation could accept personal deprivation and individual suffering with bewildered resignation. But an attack against the church represented a far more ominous threat. Conditioned by decades of warnings against efforts to persecute their sect and destroy the church, they now seemed to be witnessing the fulfillment of all the older jeremiads. This apparent assault on their religion released a tremendous psychological reaction against their per-

secutors. Moreover, to a people steeped in biblical images and stereotypes, no group seemed more the incarnation of evil than these North
Carolina guerrillas. Consequently, it is not surprising that leadership
of the home guard came largely from members of the Primitive Baptist
church such as Russell Gregory and Peter Cable.[28]

Third, resistance came as a result of the outstanding leadership and
organizational ability of Russell Gregory. Traditional leaders, such as
their squires Foute and Lemons, were Confederates; Dr. Post was in
hiding, and John Oliver, old and weakened from long illness, had died
on February 15, 1863. Widely known and respected before the war
as a rancher and herdsman, Russell had always preferred to live alone
in the wilderness for most of the year in his stone house on Gregory
Bald. An old man when the war broke out, he was staunchly loyal to
the Union but too feeble to enlist. Embittered by his son Charles's de-
fection to the Rebels, he vowed to take no part in the conflict.[29]

The desperation of the community in the winter of 1863–1864 finally changed Russell's mind. Long despised by the North Carolina
raiders "for his bold outspoken defiance of their dastardly and cow-
ardly raids on the almost defenseless old men, women, and children
of the cove," and weakened from illness and malnutrition, "his old
fighting spirit was yet strong." Not satisfied only to organize and drill
the old men in a home guard, Gregory also developed an early warning
system using all the women and children in the cove to keep watch at
the North Carolina passes used by the guerrillas and relay the alarm
throughout the cove. Morale improved dramatically, since everyone
now had a useful task in contributing to their common defense, instead
of waiting helplessly for the next attack.[30]

Utilizing this warning system, Gregory received word in the spring
of 1864 that the raiders were on their way, following their usual pattern
of entering the cove suddenly from the upper or northeast end. Sum-
moning his aged neighbors in a carefully planned strategy, Gregory led
these old men of the home guard in cutting trees across the road at the
lower or southwest end of the cove near the forks of Forge and Abrams
creeks. Here they concealed themselves behind their blockade and waited
for the raiders, who would have to use this wider route to herd their
bounty of stolen cattle and horses back to North Carolina.

At this point, one of those incidents occurred which illustrates the personal anguish caused by family divisions over the war. Unknown to his father, Charles Gregory was among the raiders entering the cove. Half a mile before they reached the blockade, Charles was stopped by his sister, who inquired after some of the family still living in North Carolina. Impatient to join his comrades, Charles was purposely detained by his sister who held on to his horse's reins and continued to make small talk. While thus engaged, Old Long Tom, Russell's famous rifle, fired, opening the battle at the blockade. "There goes Old Long Tom," Charles exclaimed as he spurred his horse to break away, "and my old Daddy is at the breech."

The battle only lasted a few minutes; no one was killed, but two of the Rebels, Jack Grant and DeWitt Ghormley, their leader, were wounded. Charles met his comrades in hasty retreat; they returned to North Carolina by another route, leaving all their booty and stolen livestock behind. This victory gave the community an enormous psychological boost; the invincible raiders had been routed by a small band of old men, and forced into an ignominious retreat. The popular exhilaration was expressed in a lengthy ballad celebrating the blockade victory composed by two sisters, Moriah and Mintie Anthony, who lived only a short distance from the scene of the skirmish. "I'd rather be a Union man, and carry a Union gun," the first stanza began, "than be a Ghormley man, and steal a cow and run!"[31]

The blockade battle thus marked a turning point in the cove's struggle to survive, since the guerrilla bushwhackers were forced as a consequence of the newly organized home guard to abandon their devastating daylight attacks, although they continued to strike sporadically at night. Correctly blaming Gregory for the community's successful resistance, some of the same band returned under cover of darkness two weeks after the battle, forced their way into his home, and murdered Russell as he rose from his bed. His martyrdom only increased the community's outrage and will to resist, however, and Russell Gregory's reputation grew to legendary proportions among the cove people after his death.[32]

Cades Cove was also an important station in the "underground railroad" which aided Union soldiers escaping Southern prison camps to reach the Federal lines in Knoxville. This underground railroad was possibly the greatest contribution of East Tennessee Unionists to the war effort — Confederate troops were tied up in attempting to prevent escapes, Union soldiers were restored to their units, and much military information on enemy troop locations and other important data were passed along to the Federal authorities by the participants and their guides.[33] One such prisoner, Charles G. Davis, a young lieutenant in the First Massachusetts Cavalry, escaped from the infamous Camp Sorghum at Columbia, South Carolina, on November 4, 1864, and making his way through the Smokies, reached Knoxville on December 5, 1864, with the assistance of the people of Cades Cove. In an excerpt from his diary he left a vivid description of the community at war:

*December 2*nd: We arose about daybreak and again started on our trip. We had some hard climbing for an hour or so, but the descent soon commenced and continued until we reached Cades Cove. We entered the Cove about 3 p. m. and very unexpectedly caused quite an alarm. A girl was on duty as a sentinel. She gave the alarm with a horn. When she blew the horn we were looking down the Cove. In an instant it was alive. The men were driving their cattle before them, and every man had a gun over his shoulder. We asked the girl to point out the home of Mr. Rowan (after telling her who we were), assuring her that we were friends. We marched in and went to Mrs. Rowan's home. She was very much frightened when she saw us, but we soon satisfied her that we were friends. She informed us that they were looking for the Rebels every moment. Rather pleasant news for us. We had not more than got seated when a woman came running up the road to Mrs. R., and informed her that the Rebs were coming. We jumped up ready to run, but we soon found out that the woman had taken us for the Rebels, and that it was a false alarm. Mrs. Rowan said she could not keep all of us, so five of us started over to the home of Mr. Sparks to whom she directed us. We soon found out that our entrance had alarmed all of the inhabitants of the Cove. The men left the fields and fled to the mountains. It soon became known who we were. They commenced to collect around us. We were resting very comfortably at Mr. Sparks' telling our story when a horseman came riding up from the lower end of the Cove and said "the Rebels are coming sure," that one of the citizens had seen them. All was confusion for some moments. The men picked up their guns and we our blankets and started for the mountains. We reached a safe place. After waiting for an hour, we found out that it was another false alarm. The report had gone down one side of the cove and up the other. We all returned to Mr.

Spark's house and ate a hearty supper. We found all good Union men here. They all have to sleep in the bushes every night, and have for the past two years. They live in continued terror of being killed. At dark we went to the bushes for our night's rest.[34]

Lt. Davis was grateful that "while on the escape from prison life, sick, tired, and foot sore," he had accidentally fallen "into the hands of the loyal, liberty-loving men and women" of Cades Cove. They not only fed and clothed him, but "sent one of their number to pilot me through to Knoxville." In that city, he reported that Union authorities, convinced of the community's absolute loyalty, were sending ammunition back with his guides "for the citizens of Cades Cove." Davis also related an anecdote about the girl sentinel in the cove which offers some insight into the bitterness and grim defiance four years of guerrilla warfare had engendered in the cove people:

The girl was the sentinel that guarded the entrance to the Cove, and at the signal from her, which was of approaching danger, the men, who were tilling the soil, drove their cattle to places of safety, and then put themselves in readiness to defend their dear ones and their homes from the Guerrillas and Bushwackers, who had invaded their little settlement many times during the War. I remember asking the girl on guard what she would do if a stranger should demand the horn of her before she could have used it, and her reply was rather a surprise to me as I had always had a great respect for women, but had met only the kind that used soft words, those who had not been on the "battle line," so to speak, those who had lived in pleasant homes and surroundings. Her reply was that she should tell him to go to "Hell!" And from my knowledge of her as a sentinel on duty, I am very sure that she would have done so.[35]

As the tide of war turned in favor of the Unionists during the last year of the conflict, the fortunes of the Confederate leaders in the cove necessarily declined. No man was more hated or visible for his loyalty to the South than Daniel D. Foute, who ironically had done more than any other individual before 1860 to improve the economic life of the community, building roads, operating a bloomery forge, and serving as legal adviser and magistrate for the cove people. Yet he had undeniably given all possible assistance to the Rebel guerrillas, spying on the community and reporting their activities and whereabouts to the Confederates. His daughter, Ethie M. Foute Eagleton, mentioned in her diary that Foute housed numerous Confederate soldiers at "Paradise Lost" throughout the war years.[36]

Trapped in a moral dilemma, Foute, basically a decent man, found it increasingly difficult to reconcile his Confederate allegiance with the atrocities committed by North Carolina guerrillas in the cove. On one occasion, he personally intervened to prevent the kidnapping of a cove youth, Noah Burchfield, and his impressment into Confederate service. Later historians erroneously have asserted that "during the stressing times of the Civil War" Foute "bought farm after farm until at one time he owned most of Cades Cove." Most of the 20,000 acres he owned at the time of his death in 1865 had been bought at fair prices from cove residents moving to the West in the 1840s and 1850s. In fact, many of these deeds specifically mention an exchange of wagons and gearage for the move West.[37]

Foute's daughter offers no explanation of why her father remained in the cove and refused to seek safety in the lower South. His friend, Sterling Lanier, who had assumed management of Montvale Springs in 1857 and purchased the resort with his brother in 1860, anticipated the end of Confederate government in the state with the surrender of Fort Donelson in February 1862 and wisely moved his family back to Alabama before Burnside's siege of Knoxville.[38]

Foute refused to follow suit, although it is clear from his daughter's diary that the entire family were well aware of the sorry tale of vengeance — harassment, libel, flogging, robbery, and even murder — which awaited Southern sympathizers in East Tennessee after Burnside's occupation of Knoxville and the political ascension of the vindictive Parson Brownlow, who became governor in 1865. Granted the opportunity for escape and the certain knowledge of retribution, it is difficult to surmise why Foute remained in Cades Cove, if not because of a deep personal attachment to his home there. At the close of the war, he was dragged unceremoniously from his sick-bed in the cove by Federal troops, who hauled him to Knoxville and threw him in jail. He died shortly thereafter, paroled but still under guard, at the Knoxville home of another daughter, Mrs. Hamilton.[39]

Shortly after peace was declared in 1865, Elijah Oliver moved his family from the Rich Mountain back into the cove. Amid the enormous devastation caused by four years of protracted guerrilla warfare, he found a community which had undergone profound changes. Gone were most of the outstanding leaders of an earlier generation: Daniel D. Foute, John Oliver, and Russell Gregory were dead by 1865; Peter Cable died in 1866, and Dr. Post lived only eight years after the close of the war. The new generation who had come of age during the war years were far less literate; deprived of the time and means of gaining an education, most of the younger leaders such as the newly elected squires, Daniel Lawson and Nathan Sparks, were provincial and introspective to a degree which would have surprised and saddened their predecessors.[40]

The average people had also changed dramatically during the war. Guerrilla warfare engendered bitterness and hatreds which lasted for many years. Many Confederates left the cove because of this hostility, among them the Foute, Bradford, Lemons, Cobb, Campbell, and Pearce families. Gradually the community resumed its prewar commerce with Knoxville, but inwardly its society became increasingly closed. In contrast to the influx of numerous immigrants from many parts of the United States and foreign countries during the 1840s and 1850s, few new families entered the cove after 1865. The kinship structure expanded to include practically every person in the community. In 1850, there were eighty-six surnames in a population of 671; by 1880, only forty-five surnames were listed in a total population of 449.[41] Intolerance of any innovation or change, suspicion and fear of strangers, and excessive reliance on the extended family—behavioral patterns necessary for survival during the war—now proved difficult or impossible to discard.

The Civil War was thus clearly a watershed for both the internal society of the cove and for the community's declining position after 1865 in relation to the rest of the state and nation. Daniel D. Foute's great dreams for the cove's economic development in the decades before 1860 were completely destroyed by the war's holocaust; no new entrepreneur of comparable ability or vision would replace him. But the community, however altered, had survived; the ties which bound the cove people to one another were stronger than ever. In the close-knit, introspective, and retrospective society which now faced the protracted economic depression of the larger region in the decades after 1865 were rich ingredients for an authentic folk culture. In that emerging culture, the war experiences furnished a model folk hero; linking the combined values of love of their mountain wilderness with unselfish service to the community was the memory of Russell Gregory.

6
The Folk Culture

Brooding over the moral and physical devastation resulting from the Civil War, fearful and suspicious of strangers, and engulfed in a protracted regional depression after 1865, the people of Cades Cove became increasingly introspective and retrospective during the Reconstruction Era. They had always been isolated from the outside world geographically. In the prosperous 1840s and 1850s, however, numerous immigrants from various parts of the nation and world had assured the community of frequent exposure to new ideas and attitudes. After 1865, the cove was no longer part of the Westward Movement; few new families entered the community, and the remaining families were related by blood and united in common values and attitudes through their shared wartime experiences.

If the war served as a crucible which burned out of the community diversity and innovation, it also left a vacuum in the lives of people who, despite their geographic isolation, had always relied heavily on commerce and news from the market centers of East Tennessee. Gradually the market economy recovered, and cove farmers resumed the familiar pattern of selling their crops in Knoxville and Maryville and purchasing various mercantile goods there. In the wake of the terrible destruction from the war, however, there was little regional unity, politically, socially, or economically; after the central goal of winning the war had been accomplished, most of the rural communities of East Tennessee became isolated units temporarily alienated by poverty and bitterness from the larger region.[1] Although a cove farmer might continue to bring his crops to Knoxville, he no longer felt any closeness or sense of community toward those outside the cove proper. The vacuum caused by this alienation and these temporary divisions within the larger region was filled by strengthening ties among themselves, thereby intensifying an already strong sense of community within the cove.

In this atmosphere, an indigenous folk culture developed which compensated the cove people in part for their economic losses and greatly enriched the quality of their relationships with one another. Cultural historians, folklorists, and anthropologists have long disputed the exact nature and definition of "folk" cultures.[2] For the purpose of this chapter, folk culture is defined simply as the totality of shared experience, knowledge, and mythology which the cove people communicated orally among themselves. The totality of this folk culture functioned almost as a foreign language inasmuch as it gave to the cove citizen both a frame of reference for interpreting new events and a code of anecdotes by which various attitudes or emotions could be immediately identified to other members of the group. Two important corollaries to this folk culture are the means by which it was expressed (regional dialect and its deviation from standard English), and the interpretation of the culture by outsiders and the representation of these interpretations in the fictional writings of such local colorists as Mary Noailles Murfree.[3]

This interpretation of folk culture is formulated only to explain and analyze the development of oral traditions within the cove and their functional value in the daily relationships of the cove people with one another. No serious study of folk culture can avoid, however, the warnings of Richard M. Dorson, who argues that the study of folklore has been "falsified, abused and exploited, and the public deluded with Paul Bunyan nonsense and claptrap collections" by money-writers who "have successfully peddled synthetic hero-books and saccharine folk tales as the stories of the people."[4]

The geographic isolation of the cove, for example, is one element in the development of their folk culture which must be examined with maximum critical skepticism. The diversity and number of immigrants moving into Cades Cove before 1860 offers patent evidence that the community was at one point neither inaccessible nor an undesirable place to live.[5] The cessation of new immigrants after the war, and the expulsion of pro-Confederate families did lead to increasing social isolation and conformity. But this isolation was always *relative*. The cove people continued to sell their crops in Knoxville, receive visitors from other sections of the country, and remain informed of major state, national, and international events through an occasional newspaper. In turning its collective attention inward, the community did not completely cut itself off from the outside world, although it is a common fallacy of local historians to envision such geographic and social isolation in absolute, either/or terms. Thus the cove people could develop their own body of shared traditions and experiences while at the same time they remained cognizant of changes and broad trends in the larger American culture.[6]

Another fallacious assumption about the origins of the folk culture in the cove was the national origins of the inhabitants, and by inference, the transmission of certain corollary national traits or characteristics. As late as the 1920s, commentators on life in the cove saw descendants of "pure" Anglo-Saxon blood there who maintained ancient English speech patterns and customs, speaking the language little altered since Queen Elizabeth reigned. Other writers confidently asserted that in these remote coves of Southern Appalachia, "blood tells," and the sturdy Scotch-Irish descendants maintained an independence of spirit and sturdiness of mind and character which made them the envy of their decadent relatives in other parts of an increasingly industrial and urban America.[7]

Such assumptions about the cultural homogeneity of the cove inhabitants resulting from common national origins reveal more about the preconceptions and erroneous assumptions of these writers than about the actual folk culture of the cove. Men like Robert Lindsay Mason and Samuel Tyndale Wilson found what they were looking for in the cove through the process of selective perception, a process cultural anthropologists now explain as the cause for such gross misrepresentation of American Indian customs by early colonial observers, who alternately perceived their red brethren as the lost tribes of Israel or the children of Satan. Wilson viewed the mountaineers both as a panacea for the ills of industrial America and as an antidote to the influx of "un-American" foreigners.[8]

Actually, non-English immigrants were numerous in the cove. German names were frequent; Myers, Headrick, Cable, Rowan, Herren, and Shuler are examples. Cable, a corruption of the original Köbel, is illustrative of the frequent Anglicization of German names which often obscures their origin. The Myers, one of the cove's largest extended families, still preserve the German Bible of their progenitors as proof of their origin. Families of French extraction were also common, bearing such names as Lequire, Foute, Fearel, Feezell, Boring, Nichol, Pastuer, Lemon, Laurens, Seay, Emmert, and Freshour. Three families of Dutch origin were listed in the 1850 census; some of their children married into cove families and lost their distinctive surnames (Lafabra, Sucan, Faurfort) but possibly not their cultural traditions from Holland.[9]

An interesting anecdote from the nineteenth century reveals the cove people's own awareness of the diverse national origins of new settlers. Before the Civil War, a stranger settled there and taught school. Several years after his arrival, another stranger visited him, and they conversed in an unknown tongue which even the German Cables could not understand. Some of the natives speculated that their strange school teacher was one of Napoleon's defeated generals living in exile among them![10]

So the most cursory look at the early census returns indicates a wide diversity in national origins of the cove people from the time of earliest settlement. Since John Oliver, the first permanent white settler, arrived as late as 1818, most of the early families had been in the United States for at least a generation before that date. The demographic picture up until 1860 reveals constant flux, waves of cove people moving further west as new immigrants from widely diverse places entered the cove. Until 1860, it would be impossible to identify any distinctive feature or indigenous pattern of cove culture, since most of the population had moved there as adults from other sections of the United States.[11] This lack of cultural consensus, however, does not preclude identifying various ingredients, such as the carpentry and engineering skills earlier noted in Peter Cable, who was of Pennsylvania Dutch extraction.

In its broadest definition, the folk culture emerged in the cove after 1865 due to wartime experiences, the expanding kinship structure, economic difficulties which drew families together, and a sense of alienation from the surrounding region. This culture was not defined by its component parts, but rather by the collective use of these ingredients, past and present, by the community. Complex as such a functional definition seems, it reflects the basic fact that the cove culture was never static, often creative, and could always use or incorporate outside experience as well as traditional knowledge passed down from father to son. To define its perimeters, for example, an authentic English ballad (and there were many of these) might be shared by the community at the same time a popular song imported from Knoxville circulated through the cove, or a group might compose a ballad to commemorate some notable event which had only recently occurred, such as the sinking of the *Titanic*. What the traditional ballad and the popular song shared in this culture, obviously, was not their respective origins, but their collective use by the community, the value assigned to the song which everyone in the cove recognized and shared.[12]

The folk culture in this sense was only a system of shared values, experiences, and myths of various origins, but each one of these oral expressions had a specific, well-defined common meaning to every member of the community. Every past attempt to analyze or dissect the folk mind of the cove has failed because no scholar has ever perceived the importance of seeing in its totality their shared knowledge within the context of such an intensive communal lifestyle. Bits and pieces were meaningless outside the context of the whole, so a wide variety of characterizations of life in the cove were made by various writers oblivious to the inherent incompleteness and internal contradictions of their observations and conclusions. Even the natives were not directly conscious of the elaborate format of their folk culture; they took these things for granted, understood them from early childhood almost intuitively, and could not explicitly identify or describe what they implicitly knew and believed, and considered common knowledge. Thus the parts were often described adequately by outside observers, but by their very fragmentation such descriptions rendered any empirical analysis invalid.[13]

As the easiest introduction into the folk mind of Cades Cove, it is probably most obvious to begin with the physical geography of the cove and surrounding mountains. Densely inhabited by comparative standards, the cove proper contained no streamlets, no meadows, fields, rocky ridges, or trees too small not to be named. Writers interviewing residents of the cove who had lived there during the last century neglected to analyze this basic, obvious phenomenon of an elaborately detailed folk geography. Cove natives could immediately identify or "home in" on specific geographic locations because everyone knew even the most minute spots by name and reputation. These tiny locales or landmarks were anthropomorphic, too, in the sense that the human history surrounding them was carefully preserved and enumerated from time to time. Corroborative evidence of this phenomenon occurs in the deeds, which often mention small and insignificant marking points by name; the implicit assumption on the part of the magistrates who drew up such deeds was that each identifying landmark would be so well known by all the cove residents that such identification could stand up in court.[14]

Much more substantive, the crux on which the entire folk culture rested, was the intimate knowledge of one another which the community shared. It began with genealogical data: all the known relatives, living and dead, parents, grandparents, aunts, uncles, cousins, and so on, of any single resident was common knowledge, frequently recited, to *all* members of the community. In such a close-knit society, secrets concerning one's personal life or family were practically impossible to keep, and an attempt to conceal any major event was interpreted in the worst possible light as both an obvious indication of guilt and an affront to and rejection of the entire community. Individuals might forgive one another such omissions readily enough in Christian charity, but the collective folk mind seldom forgave or forgot.[15]

The net result of this constant scrutiny of every individual in the community was that in an almost computer-like fashion, every variety and instance of human behavior or misbehavior were recorded and remembered. Cove children early learned, for instance, of Uncle Jack Anthony's profane reaction on being struck by lightning while riding his prize mule, even though the individual in question might have been dead for thirty years, or his family might have departed the cove several decades earlier. The important point here is that these characterizations and anecdotes on every individual who lived in the cove for the past fifty years were absolutely staggering in both their number and detail. It is likewise difficult to comprehend the fact that each rational member of the folk culture was required to recognize instantly the anecdote, its actor and context, and the moral or value reference surrounding it.[16]

This knowledge served many functions. A whole range of complex

emotions could be identified readily by reference to an incident in someone's past personal history; in this sense these anecdotes or characterizations functioned as a code or second language, often inpenetrable or
incomprehensible to an outsider. This second langauge, far more than
any supposed dialect, made adjustment difficult for those residents
moving outside the cove because in so doing they lost not only the intense sense of belonging and being cared for by the entire community,
but also this larger folk knowledge of each other which no one outside
the cove could fathom; it was almost as though one of their senses had
been removed to leave such an environment. This frame of reference
was timeless in its application because the value assigned to each incident had to remain unchanged to function as an identifying factor. The
perspective which this code gave to the average cove resident was particularly reassuring in the turbulent years after 1865, binding together
as it did the past, present, and developing future in a common, universally understood frame of reference.[17]

The folk knowledge also served a didactic purpose in socializing
their children, inasmuch as deviant behavior could be stigmatized by
reference to one of the folk characters, which was far more stinging
than customary upbraidings. This function extended to adults also,
since no one willingly incurred the risk of ridicule by odious comparisons to these types, or chanced the even greater liability of acting in
such an egregious fashion that they themselves became typed and im-
mortalized in the folk memory as an opprobrious example to future
generations. All types of variant behavior were reproduced in these
anecdotes; an unusual way of walking, plowing, and so on, might at-
tract the attention of the folk mind as well as unusual experiences.
Included in such characterizations were variant pronunciations or unusual combinations of words, a factor which often misled those folklorists collecting examples of dialect, since they seldom realized the
mimicking capacity of the folk or the enormous number and variety
of such deliberate mispronunciations that were reproduced as part of
the common store of folk knowledge.[18]

Viewing the folk culture in the context of the total cove society, it
is also important to point out that there were definite divisions within
that society which might appreciably alter or color one's perception of
the community's shared knowledge. The majority of cove farmers liv-

ing in the fertile basin shared a consensus of common ideas and values. The smaller subgroup living in Chestnut Flats, however, completely rejected the majority's condemnation of their insobriety, sexual promiscuity, disregard of the work ethic, and abstention from membership in any of the churches. This subculture in Chestnut Flats thus developed its own system of folk culture basically antagonistic to the cove majority, although there were common elements shared by both cultures which could not be ignored. Since each group defined the other in such hostile, negative terms, it is only logical that their respective interpretation of common elements in the cove culture would differ. Yet commentators on life in the cove were rarely cognizant of this very basic distinction in cove society, and frequently characterized the majority by information given by a member of the minority group.[19]

It would also be logical to assume a definite correlation between the decline in literacy and the development of a folk culture after 1865. Dr. Jobe recalled attending a school "of the most primitive order" in 1825 in the cove, but concluded that "the discipline in the primitive schools in my opinion was firmer, but more commonsense and reasonable, than we find in modern schools."[20] The emphasis on discipline and the development of basic skills which he described in the 1820s seems to have prevailed throughout the century. Before 1836, article schools were common in the cove; a schoolmaster took subscriptions, or "articles of agreement," from the people to teach school in the community. These sessions usually lasted two months, and the teacher "had to have practically no qualifications except that he could write a good hand and knew the old blue back speller and the New Testament." When the cove became the sixteenth civil district in 1836, each district elected three directors who hired a teacher. The schoolmaster thus chosen was required to pass an examination once a year administered by the county superintendent, so the standards for selecting teachers were broadened and basic or minimal qualifications were required. These free or common schools usually operated only several months out of the year and did not offer instruction beyond the fifth grade. In the period after the Civil War there is ample evidence that these free schools continued to operate, however. One extant authorization by the Cades Cove school directors in 1874 mentions paying J.C. Sprinkle $50 for teaching the free school No. 2, which indicates at least two schools were in operation at the time.[21]

So the literacy rate, or quality of the average citizen's ability to read after 1865 is difficult to measure, particularly as a function of the folk culture. From the records of the Primitive Baptist church, the handwriting and orthography seem to decline noticeably after the Civil War. Census statistics in 1870 indicate a high percentage of school-age children had attended school within the year, yet these same statistics indicate that 36 percent of the adult population could not read, and 58 percent were not able to write in that year. It seems probable to conclude that the postwar decline in the cove literacy rate coincided with the development of their folk culture, although this generalization must be qualified by pointing out that roughly half the adult population in 1870 were literate, if the census figures are not completely inaccurate. This literate half, moreover, was reasonably well informed about state and national events, and still retained the intensive, detailed knowledge of the cove's internal affairs required by the folk culture.[22]

An important function of this folk culture was entertainment in the form of innumerable folk narratives, tall tales, Märchen, jokes, proverbs, puzzles, and sayings (idioms). Examples of each of these generic types could be cited to conform to the patterns of *Volkskunde* in the traditional European classification. Three basic types of folk narratives reoccur with sufficient frequency and consistency in the cove folk culture to justify close examination: tall tales (often involving the absurd, as in the German Märchen), ghost stories, and narratives of war experiences.[23]

Possibly as a result of their wilderness environment, most of the tall tales from the nineteenth-century folk culture of Cades Cove concern extraordinary feats involving wild animals. These tales range from the absurd, Märchen-type stories primarily designed to entertain children to more involved narratives which approach some degree of credibility among the adult population. An example of the former type is the phantom cat, who chasing a man to his porch, remarked, "some footrace we had." Whereupon the exhausted man raised up and replied, "Not like the one we're going to have," and started running again.[24]

A popular tale in the nineteenth century involved a common European motif of a woman alone in the mountains escaping a pack of wolves. In the cove version, the old woman was returning home with meat for her children after assisting a neighbor in killing hogs. As the wolves neared, she dropped pieces of the meat to distract them, finally arriving safely home just as the last scrap of meat was gone. The animal most frequently involved in these tall tales, however, was the panther, whom the cove people feared and believed capable of attacking humans. Such an experience was related to Justice Douglas in 1962 about Tom Sparks, who claimed to have been attacked while herding sheep on Gregory Bald, and to have driven off with a pocket knife the panther which had jumped on his back.[25] Sparks's tale is reminiscent of most of the tall tales involving hunting and panthers during the nineteenth century.

Tall tales differed from other types of narratives inasmuch as they usually did not involve the supernatural (except in Märchen-type stories primarily intended for children) but approached some degree of credibility. The most notable such tall tale was related to Mellinger Henry, a folklorist exploring the cove area in the 1920s, and described how Hattie Carrell Herron Myers was carried off by an eagle as a small child. Hattie was playing in her back yard on Abrams Creek while her mother did the family washing there. Suddenly the eagle swooped down, fastened its talons in the little girl's clothing and started to fly off. The mother screamed so loudly, according to the story, that the eagle became frightened and dropped the child uninjured into some nearby bushes.[26]

Ghost stories were extremely popular in the folk culture, as the sheer number and variety of such extant supernatural tales from the nineteenth century testify. More than tall tales, however, these ghost stories occasionally had a specific function or didactic purpose in the culture: commemorating a notable citizen or event in the past, or marking carefully on the collective folk mind some particular crime or injustice was frequently accomplished by means of such stories. For example, a cove farmer returning home intoxicated late one night in the 1870s was angered by the cries of his newborn infant, and demanded that his wife quieten the baby. Occupied with some other task, she was momentarily unable to comply, whereupon the father seized the infant in a great rage and crushed his skull. In the area around the house where this infanticide occurred, the cove people claimed to be able to hear a ghostly baby wailing and crying for many decades afterward. This supernatural phenomenon reflected the community's sense of horror and outrage at the event, and kept the details of the murder before the folk mind as an example and warning, even though the guilty farmer soon moved out of the cove.[27]

Tales of war experiences were also popular and served to idealize and commemorate the nation's wars, particularly the Revolutionary War, in the folk mind. Lt. Davis, escaping through the cove from a Southern prison camp during the Civil War, remarked with amazement how the old-timers in neighboring Tuckaleechee Cove entertained him with Revolutionary War stories. John Oliver had a plethora of tales which he related about General Jackson and his experiences at Horseshoe Bend in the War of 1812. How determinative these stories were in molding the consensus in the cove against secession in 1861 is impossible accurately to determine, but it is undoubtedly true that such war tales, told repeatedly through the years, served to transform the early national wars into unrivaled standards of accomplishment and patriotism in the folk mind. Oliver recounted how the Cherokee chief, Junuluska, swam under water to cut loose enemy canoes at Horseshoe Bend, an action he considered paramount to their ultimate victory. Another representative tale from Oliver's experiences in this war was related by his grandson, William Howell:

The first one that I will mention was that of standing on picket guard post. He said that one of those wild Indians had killed a wild hog and skinned it and wrapped himself up in the skin of that wild hog so completely that his hands and feet was not easely detected and under that skin he had a dagger and tomahawk. He would crawl along untill he would get close enough to the man at the post, then he would throw off the skin and burst upon the sentinel without any alarm, he then killed the man and carried him off some distance and concealed him in the leaves, he then covered himself again in his hog skin and fixed for another man. This he done untill he had killed three brave men, and no trace of them could be found. This so amazed the company that the fourth man whose turn it was to take the post trembled from head to foot. The captain then stated that he would have no man against his will. A man immediately stepped from the ranks, and desired to take the post, telling the captain that if a crow chattered or a leaf fell that he would hear his muskett. My Granfather said they all shook hands with him and went away to their duty. He said that it had not been very long untill they heard his gun fire, they all went to see what he was doing, upon arrival they saw the man comeing dragging the Indian by the hair of his head. The man said he had not been verry long at his post till he seen this wild hog as it seemed to be prowling along hunting for nuts, but kept his eye upon it untill he thought he saw him give an unusual spring, upon which he no longer hesitated, took his aim, discharged his piece, and immediately the animal was stretched out before him with the groan of a human. This unfolded the mystery of what had happened to the other three men that were lost.[28]

Bearing in mind the fact that the entertainment function was only one part of the totality of the cove folk culture, it is unfortunate that folklorists in the twentieth century badly distorted this totality by selecting only certain parts of it to collect and analyze. No group was more guilty of this variety of selective perception than ballad collectors. Granted that ballads were themselves intrinsically interesting, and that from all accounts Cades Cove was an unequaled reservoir of many varieties of ballads in the Southern Appalachian mountains, collectors nevertheless ignored the historical context of these ballads and made no real effort to analyze their function within the cove folk culture. Richard Dorson has pointed out the fallacy of such researchers whose collections "include technically excellent works" but "remain on the level of text-hunting." Instead of comparing variations with the European Ur-type, Dorson argues, such ballads should be evaluated within the context of normative *American* experiences such as the Westward Movement, regionalism, and the nation's wars.[29]

In the summer of 1928, Mellinger Henry discovered in Cades Cove people who "still talk to some extent the language of Shakespeare's time and sing the songs and ballads of that period." Isolated by their mountain environment, these people of "Anglo-Saxon stock" cling "even yet to the manners and customs of the 18th century." In a series of articles in the *New Jersey Journal of Education* and in two published collections, Henry documented a vast array of traditional English and Scottish ballads from Cades Cove, including such rare songs as "Little Musgrave and Lady Barnard," "Lamkin," "Johnny Scot," "Sir Hugh, or the Jew's Daughter," "Lady Isabel and the Elf Knight," "Earl Brand," "Young

Beichan," "Lord Thomas and Fair Annet," "James Harris," "Bonny Barbara Allan," and "The Maid Freed from the Gallows."[30]

Henry doubtlessly performed an invaluable service in identifying and preserving these traditional ballads, but he ignored the larger folk culture which transmitted them and concentrated on collecting only those songs with recognizable English antecedents. Cognizant of the fact that ballad-making was a continuing process, he nevertheless ignored ballads from the later nineteenth century which reflected such signal experiences as the Civil War. Although most of the ballads came from Cades Cove, he randomly lumped them together with those from other parts of the culturally heterogeneous Southern Appalachians. If Henry was oblivious to the obvious distinctions between the cove community and the larger region, he was similarly blind to variations among individual informants who supplied the ballads. The Harmon family, his chief source, had moved to Cades Cove in the twentieth century, for instance, and were not necessarily representative of the older folk culture.[31]

Henry's scholarly myopia was partially corrected by Margaret Elisabeth Gamble in her 1947 Southern California thesis entitled "The Heritage and Folk Music of Cades Cove, Tennessee." Perceiving the vital relationship between the community and oral expressions of folk culture, she made a sustained effort to analyze the social context of the seventy-six ballads she collected from former cove residents. Descended from a former cove resident, she had an immediate entree few other scholars had previously enjoyed. Yet Gamble never quite understood what she had found, possibly due to the fact that the community had already been dispersed by 1947, and she was unable to grasp the totality of the folk culture through the eyes of individual and elderly informants.[32]

Gamble discovered that the largest group of songs, more numerous than even the traditional ballads, were hymns of the variety known as "old harp songs." Harp singing was introduced to the cove after the Civil War by various singing masters who were paid by the community to conduct a school in which interested people could learn the notes and methodology of harp singing. This type of singing, widespread throughout the area, was especially popular in Cades Cove because it had the approval of the dominant churches, particularly the Primitive

Baptist. The majority of the cove community strongly disapproved of the more salacious songs sung by the subcommunity in Chestnut Flats, and stigmatized these as "jigs," or "carnival songs."[33]

Remnants of the older folk culture were discovered accidentally by Gamble in 1946 when she attended one of these harp singings. To her amazement, former cove inhabitants called the songs by number, never by name; "they knew the book so well that the pages were even memorized." The folk culture was determined not by its ingredients, as formerly stated, but by the collective use and knowledge of whatever information was deemed necessary or desirable. In this instance, harp singing was not indigenous to the cove, since it had been imported after 1865 and was commonly practiced in the larger region. Yet the folk culture embraced these hymnals, assigning a value and identity to each song so that one had only to call the number to identify it to the entire group. This mechanism of assigning common value or identity to a wide range of phenomena functioned regardless of whether the ingredient was old or new, and meant that the folk mind was both flexible and expanding in incorporating other concepts. New ideas could also come from literary sources, since the mastery of harp singing required the participant to both read and learn the notes.[34]

An extremely important aspect of the folk culture was the dialect, or variant form of spoken English used by the cove inhabitants during the nineteenth century. Early writers believed that Elizabethan English, or at least survival forms common in the eighteenth century, were still used by cove inhabitants well into the twentieth century. Other writers such as Mary Noailles Murfree and Horace Kephart portrayed Southern Appalachian dialect in such a distorted and grotesque fashion that they completely misinterpreted regional speech patterns. Kephart, according to one critic, "seems to have been impressed particularly by what would look like good dialect on paper, and his notes and published writings scarcely do justice to the speech which he seeks to represent."[35] Even when Justice William O. Douglas, an untrained phonetician, attempted to describe orthographically the speech of Cades Cove inhabitants in a 1962 *National Geographic* article, the result "was a kind of mimicked dialect of the variety used in comic strips such as 'Snuffy Smith' or 'L'il Abner.'"[36]

The first scholarly analysis of the regional English of Cades Cove came in 1942 with the publication of Joseph S. Hall's *The Phonetics of Great Smoky Mountain Speech*. Since earlier articles by scholars interested in Southern mountain dialect such as Josiah Combs and Charles Carpenter had been primarily concerned with lexicography, Hall undertook to record and analyze phonologically representative samples of the speech patterns of all the people in Tennessee and North Carolina who were dislocated by the establishment of the Great Smoky Mountains National Park. Severely criticizing popular writers such as Kephart, who had badly distorted regional mountain speech, he found few vestiges of earlier stages in the growth of the English language which these writers had so frequently characterized as "Anglo-Saxon," "Chaucerian," or "Elizabethan." His most important discovery was "a sound system which reflects and illustrates so well the phonology of early modern English, and which helps to clarify the history of modern standard pronunciation." He concluded that Smoky Mountain speech showed "no sharp cleavage from the speech of most of America," although there were "close affinities with the speech of the rest of the South."[37]

In a more recent study, Hall attempted to analyze the folk culture of the cove people through their use of proverbial sayings and common expressions:

> Careful examination of these sayings will etch scenes and awaken echoes of the past life in the Great Smokies. These scenes and echoes reveal folk skills and the strong ties between the people and their farms and farm animals. There are also strong linguistic ties to life in the fields and forests, and in the rugged mountains; there are, too, quaint allusions to the hard work of farming, the hearty sport of bearhunting, the work of women at their tasks "never done," as the proverb goes. There are moods of weariness, sadness, joy, and pleasure, and humorous outbursts of wild exuberance. There are echoes of frontier brags and tall talk. There are occasional restrained hints of sin and sex. There are references to worn-out soil, to the lush, jungle-like growth of plants and trees, and to changes of weather. There are frank or rustic and sometimes witty characterizations of people, especially as to their oddities. There are references to the violence of moods and emotions that angered men are capable of feeling.[38]

Hall, however, made no distinction between the geographic areas in the Great Smokies, nor did he distinguish between the age of his informants or their degree of education or outside exposure. These defects were remedied in a 1972 dissertation by M. Jean Jones at the University of Tennessee. Working under the direction of Harold Orton, one of Britain's most distinguished dialectologists, she applied advanced methodological techniques for phonological research to the speech patterns of five elderly former inhabitants of Cades Cove who had remained comparatively isolated since removal from their homes during the late 1930s. She concluded that the cove people spoke a homogenous dialect characterized by a fairly persistent pattern of vowel fluctuation. More significantly, she offered convincing phonological evidence that the cove speech patterns were further characterized by forms of grammar and vocabulary common in earlier English but long discarded in modern usage.

In her study of their language, Jones was the first scholar perceptive enough to realize that a much greater need existed for analyzing the folk culture of Cades Cove, and throughout her dissertation she was sensitive to various influences and crosscurrents of this folk culture as it interacted with different types of oral communication and expressions. For example, she noted discussions of metaphors for specific ceremonial occasions, such as funerals, although none of her informants identified the normative values, or specified usages of these metaphors in differing situations.[39] In this sense, recovery of the totality of the folk culture would elucidate various phonological and lexicographical deviations, since such variations usually had a definite function or purpose of which even the speaker might not be fully conscious or aware.

The diversity and vitality of the nineteenth-century folk culture of Cades Cove are evident in the surviving language and anecdotes of former inhabitants — language elsewhere outmoded but full of earlier pictures of folk imagery. "If there is any one thing which illustrates simply and well a people's character and group personality," Hall rightfully concluded, "it is the language they use." Thus surviving language and speech patterns reflect the common bonds of the cove people united by the excruciating ordeal of the Civil War and later economic depression. The folk culture in this sense was a continuing solace; through "favorite phrases describing such common things as land, people, time and weather; oaths and profanity; humorous remarks; and aphorisms," they reaffirmed their sense of community and faith in the essential humanity of one another.[40]

At least three nineteenth-century American writers attempted to utilize this folk culture and the wilderness environment surrounding Cades Cove. Charles W. Todd, Tennessee's first novelist, used Montvale Springs and its vicinity as the setting for *Woodville; Or Anchoret Reclaimed*, published in 1832. In this rather complicated romantic tale, the hero, Allison Woodville, fell madly in love with his half-sister, unaware of the relationship. After their elopement was frustrated, the girl then yielded to the mother's wishes for an alliance with a young degenerate of blood and wealth. Woodville went to Europe to join Marco Bozzaris in the fight for Greek freedom, was pursued by the young wife's jealous husband, and killed him in a duel. Returning to America, he learned the truth about his half-sister, and left civilization to flee into the solitude of the mountains near Montvale Springs.[41]

The book is notable, as early critics pointed out, more as an "index and aspiration than from any inherent merit." But the description of mountain scenery in *Woodville* was well written if somewhat over-elaborated and placed by inference the hero's cabin retreat in or very close to Cades Cove. Little is known of Todd, other than that he was a theological student at Maryville College, was licensed to preach in September 1829 by the Union Presbytery, and later was dropped when he joined the Protestant Episcopal Church.[42] In this first effort at fiction by a Tennessean, however, it is important to note that Todd simply used the wilderness environment of the cove as a background for his own romantic plot and characterizations, and ignored the developing folk culture in the cove, a pattern that other writers would repeat with monotonous consistency.

Sidney Lanier, in contrast, stereotyped the cove inhabitants in another extremely complicated tale, *Tiger-Lilies*, published in 1867. As mentioned earlier, Lanier's grandfather, Sterling, became manager in 1857 of Montvale Springs, and Sidney was familiar with the entire area. Although *Tiger-Lilies* received a two-line review in the *Peterson Magazine* as "one of those novels, the chief wonder of which is, that they ever got published at all," critics failed to note the superficial and devastating caricature of cove society which Lanier represented in several comic, if badly distorted, vignettes of the life of the natives there. In one such scene, two German guests at Montvale Springs discussed an imaginary morning paper in Cades Cove, mirroring exactly Lanier's own misconceptions:

"A morning paper here! Imagine the local column: 'We are pained to record that our esteemed friend and neighbor, Mrs. Razor, met last night with a serious domestic calamity, in the loss of two fine chickens and a goose, supposed to have been kidnapped by a wild-cat;' or, 'It is our unpleasant duty to record an unfortunate personal recontre, which took place late on yesterday afternoon, in the streets of Cade's Cove, between a black bear and four hounds belonging to Mr. Razor, in which, though the bear was worsted, two of the dogs were badly wooled;' and then, Fraulein, the commercial column: 'The market in Cade's Cove has been exceedingly quiet the past week, and commercial transactions extremely limited. Indeed, except in the single article of whiskey, we have to report absolutely nothing doing. We have account of sales of whiskey, yesterday, amounting in all to twenty-six (26) drinks, twenty-five (25) of which being bought on time or by barter, we make no cash quotations, especially as the twenty-sixth sale might prove a false criterion and mislead dealers, it being a drink paid for, cash, by a stranger going through to North Carolina, who, not knowing the prices of whiskey in Cade's Cove, was charged double rates by our enterprising friend who runs the distillery.'[43]

Although Lanier caricatured the cove's inhabitants for comic relief, it was apparent throughout the novel that he, like Todd, was primarily interested in the wilderness environment of Cades Cove as a setting for his own romantic phantasies. He picked up the motif of contrast between "broad, level meadows . . . inclosed by precipitous ridges, behind which succeed higher ridges, and still higher, until the lofty mountains wall in and overshadow them all."[44] Unfortunately, the very wretchedness of *Tiger-Lilies'* plot and his distortion of cove society obscured the fact that Lanier was the first artist to seriously question the relationship between the wilderness and the cove people, symbolized by this geographical contrast.

The writer who had the greatest opportunity to minutely study and analyze the folk culture of Cades Cove in its fullest development after the Civil War was Mary Noailles Murfree, who, under the pseudonym Charles Egbert Craddock, achieved some fame in the 1880s for her short stories and novels set in the Cumberland Mountains of Middle Tennessee and in the Great Smoky Mountains. During the 1880s, Miss Murfree had stayed for extended periods in Cades Cove with the family of "the old 'Squire," who took her on horseback over the mountain trails because she was lame. This important detail has been missed by all her biographers, although it was fairly common knowledge in regional histories at the turn of the century.[45] Her use of Cades Cove as a setting in *In the Tennessee Mountains* (1884), *The Prophet of the Great Smoky Mountains* (1885), *In the Clouds* (1886), *The Despot of Broomsedge Cove* (1888), *In the "Stranger People's" Country* (1891), *The Mystery of Witch-Face Mountain* (1895), *The Raid of the Guerilla* (1912), and other stories is unmistakable if judged from internal evidence alone. Frequently, for example, she mentioned Cades Cove, neighboring Tuckaleechee Cove, and other familiar landmarks and geographical features, such as Thunderhead Mountain, by name. Nor can it be reasonably argued that she was not told the narratives or descriptions of their folk culture by the cove people. Her introductory description of the community after the outbreak of the Civil War in *The Raid of the Guerilla* is too accurate to have been readily obtained from outside sources. But the plot of this novel, like the rest of her stories, bears little resemblance to the actual wartime happenings.[46]

Despite these advantages, Mary Murfree was no Emily Brontë; she lacked the power to understand either the folk culture or individual motivation on any but the most superficial level. Her characters are static, unrealistic, doll-like manikins who bear no likeness to the cove people. Plots and characterizations were the product of her narrowly circumscribed Victorian world view; she remained "a Southern lady with every trait that this phrase implies." Edd Parks has pointed out that however meticulous she was "with dialect, with proper names, with the small minutiae of life that seem relatively unimportant," she nevertheless "censored the speech of her characters automatically, and she censored their thoughts and actions without any realization that she was portraying life in a distorted fashion."[47]

Critics early questioned Miss Murfree's use of dialect, in addition to the barrage of criticism directed against the weaknesses of characterization and plot in her novels and short stories. "With allowance for the fifty-five years which have passed since she wrote *The Prophet of the*

Great Smoky Mountains and the changes which dialect may undergo in that length of time," Joseph Hall remarked with acerbity in 1942, "it is still difficult to believe that the people of the Smokies ever spoke quite as she makes them speak."[48] Murfree's greatest failure, however, was her complete blindness or insensibility to the folk culture of the people among whom she lived in Cades Cove. The richness of this culture, their intricate knowledge of one another, and the enormous lore they shared were completely ignored by her, although many of these elements were precisely what was most lacking in her writings. Exposed to an almost inexhaustibly rich folk culture at its apex, she was blind to any other creative source than her own limited imagination, an unfortunate myopia to which her fiction sadly bears testimony.

Nathalia Wright concluded in her introduction to the reprint of *In the Tennessee Mountains* that Miss Murfree's "representation of the mountaineers and the mountains as by nature inseparable . . . . may be her most significant achievement." Frank Waldo argued that as she became increasingly engrossed with the physical beauty of the Smokies, Murfree adopted their geographical setting for her novels, but retained the traits of the Cumberland Mountain people, which she had earlier studied, for her fictional characters.[49] Judging from her description of the cove's inhabitants, Waldo's thesis seems far more probable. Other critics argued that her extended passages describing the mountain wilderness were overdrawn, and dominated if not overshadowed every scene. William Allen White maintained that "her mountain landscapes were done after the painting of the period, bright, lovely, gorgeous, and—alas—unreal."[50]

Regardless of whether her descriptions of the wilderness were realistic, it is evident that she became increasingly obsessed with such scenes, often to the detriment of plot or structure, and gradually the mountains assumed more identity and power than did the people living in them. It is a logical corollary to this obsession that Miss Murfree portrayed the lives of her characters as inextricably fixed and determined by their environment. Robert Love Taylor identifies this determinism, or implicit belief on Murfree's part that the mountain people were so isolated or frozen in their environment that they neither could nor should ever re-enter the mainstream of American life as her major contribution to Southern thought.[51]

Unfortunately, other modern critics continue to identify as Murfree's greatest contribution to American literature her "re-creation of life in the Tennessee mountains," wherein she "gave expression to a place, a people, and a moment in time which may never again see its duplication in the history of our civilization." Richard Cary, her latest biographer, concludes that she was "one among a glorious dozen who brought light to scattered geographic and sociological enclaves inside the United States during the last quarter of the nineteenth century." Her Tennessee community, he argues, "is a vital cell in the assimilating organism that has developed into the American character."[52] If the actual development and growth of the Cades Cove community or the folk culture which she studied there has historical validity, however, her writings *do not* reflect with any degree of realism or verisimilitude either the personal or communal lives of the people of Southern Appalachia. Along with most of the writers who visited the cove and recorded their impressions of life there during the last part of the nineteenth century, she deserves credit only for perpetuating numerous stereotypes and misconceptions which have for decades drastically impeded serious research in or study of the region.[53]

If the folk culture of Cades Cove was in reality a vital cell in the assimilating organism that has developed into the American character, it was due primarily to the fact that most of the component parts within that cell had long been fundamental elements in the larger culture. After the Civil War, certain traits or strands of the larger culture, such as the strong sense of community which had existed unimpeded from earliest settlement, were intensified. Most of the characteristics of the postwar community, in this context, were only exaggerations of existing currents in the broader mainstream of American society. Their intensified knowledge of one another and the development of an elaborate folklore gave the cove people both security and stability during the trying years of Reconstruction. Yet the difference between their folk culture and that of their fellow countrymen in other parts of the region and nation was always one of degree or emphasis, not of kind. The cove cell could arrange its atoms, or component parts, to meet the temporal and spiritual demands of its immediate environment, and still remain a fairly representative microcosm of the larger American organism.

William Howell Oliver (1857–1940), Primitive Baptist minister, grandson of the first John Oliver, father of John W. Oliver, left a remarkable history of the cove entitled "Sketches of the Olivers." *Oliver Family Collection.*

Elizabeth Jane Gregory Oliver (1855–1925), wife of William Howell Oliver, granddaughter of Russell Gregory. *Oliver Family Collection.*

Daniel David Foute (1800–1865). Foremost entrepreneur and landowner in the cove during the nineteenth century, he also served as justice of the peace and as Blount County court clerk. A staunch Confederate, he was taken from his sickbed in the cove by Union forces to Knoxville in 1865, and died shortly thereafter. Courtesy Inez Burns, copied by A. Randolph Shields.

Above left, Dr. John Calvin Post (1803–1873), physician, entrepreneur, scientist, abolitionist, was one of the most influential leaders in the nineteenth-century cove community. Courtesy A. Randolph Shields. *Above right,* John W. Oliver and wife, Nancy Ann Whitehead, 1901. John W. Oliver's inscription reads: "This picture was taken at Maryville Tenn on Saturday afternoon of January 26, 1901. Next day, Sunday, Nancy Ann and I rode horseback all the way from Maryville through the flats of Chilhowee Mountains to Cades Cove a distance of 20 miles without ever dismounting from our horses. It was a cold blue day but our hearts were warm for each other. I had on the first full

suit of clothes I ever owned. I bought them on Saturday Jan., 26, 1901 with the first money I ever earned teaching school at $23 per month. They cost me $8.50. We were 22 years old and not married. We were married Sept. 4, 1901." *Oliver Family Collection.*

Left, "Uncle John Cable, the old bear hunter at 75 years" (John W. Oliver's inscription). *Right,* Uncle Dan Myers (1854–1939), late 1920s. *Oliver Family Collection.*

Left, "Aunt Margaret Shields Myers, 1856–1940, the only living child of the pioneer baby carried in the arms of its pioneer mother, Mrs. John Oliver, in the year 1818." *Right,* "Aunt Kate Lawson, left, 82, and her sister Mrs. Rhoda Abbott." (John W. Oliver's inscription.) *Oliver Family Collection.*

Left, "Misses Susie and Lizzie Myers with their father James P. Myers," late 1920s. *Right,* "John Tipton and his bear dogs," late 1920s. *Oliver Family Collection.*

Left, "Left to right: Mrs. M.J. Whitehead, Mr. Taylor Whitehead, Mrs. Hannah Sparks, "late 1920s. John W. Oliver made an effort to photograph all the elderly inhabitants of the cove before their removal. *Right,* "Most honored citizens of Cades Cove: Aunt Sarah and Uncle Noah Burchfield, 82 and 83 years." *Oliver Family Collection.*

Left, Hugh Russell Oliver, youngest son of John W. Oliver, in hollow chestnut on the Fork Ridge, 1930. Oliver took this picture because he knew of three children who were caught in a snowstorm and took refuge in this tree until the snow stopped. *Right,* Lucille Oliver and cousin, Frank Oliver, late 1920s. *Oliver Family Collection.*

Family picture of William Howell Oliver, his wife, Elizabeth Jane Gregory, and their children, early 1900s. *Oliver Family Collection.*

Lucille Oliver Dunn (1910–1984), eldest daughter of John. W. Oliver, married, 1932, Charles S. Dunn. *Oliver Family Collection.*

Charles S. Dunn (1893–1981), at the time of his appointment as the first Assistant Chief Park Ranger in the Great Smoky Mountains National Park, 1931. *Oliver Family Collection.*

John W. Oliver in 1960 sadly surveys the remains of the community he fought so valiantly to save. In the words of Justice William O. Douglas, "Cades Cove's leading citizen served its people as no one else, bringing them enlightenment and guidance in raising their standard of living."

7
Family Life and Social Customs

If the folk culture of Cades Cove had functioned as only the collective consciousness of the community, there would have been little direct interference in the daily lives and social behavior of individuals. Yet the cove people's intimate knowledge of each other was never passive; implicit in such knowledge was a subtle form of social control. By the end of the nineteenth century, a very clear consensus about proper behavior existed, and most of the cove dwellers adhered to the unwritten rules and prescriptions imposed by the larger community. Intense scrutiny of one's neighbors meant that very little occurred which escaped public notice, and few families could avoid the opprobrium of having their most intimate private problems become widely known.

The primary instrument of enforcement for this social code was the family. By 1900, the cove population reached the greatest growth — 709 people — in its entire history. Yet despite these numbers, there were only thirty-eight surnames listed in the 1900 census.[1] With minimal migration into or out of the cove since the Civil War, most of this increase came through natural growth in the existing population. As a result, practically every member of the community in 1900 was related through varying degrees of kinship to most of their neighbors.

In this sense, the cove was actually one large extended family, bound together by myriad ties of both kinship and a common past. Some families, notably the Burchfields, Gregorys, Lequires, Myers, Olivers, Shields, and Tiptons, accounted for the largest percentage of the population, but nearly all the smaller families were interrelated to these larger kinship groups. Since most of the larger families did assist needy relatives, however remote the tie of kinship might be, membership in one of the cove families seems to have been the major reason people living elsewhere returned to the cove in the long depression years following the Civil War. Conversely, there appeared to be little incentive for people with no family connections to move into the cove. Exceptions were men with special skills needed by the community—physicians are notable examples.

This closed society contrasts strikingly with both the diversity of immigrants entering the cove in the 1850s and the ready acceptance then into the community's life of men with widely varying backgrounds and political views. The Civil War had unfortunately engendered a lasting suspicion of strangers, since these men had often turned out to be marauding guerrillas during the brutal war years. While it was true members of the same family had occasionally betrayed one another during the war, the postwar community still trusted its own kin to the exclusion of all outsiders. Practically everyone could recite the lengthy genealogies and pinpoint exactly where in the family tree his neighbor had become a relation.[2] Implicit in this knowledge was a sense of social obligation to family according to the closeness of the connection.

The larger families—collectively the whole community—exerted control over its members' social behavior primarily through the distribution of land. As a fertile basin surrounded by high mountains, Cades Cove always had a limited amount of arable land. By 1900, with a peak population, it is not surprising that 36 percent of the heads of households were tenant farmers. A careful examination of these tenants reveals 70.45 percent of them were thirty-nine years old or younger.[3]

So in Cades Cove land ownership was determined in large part by age. Some 59.62 percent of all the heads of household thirty-nine years old or younger did not own the land they farmed. Yet only 18.57 percent of the farmers forty years or older were tenants. The age group between twenty and twenty-nine was clearly the period when most young men served as tenants; 77.27 percent of all men in this group did not own their farms in 1900.[4]

These figures demonstrate that young cove farmers customarily expected to work on other people's land until they were able to buy their own farm. Usually they worked on land owned by their family or more distant relatives, with the expectation that at some point in the future they could buy their farm for a nominal price or have this land left to them in a will. During these crucial years of tenancy, ranging between nineteen and thirty-nine, the larger family or community exerted its greatest control over the young farmer's social behavior. With so much at stake, few tenants elected not to conform to community norms, particularly in the last decade of the nineteenth century before opportunities outside the cove began to open up in American industry.

Although many of the arrangements transferring land were informal, families frequently wrote definite conditions into the deeds. Usually the larger the tract, the greater were the number of conditions specified. Occasionally small tracts were conveyed for purely sentimental reasons. In 1906, for example, John and Mary Myers conveyed one acre to M.A. Lequire in consideration of their "love and affection." Much more common was the practice of reserving one-third of the rents for their natural lives, as did W.A. and Modena Feezell in 60 acres conveyed in 1905 to L.J. Myers.[5]

Often land transfers were conditional on taking care of the older couple for the rest of their lives. John and Elizabeth Anthony conveyed 170 acres in 1900 to J.T. Anthony "to take good care" of them while they lived. This deed took effect only at the death of the older couple, so presumably they could change their minds if they were not satisfied. Often the deeds specified just what services were expected, from food and clothing to a "decent burial." Usually when one-third of the rent was retained, a provision was also made for an annual payment to the grantor's widow after his death, ranging between five and fifteen dollars.[6]

Another indirect form of social control in land transfers was a note given for loans in varying amounts. In an economy with little cash, the young farmer frequently gave several notes to be paid at different times. The holder of these notes might extend or even forgive them completely at his discretion. In the meantime, the potential threat of calling these notes in made the young farmer anxious to conform to community expectations. Often a condition was placed in the deeds that if the land were resold, it must be sold to one of the original owner's other sons or grandsons. Every effort was made to keep land within the family from one generation to the next.[7]

One very tangible effect of the community's control over the lives of individuals is reflected in the average age of marriage. In 1900, 24.29

was the average age of marriage for men; 22 was the median age. For women, the average age was 20.8, with the median age at 19. These figures are surprising when compared to usual assumptions about early marriages in Southern Appalachia.[8]

In the context of Cades Cove, however, the age of marriage was determined both by the agricultural lifestyle and by the relative scarcity of land. Sons represented a vital labor pool to the family; often a farmer moved from tenant to owner status only after he had enough sons to produce larger surplus crops. Consequently, families were anxious not to lose these valuable workers through early marriages. Young men depending on their families for enough land to begin farming were forced to obey custom and to heed the preference of the family in finding a suitable mate. Usually wide latitude existed in selecting a wife; only a woman absolutely unacceptable would be vetoed.

Because children were such an important source of labor, large families were the norm. In 1900, most women forty-five or older had borne between ten and twelve children.[9] The exact number is difficult to determine because of high infant mortality. In light of the limited amount of arable land, the cove could not have sustained its high growth rate between 1890 and 1900 very long into the twentieth century. But the new century brought opportunities in factories and on lands in the West which would reduce population pressures by 1910.

The 1900 population was relatively young; 68.85 percent of the heads of household were under forty-nine years of age. Families were almost universally nuclear in living arrangements, that is, husband, wife and children with no other relatives living under the same roof. Older people remained in their own homes usually until death, as did spinsters and elderly bachelors. Most adults were married; widows and widowers usually remarried quickly. Widowers often chose younger women and began second families.[10]

Fathers usually made equitable distribution of their property among their numerous offspring. Daughters might be left money rather than land, which usually went to sons. Often daughters were given money during their parents' lifetime, or land was left to one son on condition that he give his sisters a cash payment. Provision was made for the widow in either will or deed; usually she enjoyed the use of the farm for her lifetime.[11]

Particularly revealing is the will of Daniel B. Lawson, the cove's largest landowner after the Civil War. The bulk of his estate was left to his two single daughters, Mary Catherine and Leanah, upon the express condition that they furnish "a full, comfortable and ample support and maintenance for my wife Mary Lawson" the rest of her life. If either daughter died, the other sister would inherit her share. If both sisters died without children, the land would be equally divided among the other brothers and sisters.[12]

Lawson's will reflects the community's attitude about the interrelated, or even indivisible, connection between land and family. One major function of land was to protect the interests of those unable to make their own living—widows and old maid daughters. Yet some incentive must be offered to induce other men in the family to work the land. And above all, the land must ultimately return to the family. Thus all the conditions and variations in transmitting land from one generation to the next display a subtle but profound sense of kinship not always apparent in deeds or wills.

In utilizing the land, the family was the most important unit of labor. Throughout the spring and summer an endless range of farm chores kept the entire family extremely busy. Even very small children were given tasks. Fields were plowed; crops were planted, harvested, then taken to market by the family as a group. Corn, wheat, oats, and rye were the principal crops raised for market. A large vegetable garden made the family practically self-sufficient. Orchards supplied applies, pears, plums, and peaches, usually preserved by drying. Every family kept a number of cows separate from their herd on the range for milk and butter.[13]

For meat, hogs were plentiful, running at large on free range and fattening on the abundant mast of acorns and chestnuts. Beef was plentiful in late fall and early winter, when farmers took turns killing their fattened cattle and sharing it with neighbors. Staples such as coffee, sugar, salt, and spices were obtained from the local store, usually through bartering eggs and butter.[14]

Cove families differed from other Southern Appalachian families in their ability to raise large surplus crops and in the availability of a regional market some forty miles away in Knoxville. Every fall a train of wagons left the cove loaded with a wide variety of crops. Usually the family took four days going and coming, camping along the road at night. Knoxville also offered a broad spectrum of goods not available in the local store. These annual trips accounted for the main part of the typical family's hard cash.[15]

Even more important than its function as an economic unit, however, was the family's role in transmitting values and attitudes to the next generation. In the evenings, the family which had worked together throughout the day shared their recreational, social, and spiritual needs. Cove residents often recalled a nostalgic picture of the family gathered around the fireplace in the late nineteenth century, with the mother spinning cloth while the father read aloud to the children from the Bible. This closeness and sense of common purpose shared by most cove families compensated in part for the heavy responsibilities and duties children early assumed. At a tender age, perhaps six or seven, boys began working in the fields beside their fathers. It was not uncommon to see young boys driving wagons or plowing, or being sent up into the mountains to herd cattle. Girls likewise began domestic chores very early. Occasionally they worked in the fields, hoeing corn with their brothers, but it was comparatively rare for grown women to plow or do similar work.[16]

Aunt Becky Cable, one such exception, did do her own field work and herded her own cattle in the mountains. Although never married, she was widely respected for her honesty and thrift. It was said that she could outwork any man, and that she ran her mill, farm, and herd of cattle with equal facility. She lived to be ninety-six, but never lost status in the community because she capably did a man's work.[17] Aunt Becky's life, however, was the exception rather than the rule. Usually when women other than widows or spinsters were forced to do field work, it was considered a damning indictment of their husband's laziness or mismanagement. Consequently, few men willingly risked the community's ready condemnation by allowing their wives to do such work.

Nor were the tasks allotted to women easy. Most cove wives worked from dawn until far into the night to feed and clothe their family. Usually they earned extra cash by selling eggs and butter at the local store. In 1900, most of the clothing the family wore was homespun out of flax, which involved a lengthy process of spinning, weaving, dyeing, and then sewing.[18] Practically all of the family food was raised and preserved by them; only a few staples were purchased from the local store. Vegetable gardens were usually tended by women and children. Old age did not relieve women of many of their traditional household chores. Long after their children were grown and gone, and their husbands forced by old age to leave the bulk of their farm labor to younger men, most cove women continued to work unassisted at these same tasks until their death.

Life expectancy is extremely difficult to measure from extant tombstones in the cove because the population immigration and exodus varied from decade to decade, and many monuments are no longer legible. But using these headstones, the period between 1851 and 1875 reveals the average age of death for males over the age of five was 59; for females in this category, the average age of death was 56.25[19] Since these deaths were primarily from first and second generation families who had remained in Cades Cove most of their adult lives, these figures appear valid for the nineteenth century if judged in conjunction with other data — deeds, wills, and oral genealogies — which are more difficult to quantify. A further caveat to this admittedly impressionistic generalization is the not inconsiderable number of men and women who lived into their seventies and eighties.

Tombstone data for the period between 1876 and 1900 is far less accurate, since many people in this generation outlived the dispersion of the community in the 1930s and are buried elsewhere. But within this period, the recorded average age of death for individuals over the age of five was 36.6 for males and 42.8 for females. This reduction in the average age of death must also be evaluated in light of the rapid growth — from 382 people in 1870 to 709 in 1900 — which added a much larger proportion of younger adults to the population.

The assumption of adult tasks very early in their lives seems to have had no deleterious effect on children. They accepted the obvious necessity of the entire family working together to make a living. Food was abundant and wholesome, and much of the labor was done outside in fresh air. Although the infant mortality rate remained high, the headstones for the period 1876–1900 bear out the fact that very few deaths occurred among children over five years old. Only five males and five females between the ages of six and fifteen died in these years.[20] Again these tombstones are not a complete record, but there was certainly much greater incentive to place a marker on the grave of a child over five than on the grave of a stillborn infant. So with all these qualifications in mind, it still appears that a child who survived past the age of five had an excellent chance of reaching maturity.

The community believed that farming was the healthiest occupation for the entire family. Only when cove families left to seek jobs in the burgeoning industries of the New South was their health seriously threatened. One such instance was that of George and Samantha Oliver, who went in 1903 to Lenoir City, Tennessee, to work in the textile mills. All their children were placed at an early age in these mills, following the same pattern of child labor adhered to in the cove. The unhealthy atmosphere of these textile mills, however, twisted and dwarfed their children. Nor did George and Samantha realize the anticipated bonanza of economic opportunity in these mills. With their entire family working long hours, they still could scarcely make ends meet. Periodically, George's father, W.H. Oliver, drove down from Cades Cove with a wagon load of food for the family.[21]

The intense communal life of Cades Cove manifested itself in innumerable forms of social interaction among all age groups. Families were in frequent contact with their neighbors during an average work day, and informal chains of communication were excellent. "Visiting seems to be the order Saturday nights and Sundays," wrote one cove resident in 1907. No individual could hope to keep much of his private life secret in a society where everyone knew his family and behavior since childhood, and observed his comings and goings with minute scrutiny. This scrutiny even extended to one's pet dogs or livestock; if a cow got loose in the community, she was quickly identified and brought to the attention of her owner.

The effects of this close surveillance of one's neighbor were not always negative. If a family became ill, the entire community could respond rapidly and generously. In times of crisis, childbirth, or death, many neighbors appeared to assist and do household chores until the victim recovered. Often knowledge of such need or hardship in families prompted assistance before the afflicted even had to ask for help.

If a doctor was called in for a poor family, the community made a collection to pay his fee.[22]

Some cove families remained poor for extended periods, and were consistently subsidized by their more prosperous neighbors. Usually these helping neighbors were in no sense wealthy themselves, but were simply able to raise an abundance of food which they willingly shared. Frequently these subsidies — milk, eggs, vegetables, and meat — were entirely gratuitous, since the poor farmer was struggling to plant a crop and his wife was overburdened with too many children to offer labor in return. Occasionally teenage daughters from poorer families were hired to assist in household chores; their tenure as servants always ended when they married. As was the case with tenant farmers, servitude was invariably a transitional condition. Consequently, hired hands or servant girls were treated in broadly egalitarian terms by their employers, almost as though they were members of the family.[23]

In spite of their close daily contact, the cove people were extremely gregarious and loved to congregate in many types of larger social gatherings. These meetings may be broadly classified according to four functions. First, religious meetings were historically the oldest form of social gathering in the cove, dating from the early 1820s. By 1900, each of the four churches — Primitive Baptist, Missionary Baptist, Methodist Episcopal Church South, and the Northern Methodist church called Hopewell — had adapted their meeting times to fill the social as well as spiritual needs of their members. Revivals were popular and frequent means of bringing crowds together from various denominations. The Primitive Baptist church had services only once a month, but more informal meetings were often held weekly in the homes of individual members.[24] Occasionally some members of the dominant Primitive Baptist church attended services at one of the other cove churches, but this was risky business, which if continued any length of time might constitute grounds for dismissal. The Methodists were more ecumenical and allowed their members to attend any of the other churches.

Religious gatherings also brought cove church members into frequent contact with their denominational counterparts in other communities. Every fall each Primitive Baptist church held a union meeting, and members from other churches in their association came for services and for dinner on the grounds afterward. So Cades Cove Primitive Baptists annually visited each of the eleven other churches in the Tennessee Association. There were also frequent correspondence and exchanges of ministers among these churches throughout the rest of the year.[25]

In their concern for spiritual and ecclesiastical matters, church members did not neglect the responsibility of monitoring the behavior and lifestyle of weaker members. Egregious behavior or immorality was duly noted by the congregation, and the offender was given an opportunity to publicly apologize to the church, confess his failure, and promise to reform. The threat of not only religious but social ostracism by one of the churches was a potent weapon in controlling the behavior of the congregation. Particularly in matters of personal morality — adultery or fornication — the consensus was powerful and compelling, because if a particular case came before the assembled congregation's attention, it was usually already widely known in the community, and chances of denying the charge or covering it up were minimal.[26] In more theoretical matters of doctrinal dispute, especially if more than one person were involved, consensus was more difficult to obtain.

The second category of social gatherings centered around labor which the community undertook en masse to assist a particular family. During the 1890s, barn-raisings were common examples of this type of collective activity in which all the men in the cove gathered and put up a neighbor's barn in a very short time. Other such gatherings occurred around harvest time when collective effort was necessary to preserve an abundant crop before it perished. Berry-stemming, bean-stringing, apple-peeling, and corn-husking or shelling brought neighbors together in the evenings to work and tell stories or gossip. Similar events included making molasses and quilting bees, when the women gathered to finish a quilt which otherwise would require many months for a woman working alone to complete.[27]

Another category involved what today would be called adult education, or various efforts toward self-improvement on the part of adults in the cove. Among the most popular of this type were the singing schools. A singing master would raise enough money in the community to conduct a school for ten days to teach old harp singing. Usually the school building or church was filled to overflowing. The school began at 8:00 A.M. and continued until 3:00 P.M., with a short recess at noon. The teacher would write notes on the blackboard with a staff, while pupils used a hymnal with a self-explanatory title, usually *The New Harp of Columbia: A System of Musical Notation With a Note for Each Sound, and A Shape for Each Note.*[28] The singing master sang through each song showing the rise and fall of the voice, the holds and half notes, quarter notes, and sixteenth notes as he identified their particular shape on the blackboard. Using a tuning fork to obtain the proper pitch, he rehearsed all the students until everyone could sing correctly and properly identify the shape of each note. Finally the teacher selected a particularly promising student to carry on as leader after his departure.[29] As the group continued to practice, other members of the community would join in, so the actual learning of music and notes spread far beyond the original group who had hired the singing master initially.

The almost boundless enthusiasm for this form of entertainment is reflected by the precision with which octogenarian graduates of these schools could still recite and identify the notes some fifty years afterward. Another extremely popular form of adult education was the writing school, wherein a writing teacher instructed adults on how to form and shade letters and various other skills of fine penmanship. In addition, writing teachers taught their pupils how to write deeds and wills, and how to use correct forms in business correspondence.[30] Although there is no evidence of such writing schools in the nineteenth century, the fine and often ornate penmanship used in various church records indicates that cove people traditionally placed a high premium on this particular skill. Only in the aftermath of the Civil War did penmanship noticeably decline.

Finally in this category of self-improvement were numerous school plays and recitals which drew large crowds from the community. Spelling bees were another popular form of school entertainment.[31] Gradually as the twentieth century progressed the school was used to disseminate practical, new scientific information to the larger community, ranging from new techniques in farming and home demonstration projects to lectures on health and hygiene from visiting doctors and nurses.

The enthusiasm with which new ideas and practices were received by a broad spectrum of the population offers compelling evidence that the society emerging into more prosperous years of the first decade of the twentieth century was far from static or backward looking. Membership in the singing schools, although largely composed of young adults, also contained many older people. Significantly, many of the cove's leading church families were among the most progressive advocates of both the writing and singing schools. While rigidly retaining their traditional moral values and codes of behavior, these families were able at the same time to accept new ideas and progressive developments in the secular realm. Given the frequent conflict between fundamentalism and progress in other sections of Appalachia, the adjustment of Cades Cove to the changes of the twentieth century is noteworthy.

The last category of social gatherings is that of formal life ceremonies — marriages and funerals. In a certain sense, marriage customs show the community in transition, particularly between 1890 and 1920. In the depression years following the Civil War, it was often an economic necessity to avoid a formal wedding when a couple decided to marry. The usual practice was for the bride and groom quietly to seek out a justice of the peace, who married them at a moment's notice, often late at night. Formal weddings became increasingly popular after 1900 but were never the predominant form. Elaborate receptions for the couple, called "infairs," were popular during the nineteenth century in much of Blount County, but were only sporadically seen in the cove. With increasing economic difficulties for cove farmers in the 1920s, it again became the norm for couples to seek out a justice of the peace for a brief ceremony without friends. So marriage customs varied widely from family to family, and from decade to decade.[32]

Funerals, on the other hand, retained the unchanging quality of long-established tradition. Unlike many weddings, the entire community participated in all aspects of funerals in the cove. A death was first announced by the church bell. Ringing at first to gain the community's attention, the bell was then tolled once for each year of the deceased person's life. By counting the number of times the bell tolled, practically everyone could surmise who had died, since the community knew everyone's age, and who was seriously ill at any given period.

An air of solemnity spread throughout the cove because it was considered disrespectful of the dead to continue working, to make loud noises, or to engage in any mirthful activity, even if the deceased were no kin or particular friend. The community then converged at the house of the bereaved and assumed all the necessary household and farm chores. A few older women customarily prepared the corpse for burial, a feat which needed to be accomplished quickly before rigor mortis set in. After washing the body and placing pennies over the eyes to close them, one of these women made the shroud. Men were buried in their best suits; well into the twentieth century, older women were buried in black shrouds. Children and infants were buried in white.[33]

Jim McCaulley and his son John, Witt Shields, Bud Gregory, and Manuel Ledbetter all made coffins without charge for the community. Occasionally farmers kept choice walnut boards on hand for their coffins; otherwise, someone in the community donated the lumber or the coffin-maker furnished the materials himself. Although carefully constructed, coffins were completed rapidly, since the deceased was usually buried the next day. Shaped to fit the corpse, whether a large adult or tiny infant, coffins were lined with white by cove women when the boxes were delivered to the deceased person's home.

The corpse was never left alone. Neighbors held a wake, or watch, throughout the night that the deceased lay for the last time in his own home, usually on a bed in a back room. On the following day, large numbers attended the funeral, which always consisted of preaching and various hymns sung either by groups or by the entire congregation. At the close of this service, everyone—young and old—filed by to gaze on the corpse one last time before the coffin lid was secured by wooden screws. "Hark from the Tomb," a mournful dirge admonishing the living against taking their own fragile mortality for granted, was sung as the coffin was carried from the church to the graveside. After burial, the mound would be decorated with flowers as friends took the bereaved family home.[34]

If the community claimed a person at the moment of death, they did not readily abandon his memory after the last shovel of dirt filled the grave. The folk memory clung tenaciously to much of the deceased's personality, habits, and even manner of speaking long after his death. This cataloging of innumerable individuals, living and dead, was an astonishing feat, given the sheer numbers of people involved. As long as the community existed, its members were thereby assured a kind of immortality. Reflecting their concern for absent but still full members of this community, cove people tended cemeteries with great care and decorated graves with flowers in an annual ceremony. Graves were adorned with monuments whose epigrams and iconography testify to their belief, reinforced by religion, that these friends and relatives' separation was only temporary.

At the end of the community's life when the National Park Service took over the cove, residents voiced tremendous concern over what would happen to the graves of their families. Overlooming their anxiety that these cemeteries be properly maintained, however, was the far greater fear that the memory of their dead would be lost forever to the community's consciousness. Without understanding this deeper but inarticulate fear, the new park officials would regard such anguished protests over the physical maintenance of graves as both irrational and exaggerated out of all proportion.[35]

Given the closeness and sense of community among the cove people, it is not surprising that their society was broadly egalitarian. An individual's class, or standing among his neighbors, depended almost entirely on his personal behavior and attitude. Respectability of this type was not determined by a person's family, but patterns of correct lifestyle often seemed to run in families. The cove people themselves believed that qualities of character were inherited, and that there were scrubs among people just as there were inferior breeds of cattle. Yet a man who lived uprightly was never blamed for faults in his kinfolk, and an individual could lose all the advantages of descent from an honorable family by dishonest or immoral conduct.

Religion was the single most important criterion in determining respectability. Men reverenced for longstanding piety and faithfulness had far more influence among their peers than did civil or political authorities. This influence was most apparent in times of crises, such as the Civil War, when elders in the Primitive Baptist church united the community to armed resistance against marauding guerrillas. Intertwined with religion as a second criterion of respectability was unselfish service to the community. To the cove mind, religion and assisting one's neighbor were inseparable in Christian doctrine.[36] Noteworthy, however, were the many cove citizens not especially religious who nevertheless aided the less fortunate and gave unstintingly of their time and fortune to help the community.

There were some omissions that drastically reduced a person's status within the community. Sexual promiscuity brought universal censure. Yet the community was flexible in forgiving a repentant sinner who admitted his or her error and agreed to "sin no more." Illegitimate children were an occasion for both personal and family disgrace, yet some women unfortunately caught in this one mistake later married and became respectable citizens. It was not so much an initial mistake as a continued pattern of promiscuity and an attitude of outright defiance of community mores which hardened cove citizens against an unrepentant neighbor.[37]

The community could afford to forgive a repentant sinner largely because there was little possibility of committing subsequent offenses unobserved. Close scrutiny of one's neighbor thus allowed the community to censure further offenses of a fallen woman, but more significantly, to verify the continuing resolution of an honestly reformed woman's behavior. So one mistake did not permanently cause a woman to lose all status; careful community scrutiny allowed her to be reinstated in the social order provided she make no further mistake.[38] To some outsiders, this acceptance of one-time offenders back into the fold seemed to indicate a shocking lack of communal morality — particularly in American society just emerging from the Victorian age. But they failed to comprehend the inner mechanisms of cove society — intense surveillance — which allowed a constant monitoring of everyone's behavior. Such scrutiny would have been virtually impossible in much of the United States, particularly in urban centers. In Cades Cove, however, it permitted a very humane and reasonable system of rehabilitation, while at the same time preserving high standards of public and personal morality.

Another situation which threatened loss of respectability was the manufacture and consumption of illegal alcohol, or moonshine. Quite apart from the legal problems stemming from Tennessee's prohibition laws, there existed from the Civil War onward an uneasy tension between those who drank moonshine and those who violently disapproved. All the cove churches flatly forbade and preached against the consumption of *any* alcohol — none more vehemently than the Primitive Baptist.[39] Yet the production of varying amounts of corn whiskey had begun in the 1820s at the genesis of the community, and consumption was undeniably widespread within the cove by 1900. Why did these moon-shiners — makers and consumers — not lose all respectability or status among their teetotaler neighbors?

The answer lies in their skillful application of a rule of social utility. If a cove farmer drank only moderately and if his main source of income was not from moonshining, his weakness was grudgingly tolerated. Such a person must always drink surreptitiously, however. Examples of this category were several families living in the Spruce Flats in the northeast corner of the cove. Although their moonshining activities were known, they remained part of the community and were not excluded from its social or religious life. As in the case of sexual promiscuity, everyone usually knew exactly how much moonshine was produced and by whom it was consumed. Condemnation was instant, however, if a farmer drank excessively and abused his wife and children, neglected his farm work, or became bellicose toward his neighbors. Men who made moonshine in large quantities were always in danger of becoming outcasts.[40] An excessively large corn crop or purchase of large quantities of sugar instantly alerted suspicion. And ironically, it was better for your reputation to drink alone; several men drinking together or moonshine served, however surreptitiously, as a social event greatly compounded the opprobrium and possibility of discovery.

The best loved and most highly esteemed people in the cove were not abstemious or negative personalities constantly censoring their neighbors, however. Rather they were pious and kindly couples, such as Uncle Peter and Aunt Catherine Cable in the nineteenth century and Uncle Noah and Aunt Sarah Burchfield in the twentieth. Both these couples embodied widely held ideals of selflessness and unstinting service to their neighbors. They also had the unique ability to project their kindliness to young and old alike, and were universally beloved by all segments of the community. Above their honesty, piety, and thrift was that rare quality these couples possessed of being genuinely sympathetic and compassionate to all their neighbors' problems. That the community chose these couples as their most revered models offers perhaps the greatest insight into the cove's social values and attitudes continuing intact from one generation to the next.[41]

The high respect in which both these couples were held also illustrates that personal wealth was not a determinant of social status, since neither couple had more land nor money than the average cove citizen. Before the Civil War, the enormous wealth of entrepreneurs such as William Tipton or Daniel D. Foute had given them special status, although their relations with cove neighbors were predominantly egalitarian. Daniel B. Lawson emerged as the wealthiest resident after the war, but he was a native son and related to many other cove families. His service to the community as justice of the peace and postmaster as well as faithful member of the Methodist church brought him more respect than his wealth.[42] No single individual, regardless of his income or profession — school teacher, justice of the peace, or physician — greatly overshadowed his poorest neighbors in popular esteem. Preachers were widely respected, but many of them farmed during the week to earn their living, and the distribution of power in most churches was rigidly democratic.[43] The poorest family in the cove was treated with equal respect, provided they maintained their respectability and industriousness.

In glaring contrast to the egalitarian spirit and social tranquility of Cades Cove was the alternate lifestyle of a group of families living in a remote subcommunity at the southwest end of the cove known as Chestnut Flats. The "flats" people, as they were commonly called, were outcasts shunned as virtually untouchables by the rest of the cove. Like the Eta of Japan, these people carried instant social contamination to anyone who came in contact with them. Marriage with any of the flats people was out of the question, and any man or woman seen visiting Chestnut Flats risked an irreparable loss of reputation or even of caste in the eyes of Cades Cove. Even today accounts of the cove carefully avoid mention of the flats people or their lifestyle. Yet such embarrassed silence cannot hide the fact that Chestnut Flats existed, or conceal the social wall which the rest of the community erected around it to avoid contamination.[44]

Although the locale was mentioned as early as 1836, the history of Chestnut Flats as a separate subcommunity began after the Civil War when George W. Powell moved there with his family. Later he was joined by Sam Burchfield, and these two families formed the nucleus around which other families sporadically drifted in and out. Since the population was in almost constant flux, it was impossible to determine how many people lived in Chestnut Flats at any given time. Probably not over fifty people were ever assembled there, and this estimate is not conservative. Powell had been a Union soldier and was well-educated and quite respectable in earlier days. It was later rumored that he contested with Daniel B. Lawson over land in the cove proper, and retreated to the flats after losing. In any event, there is absolutely no indication that Chestnut Flats was other than a normal part of the larger community before the Civil War.[45]

In partnership with Jules Gregg, Powell grew splendid orchards on the hilly terrain of his new home, where he legally distilled fine brandies and moonshine. In 1878, Tennessee outlawed the manufacture of whiskey, but prohibition only increased economic incentive. Powell had no intention of quitting such a lucrative business which had become his major occupation. Moonshining brought him rapidly into conflict with the law, and his notoriety spread as swiftly as his reputation for making excellent brandies. An article in the *Maryville Index* in September 1878 clearly illustrates his decline into outlaw status:

> Special Deputy Elias Cooper, while on a recent raid in Chestnut Flats, Blount County, a few days since, accompanied by eight men, visited the isolated rum-mill of Geo. Powell, where they seized eleven tubs of beer and mash, four tubs of pomace, one hundred and thirty gallons of brandy singlings, five bushels of meal, two bushels of rye and two bushels of malt. The revenue squad also arrested Powell, the engineer of the mash mill, who subsequently escaped, while the men and women of his household were abusing and threatening the officers. The captured property was destroyed by the officers, who immediately started for this city on foot. While passing an unfrequented place in the mountain, the squad were fired upon by parties in ambush, and a lively fusilade ensued. About forty shots were fired by their assailants, when the revenue squad returned the fire, but with what effect they were unable to ascertain as the attacking party remained in ambush. None of the revenue officers were wounded, though a bullet found its way through the clothing of Bennett Ledbetter, one of the revenue raiders.[46]

In time Chestnut Flats became the scene of innumerable drunken brawls. Not infrequently men were murdered in the course of these inebriated disputes over cards, cock-fighting, shooting matches, or prostitutes. Sober cove residents shuddered to think that their own sons, husbands, or brothers might be attracted to these forbidden pleasures. But in such an atmosphere of lawlessness, criminals from other parts of Tennessee and North Carolina were the ones primarily drawn to the flats. Powell willingly harbored anyone fleeing the law without asking questions. As a result, the community was periodically inundated by outlaws of all descriptions who drank, gambled, whored, and shot each other to pass the time.[47]

Although the Burchfields and Powells intermarried — George Powell had married Mary Ann Burchfield — their common profession of illicit distilling did not prevent them from murdering each other. Powell's nephew, George W. Jr., was shot and killed from ambush in December 1897 by Sam Burchfield. Another man, Burchfield's son-in-law, Hale Hughes, had been convicted and sentenced to twenty years in the state penitentiary for this crime. Hughes in 1899 claimed that both he and Burchfield had lain in ambush to kill Powell, but the victim was actually shot by Burchfield. Powell was murdered because he had earlier testified against Hughes for illicit distilling.[48] The fact that men closely related routinely betrayed and murdered one another in cutthroat competition for the illegal but highly lucrative whiskey market is illustrative of the complete collapse of all law or social order in Chestnut Flats.

Among the flats women, sexual promiscuity became rampant. Prostitution flourished as the flats became the red-light district for a much larger region. Unmarried women had numerous children, often each by a different father. One woman reportedly had three men killed over her. Occasionally liaisons lasted several years, but marriages were infrequent. The real tragedy involved children born into this environment who were outcasts in the larger community and thus trapped in a highly destructive lifestyle. If they survived childhood and various venereal diseases in this climate, daughters usually followed their mothers in becoming prostitutes.[49]

Chestnut Flats was an outcast society for many obvious reasons; the flats people completely rejected all the values of social order and morality endorsed by the larger community. The most important social institution in the cove — the family — rapidly disintegrated in the flats atmosphere of endless drunken brawls and promiscuity. Respectful cove families might be similarly threatened if their men were drawn into this snare. But what finally forced the majority to completely exclude and ostracize the flats people was the absence of that all-important mechanism of social control which worked so well in Cades Cove proper —

careful scrutiny of one's neighbor. The community literally had no way of finding out what was occurring in Chestnut Flats. They were more alarmed by what they did not know and could only imagine than by any of the horrendous tales which periodically drifted out of the flats.

Yet some of these tales were in themselves quite chilling. One of the most persistent rumors involved the fate of traveling peddlers who frequented the cove at the turn of the century. Many of these tradesmen, who sold needles, thread, lace, and other smaller household items, were never seen again after entering Chestnut Flats. Some of the flats men would subsequently be seen plowing their fields with a horse remarkably similar to that of the peddler. In a few days, the flats women would appear with innumerable ribbons and a profusion of new lace tied all around them and in their hair.[50] Whatever conjecture followed was based on purely circumstantial evidence, but it well illustrates the community's fears and imagination when confronted with an absence of concrete information. What they knew of the flats people was bad enough; what they could not see or observe worried them more.

Although completely isolated socially from Cades Cove, flats people periodically stole chickens, hogs, and cattle from their more provident cove neighbors at night. Moonshining was always extremely profitable, but the flats communal lifestyle was so sporadically extravagant and wasteful that they occasionally ran out of food or other supplies. Since agriculture was not their main support, they neglected farming techniques and machinery that appeared increasingly in the rest of the cove. Their cabins and farms reflected this retrogressive lifestyle which seemed to become more primitive and out of step with progressive developments in the rest of Cades Cove.[51]

In this context it is quite ironic that Chestnut Flats received disproportionate attention from outside journalists and writers in the twentieth century. Understandably, the lifestyle of the flats people made far more interesting reading than did the more prosaic lives of average cove farmers, who were generally indistinguishable from their counterparts in other sections of Blount County. Also, flats men closely approached the stereotype of the Southern mountaineer already prominent in American fiction. Finally, to a group so isolated and despised by their mainstream neighbors, it must have been an irresistible opportunity to justify their many idiosyncrasies and alternate lifestyle to sympathetic strangers.

Robert Lindsay Mason was one such stranger whose sympathy was exceeded only by his gullibility. George Powell and Sam Burchfield are cited throughout his book, and much of his description of mountain life and society came from them. Mason's *The Lure of the Great Smokies*, published in 1927, was widely read and perpetuated innumerable myths and distortions about Southern Appalachian society. By presenting information gathered from only a tiny outcast subcommunity, he totally distorted the lifestyle and customs of the much larger cove community. A more serious and subtle distortion was his assumption that the lifestyle of Chestnut Flats accurately reflected a much earlier way of life which, frozen in time, continued unaltered into the twentieth century. Actually, few aspects of the flats community remotely resembled the mainstream of Cades Cove fifty years earlier. The squalor and degeneracy of the flats were the direct result of a separate and intentionally retrogressive pattern of development by a few families after the Civil War.[52]

Mason's sources were mainly creative liars who told him whatever they perceived he wanted to hear. An excellent example is the eyewitness account which George Powell's wife, Ann, gave in detail of the first death of a famous Cherokee reformer and prophet, Younaguska. In 1819 at the age of sixty this Cherokee chieftain went into a trance for twenty-four hours and was presumed dead. Upon awakening, he delivered a long diatribe against the evils of intemperance, which greatly impressed his Cherokee audience. Ann Powell's vivid and detailed account of this event was uncritically repeated by Mason; he did not even question the amazing coincidence of her presence — a white woman — at such a solemn Cherokee ceremony.[53] Yet Ann Powell was born in 1834 — some fifteen years after Younaguska's famous trance which she purportedly witnessed!

In the late 1920s one cove citizen protested that the "countless stories found in magazines are gross exaggerations and gross falsifications of facts," which were written solely for commercial gain. "Such characters as 'Black' Bill Walker, Quill Rose, George Powell, Sam Burchfield, and others," he argued, "are held up and magnified and eulogized as being typical mountaineers." In reality "all of these men were public outlaws, and were never recognized as true, loyal mountaineers, or as true American citizens, by the rank and file of the mountain people."[54] Yet such protests were futile in light of the continuing popularity and durability of the Southern Appalachian mountaineer as portrayed by authors such as Mason and Horace Kephart.

Despite these enduring stereotypes, the historical record clearly shows that with the exception of Chestnut Flats, family life in Cades Cove at the turn of the century was largely indistinguishable from that of other rural Tennesseans. Whatever uniqueness may be ascribed to cove society stems from the intense sense of community shared by most of its inhabitants. Geographic isolation combined with numerous interrelated extended families contributed to the growth of community spirit after the Civil War, but the genesis of such close cooperation extends far back into the nineteenth century. By 1900, a cove citizen might resent close scrutiny of his behavior, but most welcomed the pervasive physical and moral support during times of crisis, sickness, or death. In later years people would look back with great nostalgia at the social peace and harmony of their community at its zenith between 1890 and 1910. Thereafter, all its traditional strength and flexibility would be severely tested by the challenges and upheavals of the twentieth century.

8

Government, Law, and Politics

Nothing else in their lives connected the people of Cades Cove to the outside world so completely and inextricably as their civil government, frequent recourse to the law to settle disputes, and not least of all, their avid participation in politics. Quite contrary to Horace Kephart's dictum that Southern Appalachian courts were "feeble to puerility," and every mountaineer "a law unto himself," both the Cades Cove justice of the peace dockets and the Blount County Circuit Court minutes reflect vigorous and frequent judgments involving cove citizens, particularly in the decades after the Civil War when county government was presumably eclipsed by local concerns.[1] Throughout these decades covites submitted to numerous taxes on their time and wealth levied by the county court, but they also made their own frequent and often vociferous demands on the county for services and benefits.

Central to both county and local government was the justice of the peace. After Cades Cove became the sixteenth civil district in 1836, two justices were elected every six years by popular vote. A constable was also chosen to execute judgments of the magistrates, but real power belonged to the justices themselves.[2] Usually men of considerably more wealth and education than their constituents, justices nevertheless had to be natural leaders — men held in high esteem by the whole community — to be elected. Although none of the cove justices had any formal training in the law, their legal knowledge and skill were often surprisingly sophisticated. Deference to such a magistrate was both voluntary and supported by previous knowledge of and respect for the individual.

The actual powers of the justices were enormous; judges within their own civil district, collectively they exercised much judicial and all executive and legislative power in county government. As local judges they tried both civil and criminal cases within their district in which the penalty did not exceed a fifty-dollar fine or thirty days in jail. Forcible entry, assault and battery, recovery of stolen property, and a wide variety of penalties and fines under statutory law fell within the jurisdiction of these local magistrates. They could issue warrants for arrest, appoint special temporary officers for making arrests if the constable was not available, and convene their courts at their own discretion. The law required each justice to keep a docket of his cases, to provide proper transcripts of cases transferred to higher courts, and to designate one day each month when his court would be in formal session. Each justice's power, however, was county-wide, and any justice could "try any cause that may be brought before him at any time and at any place within the county." Tennessee law additionally reinforced the authority of these amateur judges by a strongly stated "presumption" in favor of the "sufficiency and validity of proceedings" before justices of the peace, regardless of "any informality whatever" in such trials.[3]

Cases outside their jurisdiction could be bound over to the appropriate higher court by these magistrates, so practically no offense occurred within the county where their power was not determinative. Ironically the next higher court, called the county court of monthly sessions, was presided over by three justices of the peace elected by all the justices within the county. After 1875, the chairman of the Blount County Court became the de facto county judge, but he was still himself a justice, elected by other justices.[4]

Even more significant was the county court of quarterly sessions, composed of all the justices within the county. Despite its confusing name, the Blount County Quarterly Court was the actual governing body of the county, entrusted with all executive and legislative functions from taxation to building roads. This quarterly court met four times a year to govern the county, and the two justices from Cades Cove were then present to represent the interests of the sixteenth civil district.[5] Participation in county government by Cades Cove justices meant that the cove always had direct access to and information about any new laws being considered by Blount County.

Outlining the formal duties and responsibilities of their magistrates illustrates how vitally involved they were in county government, but it gives a very distorted picture of how these justices actually functioned in the cove. Occasionally stern prosecutors and formidable enforcers or representatives of the law, more often they were kindly legal and financial advisers who spent countless hours assisting the cove people in solving a wide variety of problems. Their names frequently appear as preparers of wills, deeds, or applications for bounty lands or government pensions.[6] Although covites saw their magistrates more as friends and counselors than as stern judges, this relationship in the final analysis strengthened rather than detracted from their ultimate respect for the law.

Justices of the peace for Cades Cove during the nineteenth century were Robert Shields, Curran Lemons, Daniel D. Foute, Daniel B. Lawson, and Nathan H. Sparks. In the twentieth century, James E. Gregory, Russell D. Burchfield, A.W. Shields, George D. Roberts, Albert Hill, and A.W. Shields Jr. served, the latter two from 1918 to 1924. Lawson and Foute were among the largest landowners in the history of the cove; the other justices usually owned far more land than their neighbors. Daniel D. Foute, justice from 1856 to 1862, was also very active in county government, serving as clerk of the Blount Circuit Court from 1822 to 1836, and from 1840 to 1848. George D. Roberts, a native of the cove, served as justice from 1912 to 1918, then as the county court clerk from 1918 to 1930, and was finally elected county judge in 1934.[7] So Cades Cove magistrates were involved from the beginning to the end of the community's life in the broader functions of county government.

One constable was elected every two years for each civil district under the Tennessee constitution of 1870. They were minor peace officers who attended the justice of the peace courts and also served certain processes for other courts. Since they were popularly elected and were almost always natives of the cove, constables were regarded by the community in generally friendly terms. The bitter hostility between cove moonshiners and revenue officers after the Civil War usually did not involve the local constable. Nor was the constable ever wounded or shot at from ambush, as often happened to the sheriff. A cove correspondent to the *Maryville Record* in 1904 reflected this attitude of familiarity and affectionate tolerance toward the constable: "We do not yet know who will run for constable on either side, but if Jessie Brown should, we would all be glad to have him elected. Not that he is a coward, but we could get him to laughing and run a quarter of a mile uphill before he could hush enough to try to halt anyone!"[8]

Among the duties which cove citizens owed the state was service in the militia, composed of all able-bodied men between the ages of eighteen and forty-five. Each county formed a militia regiment, and each civil district formed a company whose soldiers elected their own captain. Jacob Tipton was the first captain of the Cades Cove militia district, which preceded division of the county into civil districts in 1836. Although attendance at the militia muster four times a year was initially a serious responsibility involving the protection of the whole community from Indian attack, by the 1830s it had generally deteriorated into a festive occasion including pageantry, feasting, socializing, and rifle shooting matches. The old muster field was located on the south side of the cove opposite Joe Lequire's farm; in the twentieth century covites used this field to play baseball. An 1841 notice from Major J.C. Murphy to elect a captain, first lieutenant, and ensign in Cades Cove "at the usual muster grounds" indicates the early use of this muster field for militia assemblage and drill.[9]

Every able-bodied male between the ages of twenty-one and forty-five was also required to work on the public roads in his district from five to eight days each year or to pay the road commissioner of his district one dollar for each day he did not work. Cove citizens, handicapped by bad roads throughout the nineteenth and much of the twentieth century, frequently appealed to the county court for more work days and an increased road tax. A 1907 cove correspondent to the *Maryville Times* summarized their arguments cogently and plaintively:

> Our roads are in bad condition in this district and reports from all over the county show like conditions. Now my dear friend, you argue that the poor man, who has not wagon or team have roads to work and that he does not realize any benefits of his labor and therefore you are not in favor of him working the roads but 5 days per annum. My brother, you must have been coming up the Rich Gap Mountain sound asleep when Satan told you that. The poor man referred to, must pay some fellow to haul his meat and flour

over these bad roads too. And you bet the merchant don't loose anything on account of bad roads. He just adds another dollar per hundred for bad roads, and the poor man just has to go down in his jeans and fork out the kale. Now who is the loser in the end? The poor man has just simply paid the dealer for 20 days work on the road per annum and the roads are in worse condition than we found them. Mr. Squires give us 7 days work to each hand per annum and we will not have to prove our argument.[10]

No other obligation to the government evoked such an anguished outcry from cove citizens as taxes, particularly the property tax, which was based on the assessed value per $100 of land. "Don't know that the tax can all be paid for in 1886 without great distress" is a typical cove citizen's lament which echoes through each decade. Just how difficult this tax burden actually was is difficult to measure. Elijah Oliver's total tax payment on 225 acres was $1.40 for 1880; $4.68 for 1886; $7.32 for 1895; $4.42 for 1899; and $6.53 for 1905. The Blount tax rate per $100 of assessed property grew from $1.30 in 1899 to $2.00 by 1911, although the assessed value of cove property seems relatively stable during this period.[11]

Perhaps what irritated cove taxpayers most was their growing sense of frustration at public expenditures for improved roads and railroads in other parts of Blount County. "The sixteenth district pays as much or more land tax than any other district in the county," complained one angry cove citizen in 1918, "and has not a foot of graded road. Is it not time for us to begin to get some road?" There were also various additional tax assessments for special projects which were collected separately: on December 4, 1875, for example, Elijah Oliver paid $2.50 in railroad taxes directly to the railroad revenue collector. When revenue bonds were placed on the ballot, however, the only such measures generally approved in the sixteenth civil district involved road improvements or extensions directly connected with the cove.[12]

If the government made demands on them, cove citizens had comparable expectations of what services and benefits their government should provide them, and they pursued these claims with persistence and vigor even during the decades of comparative isolation immediately after the Civil War. No single example better illustrates their knowledge of current national legislation and their willingness to pursue their claims through an amazingly complex and protracted maze of federal bureaucratic regulations and paperwork than Lucretia Oliver's application for a widow's pension in 1873.

Lucretia, who was seventy-seven years old at the time, could neither read nor write, and her family, never wealthy, was impoverished in the years after the Civil War. Nevertheless, still showing signs of her old indomitability, in September 1873 she applied through a Maryville lawyer, Robert N. Hood, for a pension from the federal government based on her husband John's service in the War of 1812. John Oliver had died in 1863, but during the 1850s he had received two grants of bounty land for his military service.

Complications arose immediately in her application. Although Lucretia furnished written statements from her neighbors attesting to her loyalty during the Civil War, she had difficulty remembering the captain's name of her late husband's militia company. She thought it was Bartley Boyd, but the Pension Office could locate no such record. Next came a letter from James Bradley, clerk of the Carter County Court, stating that her marriage license could not be found because "there was no record kept in the office of that day." Bradley had discussed her problem, however, with an old man, James Taylor, who happened to be in the courthouse that day. Taylor well remembered the Olivers, recalling that "he once went with Oliver when he went acourting the lady that he afterwards married."

Taylor's sworn testimony along with that of another old Carter County acquaintance of the Olivers was promptly forwarded to the commissioner of pensions. In the meantime, Hood pointed out that Lucretia was an elderly lady and had difficulty recalling the name of Oliver's captain. Perhaps it was Captain Vincent or Vinson or Captain Daherty or Daugherty. But the pension office remained skeptical about the marriage and after further inquiry could find no record of Oliver's service under either captains. On July 19, 1875, the pension examiner formally rejected Lucretia's claim.

Undeterred by this rejection, Lucretia began the whole application process again in May 1876. New character witnesses—Elijah Oliver, Smith Campbell, Nathan Burchfield, and Henry Shields—were forwarded with certification of their past loyalty, reputations, correct ages and addresses. Another lengthy affadavit on May 19, 1876, from John and Elizabeth Thomas of Maryville stated they were neighbors of Lucretia in Carter County, were well-acquainted with her marriage to John Oliver in 1814, and that both Thomas and his wife "have been intimately acquainted with the said Lurena Oliver almost all their lives." Finally the pension office discovered Oliver's service record under Captain Adam Winsell, and also the record of his two warrants for bounty land. The triumphant Lucretia was at last "admitted December 8, 1876, to a pension of eight dollars per month, from February 14, 1871."[13]

Possibly the most important service which the cove people expected from the federal government was delivery of their mail. Cades Cove was established as a post office on June 28, 1833, with Absolom C. Renfro as the first postmaster. In 1839 the mail came from Sevierville and was delivered once a week in the cove; residents received their mail at the post office which was usually in the home of the postmaster. Writing to Robert Burchfield in the cove in January 1839, Philip Seaton of Sevierville stated that he would "take it as a great favor if you will let my mail boy stay one night in each week with you, and if you will do so I will pay you at the rate of twenty dollars a year." The man who delivered the mail carried a bugle which he blew when he reached the top of Cades Cove Mountain to let the people below know he was coming. After the Civil War, the cove mail came from Maryville; by 1897 delivery had increased to three times a week. In 1904 rural free delivery began with John W. Oliver delivering mail six days a week directly to the homes of patrons.[14] Regardless of the routes or delivery schedule, however, throughout the community's history the cove people enjoyed writing and receiving letters from friends and relatives who had moved west. Various mail order catalogs were extremely popular by the 1890s, and many people subscribed by mail to Knoxville and Maryville newspapers, particularly the *Maryville Times,* from the 1870s through the 1920s.

If the cove people had clear expectations of what the county, state, and national governments owed them, they were no less demanding with one another. Their willingness to seek legal remedies for any grievances against their neighbors marks them as rather surprisingly litigious, given their comparative geographic isolation. Careful scrutiny of the cove justice of the peace dockets reveals the frequency of such disputes taken to their local magistrates. While some clear instances of crimes like assault, larceny, or malicious shooting occurred, most of their disputes involved various exchanges of property or services. These ubiquitous barter negotiations often left one party feeling cheated.[15]

The other rather surprising feature about these disputes settled by the justice of the peace is the wide diversity of people either accusing or being accused. Evidently no opprobrium in the least attached to being thus involved in litigation, not did the disputants apparently suffer any ill-will toward one another after settlement occurred. Not only did large numbers of the respectable middle class appear in these dockets, but even on occasion the names of other magistrates! The outlaw subcommunity of Chestnut Flats might dominate the circuit court's docket with murders and drunken fights, but the flats people appear very seldom in any of the cove justice of the peace dockets. Petty disputes were almost the sole prerogative of the broad middle class or ordinary small farmers, who apparently suffered no diminution in their social or religious standing by such litigiousness. In fact, the church records never show censure of any member for involvement in civil disputes; many of the clergy were often thus engaged themselves. Cove people also appear occasionally in the dockets of neighboring Tuckaleechee Cove's magistrates, so evidently their legal contentiousness extended as far as their trade or business dealings.[16]

Aside from frequent brawls in Chestnut Flats, murder was rare in Cades Cove. The Blount County Circuit Court, to which jurors from the sixteenth district were required by law to attend each session, usually considered cases involving stolen property from the cove. The infamous raid of North Carolina guerrillas in the summer of 1864 which resulted in Russell Gregory's death came before the Blount Circuit Court in 1865 not because of his murder, but because one member of the guerrillas, Ezekiel Burchfield, received two horses belonging to Mary Burchfield, "well knowing that the same had been shortly before that time feloniously stolen."[17] Burchfield was sentenced to five years at hard labor in the state penitentiary as a result of his conviction for this crime.

In more common cases from the cove, the legal proceedings were often out of all proportion to the actual property involved, and betrayed a tendency to sustain litigation for its own sake. One such example involved "a certain red steer eighteen months old," whose ownership was bitterly contested by two cove farmers in 1885–1886. J.D. Gregg had finally obtained a favorable judgment before the justice of the peace, who issued a writ of replevire which allowed him to take immediate possession of the steer from A.J. McCulley. McCulley appealed this decision to the Blount Circuit Court, which ruled that as no bond had been executed by Gregg for the writ of replevire, it was invalid. McCulley was therefore entitled by the circuit court to recover his steer from Gregg under a writ of restitution.[18]

In the next scene of this unfolding legal drama, McCulley appeared before the circuit court complaining that when he went to recover his steer, Gregg "denied having any such steer" and furthermore maintained "the steer was in North Carolina" where it "cannot be reached by the process of this court." An angry judge commanded the sheriff to apprehend the "said J.D. Gregg" and bring him before the court to answer the alleged charges and to "purge himself of said contempt."[19]

A querulous Gregg next appeared before the circuit court to "quash the affidavit filed herein by A.J. McCulley." His attorney presented a long and disingenuous argument. Seizing the person because of failure to recover property "replevied after judgment," he maintained, was "an irregular proceeding and a remedy unknown to the law." The information given to McCulley for his affadavit was not given under oath, and "therefore is not sufficient to justify an attachment in any event." Finally, Gregg's attorney argued, the original replevin bond was not "sufficient in form, amount of penalty, or in respect to the solvency of the sureties."[20]

The weary circuit court judge finally ruled that Gregg was not, after all, in contempt of his court. Dismissing McCulley's attachment, he allowed Gregg to "recover of the plaintiff all the costs of the attachment."[21] It must have appeared a Pyrrhic victory to Gregg, however, when he considered the time, energy, and money expended in attorney's fees. No red steer could be worth so much, but this case is illustrative of how legal battles between ordinary farmers over relatively minor incidents or property often escalated out of control.

The Blount Chancery Court saw the largest number of lawsuits from the cove because most such cases involved title or boundary disputes. In 1874, for example, Mary Ann Sands argued before this court that she and her husband, Alexander Sands, were forced under duress to deed their land in May 1861 to George W. Feezell. Although the chancellor did not believe her charge of duress was fully proved, he ordered the deed "declared void and of no binding force" because no money or any "valid consideration" had been received by either of the Sands in exchange for their land. Occasionally the title to property was brought into question because the owner had "abandoned said land and left the country." Such was the case in an 1871 suit involving land purchased earlier on installment by George Blair. This farm, "the Sparks' place," was ordered by Chancellor M.S. Hall to be sold at public auction.[22]

Although the chancellor in such cases was forced to make difficult and often unpopular decisions based on statutory law, he always went to great lengths to achieve some degree of equity or fairness between the claims of the disputants. In 1892, for example, Chancellor Henry R. Gibson was forced to rule that an 1868 sale of a farm by Alfred Potter to Nathan Sparks was invalid because it was "a parole or verbal sale," which did not involve written transfer of title. But Sparks's heirs were entitled to recover from Potter's heir the purchase price with interest in addition to "the present value of any permanent improvements that may have been placed on said land."[23]

In many cove land disputes the chancellor ordered a surveyor to mark the boundary between the tracts being contested. Such was an 1887 lawsuit involving a 300-acre tract of land owned by G.W. Shields. In 1873 George W. Powell purchased 160 acres of this tract; in 1880 Wilson and Samuel Burchfield purchased the remaining 140 acres. Since the boundary of these two tracts had never been "definitely fixed," Chancellor Gibson ordered a survey to be made "making as straight a line as possible but including all of Powell's improvements on the southeast side of said 300-acre tract but not including any of the plaintiffs' improvements." Chancellor Gibson was somewhat irritated to learn, however, that the plaintiffs, the two Burchfields, had never finished paying Shields for their tract. He therefore gave them until June 1887 to pay the remaining $156.[24] Actually, it was not all that uncommon among cove litigants to bring a lawsuit involving property still being paid for, or to sue for issues involving a tract in which they had only a small fractional inherited interest.

The very diversity and complexity of problems which covites submitted to the chancery court for adjudication is also apparent in many cases involving the rights of widows and minor children. Typical was the court's consideration of widow Mary Myers and her five minor children, who inherited partial interest in two tracts of land from their late father, L.J. Myers. After carefully investigating this family's situation, Chancellor Hal H. Haynes ordered the smaller tract of 22 1/5 acres to be sold for $700. This money he then ordered used to purchase the remaining interest for the family in the larger tract of 38 acres. This latter tract had "a house and barn on it, both in good condition, also a good orchard, and the most of it is timbered, part of the timber being a good grade of saw timber." Additionally, the chancellor pointed out, this larger tract adjoined the Myers's farm, contained the family's access to the public road, and also contained their water supply. If an antagonistic third party should ever become owner of the 38-acre tract, the solicitous chancellor reasoned, the Myers children "might be cut off from outlet to the public road except by a very inconvenient way, and also be deprived of the privilege of getting water."[25]

Community-wide problems were also addressed by chancery court. In 1901 A.C. Caughran and Thomas Frye were sued by John Myers and his neighbors for "putting saw dust into the Potato Branch a running stream and thereby befouling the water of said branch and rendering the waters unfit for use, and thereby also causing sickness by the decaying of said saw dust along the banks of said stream." The chancellor ordered an immediate and permanent cessation of this pollution and further prohibited the defendants from placing saw dust anywhere near the Potato Branch "where it will be carried by the rains or otherwise into said stream."[26]

Lawsuits involving several family farms could arouse enormous hostility and enmity within the cove. One such lawsuit involving complex overlapping claims between original land grants was brought in 1904 by James W. Post and H.B. Beecher against land owned by Daniel B. Lawson, W.H. Oliver, and F.D.D.F. Shields. "It would hardly do to hold a revival here in Cades Cove until most of the land suits are settled," noted one covite with acerbity, "as some of our citizens are greatly disturbed in their minds over the run of affairs." So complicated were the issues involved in this lawsuit that an elaborate map of the overlapping original land grants was added to the chancery court record. The chancellor finally ruled that the title of Oliver's small farm, although admittedly based on an inferior claim, was nevertheless perfected by "long and continuous possession." Beecher and Post did receive other tracts, however, which were either not occupied or only recently purchased, based on the older Callaway grant.[27] Such a compromise was actually very fair to all parties, but bitterness over this lawsuit lasted for many years.

Politics, elections, and debates over political issues were pursued with avid interest by the cove people throughout their history. Even before Cades Cove became a voting precinct, two cove men, Thurman and Wiseman, got into a heated argument over politics as they were returning from voting in neighboring Tuckaleechee Cove, whereupon Thurman murdered Wiseman. Cove records contain innumerable references to attendance at various conventions of both the Republican party and the Democratic party after the Civil War. Candidates for different state and local offices frequently spoke in the cove. Comments from the cove on political debate over issues ranging from constable and justice of the peace races to state laws involving prohibition, fence limitation, or new revenue bills abound in the *Maryville Times*.[28]

Often local political events were recorded with great humor, if not acerbic wit. Following the 1884 election of Democratic President Grover Cleveland, the Republican postmaster since 1868, Daniel B. Lawson, lost his job, first in February 1886 to James McCaulley, and then shortly thereafter in June of the same year to William A. Feezell. "We understand there is great complaint by some of our democratic friends on account of the post office being moved from where it was to a radical's, not a true, well-tried democrat, as the Blount County *Citizen* calls him," noted one obviously Republican covite in April 1886. "Go a little slow, Mr. Vilas, in making appointments," this commentator further admonished the postmaster general. "It's likely to weaken the Democratic party!" An even more acerbic comment regarding the spoils system followed Feezell's appointment in June:

> We hope to get along better when our post office stops rolling. I think it will stop when it gets to Wm. A. Feezell's; as there is no public road leading there, he will shut his gate, stop it up south the mountain, and north is so steep it cannot roll that way, so it will have to stay, unless he will suffer his gates to be opened. I have heard of things being run in the ground, but our post office is run in a hollow in the side of the mountain. Hurrah for Democ-

racy! It runs offices in strange places since its advent into the world. We don't wonder at the move of our office to where it is going, for to the victors belong the spoils.[29]

In a broader context, the cove was the sixteenth district within one of the most strongly Republican counties in East Tennessee. Following its unsuccessful attempt to secede from Tennessee at the outbreak of the Civil War, East Tennessee after the war remained staunchly Republican. Part of this Republicanism was engendered by the bitter guerrilla warfare suffered during the Civil War, but after Reconstruction, East Tennessee continued its conscious political dissent within an otherwise solidly Democratic state because of both real and perceived economic discrimination.[30] Logic would suggest that Cades Cove, which had suffered not inconsiderably herself from guerrilla raids during the war, would follow the same pattern as Blount County and East Tennessee in voting a Republican ticket.

Yet surprisingly, the cove was one of only two civil districts in the county where the Democratic party remained strong. The single most important political pattern in the cove after the war was vigorous two-party competition, with the vote dividing astonishingly even between the two major political parties in local, state, and national elections. There were of course aberrations in this pattern, but the cove's political equilibrium remained consistent over time.[31]

Reasons for this equilibrium vary from one decade to the next. Many of the extended cove families were closely related to families in the fifteenth civil district, Tuckaleechee Cove, which frequently had a heavy Democratic majority. The most important reason, however, was the cove's conscious resentment at being shortchanged over funds for roads, schools, and other improvements common in other sections of the county. Whether this discrimination was deliberate or due only to the cove's geography is a moot point in terms of politics: the cove people thought they were being discriminated against and their anger and ensuing complaint were ubiquitous yet remarkably consistent in the decades after the Civil War. "We learn, with regret, that the schools of this district will have to close in about two weeks for lack of money," complained a cove correspondent in 1878 to the *Maryville Index*. Twenty-eight years later in 1906, another covite expected the county superintendent "to visit our schools in the near future and to see after matters like that for us if we do live back in the mountains." Why should the cove people, he argued plaintively, not "have a systematic schooling as elsewhere?"[32] In the final analysis, the strength of the Democratic party in Cades Cove was as much a manifestation of dissent against Blount County as the larger section's Republicanism was an indication of dissent against Nashville.

As a rule, covites did not usually split their ticket but voted the same party in local, state, and national contests. Party loyalty was most likely to waver in local or county elections involving a candidate personally known in the cove. Such an instance occurred when Sam H. Dunn, a Democrat, ran for representative in the Tennessee General Assembly in 1912. He polled 74 percent of the cove vote primarily because he was the son of a well-known justice of the peace in neighboring Tuckaleechee Cove and related to many families in the cove. Popular sheriffs and judges could also cause cove voters to split their ticket, as happened in an 1886 election where Chancellor Gibson, a Republican, received 68 percent of the cove vote and Sheriff M.H. Edmondson, also a Republican, received 77 percent of their vote.[33] Otherwise it was extremely rare for the cove vote to reflect the large Republican margins usual in Blount County.

In presidential elections Cades Cove maintained its political equilibrium and fierce independence from Blount County. Even an extremely popular candidate like Theodore Roosevelt in 1904 gained only 54.7 percent of the cove vote, as compared to 75.5 percent of Blount's vote. Voter turnout was always highest for presidential elections, followed by congressional and gubernatorial contests.

The first extant return for the sixteenth civil district was in 1867, when William G. Brownlow received no votes at all in the cove compared to 80 percent of Blount County's vote. Republicans gained the ascendency thereafter during the 1880s until the 1890s, when gubernatorial candidates came close to splitting the vote evenly. This rough equilibrium would continue until the last important cove election in 1924, again in striking contrast to Blount County's strong Republicanism in gubernatorial contests.

Contests for the second congressional district of Tennessee follow a similar pattern. In 1868, the ticket was split 11 to 10 between L.C.

Houk and Horace Maynard. By the 1880s, Houk had a commanding lead of usually twice his democratic opponent's tally in the cove vote. Houk was a native of Sevier County and was personally known to some of the cove people. By the 1890s, equilibrium was restored and remained roughly balanced between Democratic and Republican candidates through 1924.[34]

Although the rhetoric in the *Maryville Times* between 1868 and 1924 was often partisan and occasionally vituperative, it is difficult to gauge how cove citizens regarded the salient political issues of their time, particularly the intricate maneuvering common within Tennessee state politics. It is very clear from their voting record, however, that Populism had disproportionate appeal to them after 1890. Throughout the 1880s Cades Cove regularly sent delegates to the East Tennessee Farmers' Convention, which was neither politically radical nor controversial initially. This organization, dedicated to improved farm methods, attracted an unusually large and bipartisan group of leading cove citizens to its annual meeting in May 1886: Calvin Gregory, John Cable, A.W. Shields, N.H. Sparks, and Daniel B. Lawson.[35]

Trouble was apparent in 1890 when 60 percent of the cove voters cast their ballots for John P. Buchanan, the Farmers' Alliance leader who had used his Alliance following to seize the Democratic nomination for governor from more conservative Democrats. In contrast, Buchanan polled only 33.4 percent of the total Blount County vote. In 1892 when Buchanan ran on a separate Populist ticket, he polled 9.9 percent of the cove vote in contrast to only 2.6 percent of the Blount total vote. Likewise James B. Weaver, the Populist candidate for president, drew 9.9 percent of the cove vote but only 2.2 percent of Blount County's total.[36] Such radicalism in the cove surprised Blount party regulars, but it was in reality only a logical extension of the growing frustration Cades Cove farmers felt over poor roads and inadequate services from county government. In the Farmers' Alliance's rhetoric of dissent, cove farmers had heard remarkably similar echoes of their own dissatisfaction as a neglected minority within a larger political entity.

The fortuitous survival of a 1900 list of voters from the sixteenth district combined with the more detailed 1900 census allows a careful analysis of voter participation in Cades Cove at the turn of the century.

Table 1. Presidential Elections, 1868–1924

Year	Candidate	Party*	Sixteenth District		Blount County	
1868	Grant	R	10	(41.7%)	1361	(92.4%)
	Seymour	D	14	(58.3%)	112	(7.6%)
1892	Harrison	R	50	(49.5%)	1935	(66.8%)
	Cleveland	D	41	(40.6%)	821	(28.3%)
	Bidwell	Pro	0	(0.0%)	77	(2.7%)
	Weaver	Pe	10	(9.9%)	64	(2.2%)
1896	McKinley	R	55	(50.9%)	2634	(73.4%)
	Bryan	D	53	(49.1%)	953	(26.6%)
1900	McKinley	R	58	(53.7%)	2067	(71.9%)
	Bryan	D	50	(46.3%)	806	(28.1%)
1904	Roosevelt	R	58	(54.7%)	1986	(75.5%)
	Parker	D	48	(45.3%)	645	(24.5%)
1908	Taft	R	52	(54.2%)	2568	(75.2%)
	Bryan	D	44	(45.8%)	847	(24.8%)
1912	Taft	R	13	(14.8%)	870	(27.6%)
	Roosevelt	Prog	33	(37.5%)	1410	(44.7%)
	Wilson	D	42	(47.7%)	836	(26.5%)
	Chafin	Pro	0	(0.0%)	39	(1.2%)
1924	Coolidge	R	20	(54.1%)	2760	(73.2%)
	Davis	D	17	(45.9%)	976	(25.9%)
	La Follette		0	(0.0%)	37	(1.0%)

Table 2. Tennessee Gubernatorial Elections, 1867–1924

Year	Candidate	Party*	Sixteenth District		Blount County	
1867	Brownlow	R	0	(0.0%)	1381	(80.1%)
	Etheridge	C	19	(100.0%)	344	(19.9%)
1869	Stokes	C	1	(2.7%)	1272	(60.8%)
	Senter	R	36	(97.3%)	819	(39.2%)
1878	Wright	R	1	(2.8%)	987	(56.1%)
	Marks	D	35	(97.2%)	773	(43.9%)
1882	Hawkins	R	35	(64.8%)	1625	(70.1%)
	Bate	D	19	(35.2%)	692	(29.9%)
1886	Alf Taylor	R	51	(64.6%)	1863	(69.4%)
	Bob Taylor	D	28	(35.4%)	822	(30.6%)

Table 2. Tennessee Gubernatorial Elections, 1867–1924 (*continued*)

Year	Candidate	Party*	Sixteenth District		Blount County	
1890	Baxter	R	42	(40.0%)	1526	(63.7%)
	Buchanan	D	63	(60.0%)	801	(33.4%)
	Kelly	Pro	0	(0.0%)	69	(2.9%)
1892	Winstead	R	50	(49.5%)	1953	(67.5%)
	Turney	D	41	(40.6%)	800	(27.6%)
	Buchanan	Po	10	(9.9%)	74	(2.6%)
	East	Pro	0	(0.0%)	68	(2.3%)
1894	Evans	R	47	(50.5%)	2232	(77.6%)
	Turney	D	46	(49.5%)	643	(22.4%)
1898	Fowler	R	33	(46.5%)	1312	(72.4%)
	McMillin	D	38	(53.5%)	500	(27.6%)
1900	McCall	R	59	(54.1%)	2072	(72.0%)
	McMillin	D	50	(45.9%)	805	(28.0%)
1902	Campbell	R	32	(46.4%)	1361	(69.1%)
	Frazier	D	37	(53.6%)	608	(30.9%)
1904	Littleton	R	57	(54.3%)	1940	(76.2%)
	Frazier	D	48	(45.7%)	606	(23.8%)
1908	Tillman	R	48	(52.2%)	2523	(74.6%)
	Patterson	D	44	(47.8%)	861	(25.4%)
1910	Hooper	R	45	(50.0%)	2210	(72.2%)
	Taylor	D	45	(50.0%)	853	(27.8%)
1912	Hooper	R	29	(38.2%)	2158	(70.8%)
	McMillin	D	42	(55.3%)	776	(25.4%)
	Poston	Prog	5	(6.6%)	116	(3.8%)
1914	Hooper	R	32	(59.3%)	1750	(73.3%)
	Rye	D	22	(40.7%)	636	(26.7%)
1918	Lindsay	R	20	(46.5%)	1766	(76.9%)
	Roberts	D	23	(53.5%)	529	(23.1%)
1922	Taylor	R	12	(31.6%)	1461	(66.5%)
	Peay	D	26	(68.4%)	735	(33.5%)
1924	Peck	R	16	(55.2%)	2310	(69.2%)
	Peay	D	13	(44.8%)	1030	(30.8%)

*R = Republican, C = Conservative, D = Democrat, Pro = Prohibition, Pe = People's, Prog = Progressive

Out of a possible 141 eligible males twenty-one or older, 109 voted, or 77.3 percent, which is rather high for both Blount County and Tennessee in general. Voter participation as a percentage of the total cove population was 6 percent in 1870; 8 percent in 1880; 17 percent in 1890; 15 percent in 1900; 16 percent in 1910; and 7 percent by 1920.[37] So in comparative terms the two decades between 1890 and 1910 were the years of greatest voter participation in the cove.

According to the 1900 census, male voters can be divided into three categories: property owners who were heads of household, tenants who were heads of household, and those living in a home where another person was head of the household. Such dependents in this latter group were usually young sons of the family, but they might be servants or poor relations; one such individual listed himself as a "pauper." Some 80.28 percent of the property owners voted in 1900; 77.78 percent of males living as dependents in someone else's household voted. The really surprising statistic is that 72.09 percent of farm tenants, i.e., propertyless farmers renting land, participated in the 1900 election.

Dividing voters by age groups, 27.4 percent were between twenty-one and twenty-nine years old; 23.6 percent were in their thirties; 25.5 percent were in their forties; 10.4 percent were in their fifties; 8.5 percent were in their sixties, and 4.8 percent were in their seventies. Comparing voter participation within each age group, 70.7 percent of cove men in their twenties voted in 1900; 89.3 percent in their thirties voted; 81.8 percent in their forties voted; 84.6 percent in their fifties voted; 90 percent in their sixties voted; and 62.5 percent of cove men in their seventies voted in the 1900 general election. These figures indicate that with the exception of young men in their twenties, cove citizens consistently exercised their right of franchise each decade of their lives. Despite the lower ratio in their age group, many examples occurred of men voting who had celebrated their twenty-first birthday only months before the 1900 election. Such younger sons tended to be members of one of the cove's large extended families which encouraged or placed a high premium on voting.

Even more surprising is the high number of cove voters who, although unable to read, nevertheless voted in 1900. Some 82.6 percent of all adult males voting were literate; 17.4 percent were illiterate. But a surprisingly high 63.3 percent of all illiterate males voted in 1900, in comparison with 81.1 percent of all literate males who voted in that year.[38] One can only speculate that illiterate voters heard enough about political issues and choices through innumerable conversations within the community. Occasionally the postmaster or one of the justices would read aloud from a newspaper to his assembled friends and neighbors.

In conclusion, both democracy and "the Democracy," the cove Republicans' epithet for the Democratic party, were alive and well in Cades Cove. Neither age, poverty, tenancy, nor illiteracy effectively prevented cove farmers from routinely exercising their right of franchise. Although covites were frequently frustrated or unsuccessful in their struggle to obtain better roads and schools, most continued to actively seek solutions to these problems through the political process. Increasing numbers after 1900 joined voluntary clubs or associations of a semi-political nature, like the Junior Order of American Mechanics.[39] In the broader context of all the political activity and interest in political questions in the cove during the 1880s and 1890s, the progressive accomplishments of the community during the twentieth century would appear to rest on a solid foundation of past experience.

9
Progressivism and Prohibition

In September 1899 John Walter Oliver, a great-grandson of the first John Oliver who settled in Cades Cove, packed all his clothes in a bundle and hiked over thirty miles out of the mountains to attend Maryville College. His journey was in a certain sense an act of faith. Only twenty at the time, and with practically no money, he believed education was the key both to his own future and to the progressive development of the entire cove community.

Maryville College, an old Presbyterian school with a long eleemosynary tradition, did not disappoint him. The administration arranged for him to work out his tuition on the campus Saturdays at 7½ cents per hour. He and three other students in similar circumstances managed to rent a small, two-room cottage near the campus. Here they lived in very primitive conditions, cooking their own often meager meals. Despite these hardships, Oliver managed to complete one full year in the teacher preparatory department.[1]

Returning to Cades Cove the following spring, he began teaching school in the upper end of the cove on July 16, 1900. With money thus earned, he returned to Maryville College for additional study. Returning again to teach in the fall of 1901, he married Nancy Ann Whitehead. He continued teaching in the cove throughout the fall and winter of 1903 and 1904. Dissatisfied with his own preparation, he moved to Louisville, Kentucky in January 1904 at the close of his school to attend the Massey Business College. The practical, business-oriented training provided in this commercial school seemed more useful than the still largely classical curriculum at Maryville College. So despite many deprivations, he and his wife remained in Kentucky until he earned his diploma.[2]

Oliver had received several lucrative job offers from banks after graduation in Louisville, but he was determined to use his new knowledge to improve the living standards of his native community. His commitment to Cades Cove was characterized by an almost missionary zeal and enthusiasm. In September he returned to the cove and took the civil service examination for rural mail carrier. Passing the exam with a score of ninety-eight on October 15, 1904, he began a career as rural mail carrier that would last thirty-two years.[3]

John Oliver personified the *Zeitgeist* of American progressivism in all its ramifications. He had an unquenchable faith in modern science and the new technology emerging at the beginning of the twentieth century. Benefits from scientific discoveries, he believed, could be directly harnessed to solve all the practical problems of ordinary citizens, whether in the area of health, agriculture, or industry. This idealistic optimism gave him both a restless energy and a profound conviction that the physical environment of Cades Cove could be constantly improved as new discoveries were made. Like other progressives of this period, he was also deeply committed to a wide spectrum of political, social, and economic reforms which were part of a larger faith in the improvability of the human condition. But the quintessence of all his progressivism was an almost mystical faith in education as the fulcrum by which the broad masses of Americans would be lifted to a more prosperous life.[4]

Despite his progressivism, Oliver remained a staunch member of the most conservative and fundamentalist cove church, the Primitive Baptist. He was liberated to speak in public in December 1901 by this church. Following its rigid prescriptions, he was licensed to preach in 1903, ordained a deacon in 1907, and ordained to the full work of the ministry May 21, 1916.[5] Ironically, the principal feature of the Primitive Baptist church was its total unwillingness to admit any change in doctrine or practice. But in Oliver's instance, the fluidity of progressivism and the rigidity of his religious beliefs caused no inner turmoil. Each sphere was separate in his mind, and the benefits of modern science complemented the religious impulse to assist his less fortunate neighbors.

This distinction is crucial in understanding why fundamentalism never obstructed the adaptation of modern technology in Cades Cove. The absolutism of their theology and the confidence they held in the completeness and perfection of their particular creed erased any insecurity church members might have had about changing conditions in this world. The church continued to exert a powerful impact on the spiritual lives and morals of its members, but it never attached any religious value or significance to outmoded or old-fashioned ways of farming or any other temporal way of making a living. And although the cove Primitive Baptists continued to reject the idea of religious seminaries to educate their clergy, they heartily endorsed secular education for their children and enthusiastically supported Tennessee's public schools. "Hollering amen," noted one such cove resident in 1909, "does not fully express our gratitude for the new compulsory school law of Blount County."[6]

So unlike other areas in Southern Appalachia, the cove never suffered from a debilitating conflict between fundamentalism and progressivism. As long as change did not directly involve church government or what were considered primarily spiritual matters, every new innovation was judged largely on its own merits. This is not to say that "kickers," reactionaries or backward people unwilling to change, were not present in the cove society. But they were always isolated from the consensus of the larger community, which welcomed progressive changes, and their ignorance received neither official support nor unofficial sanction from the cove's leading churches.[7]

Fate could not have selected a better representative of progressivism than John Oliver, nor a more effective means of spreading the new secular message than through a rural mail carrier. As a member of the cove's oldest family, his acceptance by the community was already assured. Indeed, he was actually related to most of the cove inhabitants through myriad ties of blood; even some families among the outcasts of Chestnut Flats called him "cousin Johnny." As a minister of the dominant Primitive Baptist church, his credibility was doubled; the nineteenth-century pattern of according such ministers enormous respect and influence continued unaltered into the first decade of the new century. Combined with these credentials were his daily contact and intimate knowledge of the community while delivering the mail. He personally knew every individual in the cove, from the oldest patriarch to the most recently born infant.

Often Oliver was called on to comfort or assist his customers in the capacity of minister. He later recalled having "gone so far as to leave my route and hold funeral services with my mail bags hanging on the pulpit beside me."[8] Whatever the emergency, he routinely stopped to aid his patrons, visiting the sick and comforting the bereaved. Side by side with these spiritual ministrations, however, he also preached the gospel of progressivism. He told scores of farmers how to improve their yield — seeds, farming techniques, and improved breeds of livestock — and explained in terms they could understand exactly how new scientific methods were supposed to be implemented. Often he gave new varieties of seed to his neighbors on the mail route, and at his own expense brought them eggs of thoroughbred chickens to hatch. His own farm was a model of scientific agriculture, and he invited all the cove people to visit and observe these new techniques for themselves.[9]

The community to which Oliver returned in 1904 was receptive to new ideas and was far from isolated from the mainstream of Tennessee or national currents. Although the cove population steadily increased each decade after the Civil War to a peak of 709 in 1900, thereafter it declined each decade. This decline occurred within the context of a rather dramatic increase in Blount County's total population, from 19,206 people in 1900 to 28,800 in 1920. Both urbanization and new industry accounted for Blount's rapid growth, which centered around Maryville. The activities of the Little River Lumber Company in neighboring Tuckaleechee Cove (the fifteenth civil district) almost doubled that community's population from 876 in 1890 to 1705 in 1910.[10]

Young men and often entire families moved out of the cove in increasing numbers after 1900. Although some of these emigrants settled in neighboring states, a surprisingly large number went to the Far West. During the 1850s, most families left the cove for Missouri. In the twentieth century, the most attractive state for emigrating covites was California. These families kept in touch with their relatives back in Cades Cove, and visits to the home community were not infrequent. Occasionally a cove couple, after a successful career in perhaps Kansas or Oklahoma, returned to buy a cove farm in their later years.[11] This network of relatives throughout the United States insured a flow of new ideas and information which played a significant role in keeping the cove abreast of national events.

Modernization was a complex process of accretion, often piecemeal and never completely replacing older ways. For example, traditional methods of quilting and weaving continued to be practiced at the same time many cove women were buying modern Singer sewing machines.[12] Much descriptive material has been written about daily life and farming in the cove during the first two decades of the twentieth century. Yet it is important to bear in mind that most of this traditional knowledge — ways of killing hogs, preserving food, and so on — was not unique to the cove but rather was widely employed throughout rural Tennessee and the South. After 1900, these traditional modes of life were still evident, but the dynamic adaption of new technology was rapidly gaining momentum throughout the community.

Limitations or backwardness in one realm did not necessarily limit cove residents in other areas. Despite roads in poor repair much of the winter, for example, a battery telephone system connected the cove with the outside world as early as the 1890s. Although local stores stocked mainly very basic goods, covites might buy exotic items or the latest products from America's burgeoning factories in Maryville or Knoxville, or from numerous mail order catalogs. At least one local store owner, R.D. Burchfield, was fully insured by a London company. Newspaper accounts also document frequent travel out of the cove by residents for a wide variety of services in major cities. Many sought medical treatment in special clinics or spas in distant parts of the country. Sam Blair, for example, sought a cure for rheumatism in Hot Springs, Arkansas, in 1911. Devero Sands returned in 1912 from Colorado, where he unsuccessfully sought a climate which would alleviate tuberculosis.[13]

A persistent theme constantly repeated throughout the first two decades of the twentieth century was the urgent need for better transportation out of the cove. In a real sense, better roads tied together a wide range of economic expectations of modern development within the community. New scientific methods of farming would produce far greater surplus crops than could presently reach the growing markets in Maryville or Knoxville. Cove farmers were particularly frustrated during the prosperous years before America's entry into World War I, when high prices and steady demand for their crops were thwarted by bad roads in frequent disrepair. The better the outside market, the more vociferous were farmers' demands for improved transportation.

One perceptive cove citizen pointed out in 1907 that the entire community was harmed by inadequate roads. Even a farmer too poor to own his own wagon and team must pay an additional fee to have his meal and flour hauled over these bad roads. The merchants, he argued, simply added the additional costs of transportation to their retail prices. Ultimately everyone, rich and poor, paid a hidden tax for poor roads which remained "in worse condition than we found them." This citizen begged the county court for seven days work to each hand per annum instead of the customary five days.[14] With the advent of the automobile and concurrent promises of a lucrative tourist industry, demand for better roads continued to accelerate.

Another great expectation never realized was the extension of a railroad into the cove. The *Maryville Record* reported in 1904 that "the Little River Lumber Company is about to extend its line over into Cades Cove to provide an outlet for a lot of logs and lumber on that side of the ridge." Immediate benefits from this railroad were also assured to farmers, who "now cannot market their produce without a long and hard haul over rough roads." Twelve years later cove residents were still "elated over the possibility of a new railroad."[15]

So plans for a railroad into the cove kept the residents in a constant state of expectant optimism between 1904 until after World War I, when new improvements in macadamized roads and the explosion of American automobiles made conventional highways a more attractive alternative. But their anticipation of a railroad into the cove before 1915 was not without considerable justification. Sawmilling was already booming within the community by 1900 as the inhabitants built new houses and modified older structures. Many timber tracts surrounding the cove were bought by several large outside lumber companies. Morton Butler Company of Chicago was the largest owner of timber land around the cove; from the early 1900s until 1936, this company alone accumulated 25,244 acres. But numerous other lumber companies of intermediate size were also buying timber land during the period, and cove farmers operating small sawmills also speculated periodically in mountain land.[16]

Although it was never economically feasible for the Morton Butler Lumber Company to extend a railroad into the cove or to begin large-scale cutting, neighboring lumber companies had an important impact on the economy. Sawmilling and timbering gave permanent jobs to many men, and even cove farmers might supplement their income by part-time work on these projects. The rising demand for timber lured some residents into establishing sawmills on a much smaller scale; lacking capital to buy much land, however, these local ventures were always ephemeral. "Saw milling is all the go now," commented one resident in 1907, noting how many of his neighbors were thus occupied and "doing a lively business."[17]

Farming remained the primary occupation for most cove inhabitants, however. In the development of scientific agriculture, John Oliver wrought a minor revolution in the community after 1904. Many of his initial ideas came from farm journals, but by 1910 he turned increasingly to the College of Agriculture at the University of Tennessee for advice on an amazing variety of horticultural problems. From their literature he learned how to vaccinate hogs to immunize them against cholera, and cattle and sheep to prevent black-leg. He willingly vaccinated any of his neighbors' livestock without charge.[18]

Oliver's tireless efforts to propagandize scientific agriculture would have been pointless had the community not shown an instant receptiveness to his ideas. Repeatedly he was praised by other covites for his "model" farming. One resident summed up the community's admiration for his success as an "up-to-date" farmer in 1914 by pointing out how such an "educated farmer can enjoy life to a greater extent than the one who does not keep up with the times."[19] With this communal respect came widespread imitation, and since Oliver was always ready to share his knowledge with neighboring farmers, he was directly responsible for raising standards and productivity throughout the cove.

One of the most tangible benefits came through Oliver's introduction of new purebred livestock. In 1914 he bought a thoroughbred Aberdeen Angus bull from John Hitch, the outstanding breeder who first introduced this splendid breed into Blount County. Since he kept meticulous records of "Black Joe's" stud fees ($1.00 if successful), it is evident that practically every farmer in the cove bred their cows to this fine new specimen which was so obviously superior to any native stock.

"Black Joe" led a busy life. In 1917 alone he serviced eighty-four cows. By the time his successor, "Nosegay," took over in 1924, "Black Joe" had improved the breeding stock of cattle throughout the cove.[20]

Oliver also imported a registered Berkshire boar in 1914 from J.W. Robinson Company in Loudon, Tennessee to upgrade hogs. "Old Berk" was widely employed by the community and produced a superior grade of pork in much of the cove breeding stock in a relatively short time. Further, Oliver introduced purebred Shropshire and Southdown sheep to the cove and unsuccessfully attempted to organize a collective plan among neighbor sheepowners to send a large number of lambs to market each year in Kentucky. In 1907 Oliver brought "a fine lot of Brown Leghorns" from a breeder in Maryville; in 1909 he imported "a fine Rhode Island Red cockrel" from East Point, Georgia. The first farmer in the cove to caponize chickens, he also was the first to use incubators fueled by kerosene to hatch larger quantities. He continued to give many of his neighbors fertilized eggs from these thoroughbred chickens so that they could also enjoy the advantages of superior breeds.[21]

The implementation by Oliver of such a far-ranging catalog of scientific farming techniques almost staggers the imagination, particularly when viewed in the context of his job delivering the mail six days a week. New types of seed, methods of farming, and the latest mechanized machinery — tractors, threshing machines, and so on — were utilized by him as soon as they appeared on the market. Before long Cades Cove's larger and more progressive farmers were using such new inventions as soon as they appeared in Blount County. Esquire A.W. Shields bought a gasoline engine, thrasher box, and feed crusher in 1911, for example, and operated these machines for the public every Saturday.[22]

Oliver also built the first modern silo in the cove to store much larger amounts of feed than was heretofore possible. He imported many varieties of fruit trees and carefully studied new techniques on how to improve their yield. He also imported three-banded Italian queens to upgrade his bees, and built modern hives to triple the production of honey.[23] He was in fact so successful in the study of apiculture that after his retirement as rural mail carrier the state of Tennessee offered him a position as bee inspector.

Oliver also crusaded for better health care in the community. The cove was fortunate in having a physician in residence almost continuously from 1902 until 1914. John McGill, M.D., lived there between 1902 and 1905. After 1905, James M. Saults, M.D., served the community until his death in 1914. He moved to the cove from Wear's Valley in 1910. Although the community was generally healthy, periodic epidemics of highly contagious diseases such as typhoid, diphtheria, and influenza took a high toll of infants and small children. After losing a daughter to diphtheria, Oliver invited another physician, Dr. K.A. Bryant, to his home in 1915 to inoculate his other children as an example to the community.[24]

Health care remained spotty, however, despite the presence of these qualified physicians and the increasing availability of immunization. Some women continued to use midwives, and infant mortality remained high. A small minority relied exclusively on folk remedies and occasionally concocted elaborate theories to explain epidemics.[25] At the other end of the spectrum, some cove residents sought advanced medical care in distant clinics. The problem of health care, like that of modernization of agriculture, seemed basically a question of education to Oliver. Improved public education continued to be the key to unlocking all other problems facing the community.

In the progressive chain of thought, reform followed closely after education. Oliver's initial efforts toward reform were channeled into conserving the cove's physical environment. He attacked wasteful methods of farming, and particularly deplored periodic forest fires which ravished the surrounding mountains. The benefits of conservation — land, water, or timber — were not readily apparent to most cove citizens, however, and in these efforts Oliver often labored alone. He did manage to organize an agricultural club for young boys, and taught them conservation as well as new techniques of farming.[26]

Among the most memorable of his myriad conservation efforts was the stocking of Abrams Creek with rainbow trout. In response to Oliver's request, Congressman Henry R. Gibson had a few thousand fingerlings shipped in 1907 from the fish hatchery in Erwin, Tennessee. When he was unable to meet the train in Townsend to pick up the first shipment of these fingerlings, they were dumped there in Little River. Oliver thus inadvertently stocked rainbow trout for neighboring Tuckaleechee Cove. When in 1908 he got the second shipment in time and hauled these fingerlings back to Abrams Creek, he met widespread skepticism and scorn from the rest of the community. "They'll all go over Abram's Falls," his knowing neighbors concluded, "and be deader'n four o'clock!" Yet these beautiful trout flourished and multiplied in their new habitat, and furnished great enjoyment to future fishermen.[27]

The progressive thread of conservation in Oliver's character was not limited solely to the physical environment. As early as 1901 he began collecting local history and genealogies, and interviewed many elderly residents in order to get a written record of the cove's history and heritage. He encouraged his father, William Howell Oliver, to write a lengthy sketch of the family. Writing the war department, he obtained exact information about the original John Oliver's record in the War of 1812. Beginning what eventually became an enormous collection of manuscripts, justice of the peace docket books, and store account books, he traveled widely to seek out cove history in other libraries and collections. Through these efforts and with his own intimate knowledge of the cove, he succeeded in leaving a documented and detailed record of most of the cove's history from 1818 through the twentieth century.

In this task of historical preservation he was greatly aided by the unbroken oral tradition or community consciousness still alive and active in Cades Cove during the first decade of the new century. He was even able to organize young people periodically to clean up existing cemeteries. Although primarily a social occasion, like logrolling or a "brush burning," this group effort greatly improved the appearance of the cove graveyards.[28] In later years Oliver furnished at his own expense many tombstones to graves which otherwise would have been lost.

The high point of progressivism occurred on August 16, 1915, with the opening of a model consolidated school in the cove. The support and enthusiasm of the entire community is reflected in an article from the *Maryville Times*:

> In Cades Cove, where the first consolidated school building in the county was completed, the public-minded men and women and progressive teachers who have been assigned to that school have underway the organization and establishment of such a model school. Far off in the mountain cove, ten miles from a railway, away from the conveniences that we of the towns and cities and rural communities in close touch with the town have, is this modern school building complete in every detail, modernly built, modernly lighted and heated, with water from a mountain spring quite a dis-

tance away, and with educational advantages equal to those of the boys and girls in the towns. A preachment of educational leaders that has become a kind of ark of the covenant, is that the public school building should be a community social center. Some communities in other counties and in other states, and school buildings in larger cities have adopted this community idea in the operation of their school, and it has proved most successful. The patrons and teachers of the Cades Cove school are planning to make that building the community center. To this end the boys and girls already have underway the organization of ball teams, debating societies, reading circles, etc. The building is a convenient place for the assembling of the patrons of the community, and it is the hope of those heading the movement that a library can be established, literature placed on the reading tables, and the place made as attractive and fascinating that patrons will want to assemble there to spend their leisure hours in the reading of good books, good papers, the enjoyment of the contests in which the boys and girls will engage, and become better acquainted with the teachers, parents of other pupils, the pupils themselves, and to see their own children at work in the school. A splendid example which others would do well to emulate has been set by the patrons in Cades Cove. The first week of the school, more than 200 patrons, or about all there are in the cove, visited the building. The work is progressing harmoniously, and there is a "work together" spirit here.[29]

The *Maryville Enterprise* further asserted that "the people of Cades Cove are among the most progressive in the county." Every question of progress before the community was supported "as a unit" there, concluded one editorial.

The consolidated school and all it represented in terms of expanding service to the wider community was a personal triumph for Oliver. Speaking "very enthusiastically" at its opening, he said the school about which he had dreamed fifteen years ago at Maryville College had finally become a reality.[30]

Oliver practiced what he preached with his own children. His eldest son, W. Wayne, was sent out of the cove at the age of eight to a private preparatory school in Maryville. In later life this son became a distinguished jurist, serving for many years as judge of the Fourth Judicial Circuit of Tennessee and finally as an eminent judge on Tennessee's Court of Criminal Appeals. Many other cove families followed Oliver's example in sending their children out of the cove to preparatory schools which would qualify them to enter college. Further, Oliver would not tolerate local prejudice against educating women. He sent both his daughters to Montreat, a Presbyterian junior college and preparatory school for girls at Black Mountain, North Carolina.[31] He was always greatly angered by the prevailing notion that higher education was somehow "wasted" on women.

America's entry into World War I transformed most of the cove's progressive idealism into ardent patriotism. Not since the Civil War had the community been so galvanized by national affairs. The years immediately before 1918 were probably the most prosperous ever for cove farmers. The demand of Great Britain and France for American food brought extremely high prices, and even greater production was urged after the United States declared war on Germany. Cove farmers doubled their efforts to produce record harvests. Many bought liberty bonds to support the war effort, and other families joined the Olivers in observing national "meatless" and "wheatless" days. As early as April 1915 the cove reported that seven-eighths of its citizens supported Britain.[32] Although much of the cove's population was of German extraction, all these families had been in the United States over a hundred years. In an atmosphere of moral unanimity and patriotism, many young cove men volunteered for the army.

One such cove soldier, Willie E. Roberts, wrote a lengthy letter from France to his mother in Cades Cove, and the letter was published on June 13, 1918, in the *Maryville Enterprise.* His rhetoric was an almost perfect repetition of Wilsonian idealism. The barbarism of the "Huns," the struggle to "make the world safe for democracy," and the faith in America's unselfish sacrifices to safeguard humanity and independence for all peoples seem concepts jaded and stereotyped from overuse.[33] The significance of Roberts' letter, however, lies precisely in its unoriginality. Cades Cove had become a national community, vitally concerned with America's national and international problems. For once, Americanism was far more important than any state or regional identity. And these ideas were interchangeable; Roberts' letter would have been applauded in practically any section of the United States at that time.

How ironic that out of the great unity and idealism of this national crusade would emerge a law destined to divide and fragment the community: national prohibition. Moonshining had been a growing problem throughout the years of greatest progressive achievement in Cades Cove. As illicit distilling steadily increased during the first decade of the twentieth century, it cast an ominous shadow over every progressive accomplishment. Yet during these years, moonshining was not completely out of control; the majority of cove citizens condemned both its manufacture and consumption.[34]

Before Tennessee's state prohibition laws, moonshining for commercial purposes was mainly confined to Chestnut Flats. There were exceptions, but romantic notions by writers such as Mary Noailles Murfree, who idealized the moonshiner as trapped in the only possible occupation available to support his starving family, are nonsense. Too frequently a family starved *because* the father was moonshining. Too many other honest occupations existed, and the cove land was always fertile enough to supply ample food to any farmer willing to work. Emigration was an option open to all and taken by many to improve their status. Jobs were plentiful in many neighboring sawmills, and tenants on marginal or peripheral land still managed to provide the basic necessities for their families through hard work. "Anyone wanting work to do can find it by coming to Cades Cove," noted the *Maryville Times* in 1907.[35] So the popular notion that moonshining was somehow forced on otherwise honest people against their real inclination ignores overwhelming statistical evidence to the contrary.

Actually, making whiskey was an easy way out. Unfortunately it proved impossible to pursue moonshining and remain either respectable or honest. Brawling and thievery followed as the distiller became more and more enmeshed in an outlaw subculture. Since there was absolutely no socialization in moderate consumption of alcohol among the cove people, social drinking was impossible, and few men actively engaged in manufacturing whiskey avoided excessive personal consumption. No middle ground seemed to exist between teetotalism and drunkenness.

"Whiskey is said to have caused the murder of Fayette Myers in a fight that followed a drunken row up in Chestnut Flats," reported the *Maryville Enterprise* on January 22, 1914. Accounts of such murders and of battles between cove distillers and revenue officers multiplied. By 1917, one covite complained that "moonshining in and around Cades Cove is as bold and open as going to mill."[36]

The wives and children of moonshiners often faced starvation or brutal abuse. Frequently they sought advice from John Oliver on his mail route, and begged him to report their husband's stills to the revenue officers. Oliver was placed in a real dilemma. Community norms mitigated against exposing a native son to outside harassment. This norm often forced reluctant residents, quite decent themselves, to warn moonshining relatives when revenuers were in the cove. "I am told," lamented one cove citizen, "that a man who has his name on the church roll ran to tell the moonshiners to look out."[37] For this reason, although many stills were periodically captured and destroyed, the operators were seldom caught. This system of warning was reminiscent of a similar network developed during the Civil War as protection against marauding guerrillas. And the internal system of communication by word of mouth had remained quite effective far into the twentieth century.

Yet it was apparent to Oliver that illicit distilling was tearing many families apart and might eventually threaten the fabric of the entire community. National prohibition in 1919 combined with rapidly dropping prices for farm products further exacerbated the situation. Because of the cove's relative inaccessibility, economic opportunities from distilling mushroomed after 1920 as federal officers seized distilling equipment in more settled areas of the state. Many mainstream cove farmers, even respected church members, were now tempted to ply this old trade which had suddenly become so lucrative. Law enforcement officials commented on the growing size of stills and the increased volume of whiskey seized in 1921 in and around the cove.[38]

The sight of one murdered moonshiner's family of small children forlornly gathered around their father's open coffin finally persuaded Oliver that he must actively fight the moonshiners, regardless of the personal consequences or danger.

Privately he began informing both federal and state law enforcement officials of the exact location of these stills. Such knowledge was widespread among the cove people, but Oliver had the additional advantage of scouting out concealed stills unobtrusively on his mail route. Telltale smoke or other signs, combined with his intimate knowledge of the cove's geography, made possible extremely accurate and timely information. Law enforcement agents also used his home as a base, arriving there secretly in the early hours of the morning to plan their attack.[39]

Because Oliver was so outspoken in his public condemnation of moonshining, he was increasingly blamed by the distillers when their equipment was captured. One such incident occurred in December 1921. Josiah Gregory, known as Joe Banty because of his short stature, had been convicted with his sons in the Blount County Criminal Court at different times for manufacturing and storing whiskey for sale. Joe Banty Gregory had a reputation for making a very high grade of corn whiskey which was in great demand.

On December 8, 1921, officers from the Blount County sheriff's office and local officers raided Joe Banty's still, which was located near his home. In order to transport the large copper pot and other confiscated paraphernalia to the nearest railroad station in Townsend, the two local officers, Deputy Sheriff John A. Myers and Constable George Brown, borrowed a team of mules and wagon from John Oliver's father, William Howell Oliver, also a Primitive Baptist minister. Myers was the son-in-law of the elder Oliver; Brown was working for John Oliver on his farm at that time. Because of these relationships and circumstantial evidence, Joe Banty and his family accused John Oliver of reporting his still. Actually, a surveyor, Andrew K. Gregory, had reported the still, but the Gregorys were infuriated at John Oliver and determined to seek revenge.[40]

On December 9, 1921, Oliver and his two oldest children, Lucille, eleven, and Wayne, fourteen, attended a program at the consolidated school to raise money for new books in the library. Returning home at 9 o'clock, Oliver put the horse and buggy up and retired with the rest of the family soon after. At about 10:30 the whole house was illuminated by a bright light. Running to the door in his night clothes, Oliver saw that his whole barn was ablaze.

Oliver's immediate concern was to save his five horses. Duncan was in the first stable as he entered the barn; Frank and Tice were at the other end in different stables. These three escaped unharmed when the gates to their stalls were opened. The two big farm horses, Gibb and Joe, presented problems because their stalls were in the center of the barn, already engulfed in flames. Reaching Joe's stall after a desperate struggle, Oliver could not get the frightened horse to come out. By taking off his undershirt and putting it over Joe's head, he finally led the frantic horse out to safety. This maneuver worked well because with his eyes thus covered, the horse could not see the flames rapidly growing around him.[41]

By this time, Gibb's stable was a solid sheet of flame. Oliver made repeated attempts to reach this horse, and suffered severe burns as a consequence. The horse kept neighing to him over the din until finally Oliver heard him fall. At that point he knew Gibb was dead. Then he hastened around on the back side of the barn to a shed and opened the gate to free about a dozen young cattle.

In the meantime many neighbors had come over and began trying to save the crib which stood close to the barn. This crib contained a year's harvest of corn and all the farm machinery. Lucille and Wayne carried dozens of tubs of water from the branch as the neighbors placed wet tow sacks on the crib roof, putting out the flames and wetting it down. They said that if the barn fell in the direction away from the crib, they could save it.[42]

After the barn had fallen and the crib had been saved, John Oliver came back to the house. His wife, Nancy Ann, was sitting on the bed crying. Almost immediately, a neighbor, John Burchfield, came to the door and said, "John, your other barn in the upper end of Cades Cove is on fire." The family all ran outside again. They could hear Grandfather and Grandmother Oliver screaming across the open fields. "That's my father's barn," Oliver said in a moment of supreme agony.[43]

The elder Olivers slept like children with the shutters on their windows closed. When they were finally awakened by their dog barking, the fire had advanced to the point that nothing could be saved. They lost all their livestock — cattle, milk cows, horses, mules — in addition to plows, mowing machine, hay rake, harnesses, bridles, saddles, and a barn full of hay. "The fire destroyed about twenty-five years of our hard labor," William Howell Oliver later recalled. Because this barn was a solid log structure it took much longer to burn; for hours its flames could be seen all over the cove.[44]

More lasting than the loss of property, however, was the emotional trauma the family endured. For years afterward, they dreaded to see nightfall. Grandmother Oliver suffered a fatal stroke four years later, which her husband attributed to the enduring shock of the barn burnings. Fearing a return of the arsonists, John Oliver slept with his rifle for months in his other barn with the silo which had been built in 1920 on property next to his father's barn. It was this latter barn which the neighbors had mistakenly thought was on fire while his first barn was burning.[45]

On Christmas Eve, 1921, Joe Banty Gregory's son Earl and a friend, Perry Tipton, went up to Dave Sparks's home to visit John and Francis (France) Sparks. Advised by Dave and his wife that the two Sparks sons were away but would return shortly, Earl and Perry waited. When they heard the Sparks brothers coming, Earl and Perry decided to play a prank on their friends. Pretending to be officers Myers and Brown, they attempted to place the two Sparks brothers under arrest.

John and France Sparks immediately thought something was wrong because both Perry Tipton and Earl Gregory were very short men, under five feet tall. The Sparks brothers knew that both Deputy Sheriff John Myers and Constable George Brown were large men well over six feet. So the Sparks resisted arrest and in the dark one of them beat up Earl Gregory badly, striking him several times about the head and face with a heavy flashlight. When after the melée Earl and Perry identified themselves, John Sparks took them into the house where his mother bandaged Earl's wounds.[46]

Earl's injuries infuriated the Gregorys; they could not let this injury or blow to their family honor remain unavenged. On Christmas morning, Sunday, 1921, Earl's father and brother, Joe Banty and Dana Gregory, saddled their horses and set out to find the Sparks boys. They found all the Sparks gathered at the home of Dan Myers, whose wife was a daughter of Tom Sparks and Asa Sparks's sister. This home was located in the upper end of Cades Cove about a mile from the Sparks home.

At the Dan Myers home, a family Christmas celebration was in progress. Tom Sparks, his son Asa, and his nephew John Sparks were all there with other relatives. Joe and Dana Gregory joined these festivities, entirely congenial and in apparent good humor. Late in the afternoon, after participating for quite some time in the merriment, Joe Banty remarked that it was time for them to go home and do their evening chores. As they were leaving, Dana picked up a wooden fire poker and without warning knocked John Sparks out of his chair into the fireplace. At this point, both Dana and Joe Banty pulled out their pistols and began shooting, seriously wounding Asa and John Sparks. Calmly reloading their guns, the two Gregorys backed out of the house, mounted their horses, and rode away. Shortly thereafter they disappeared from home; nobody knew where either of the Gregorys had gone.[47]

On New Year's Day, Sunday, 1922, Tom Sparks rode up to the Oliver home and asked for John. Wayne told him his father was feeding cattle at the new barn. There Tom asked John to bring Constable Brown and the two justices of the peace, Albert Hill and Andrew Shields, and meet him at the home of Deputy Sheriff Myers. When Oliver and these men arrived, Tom, Wade, and Sam Sparks had built a fire in a small clearing near Myers' barn. When the group assembled there, warming themselves on this bitterly cold day before the open fire, Tom ordered his grandson, Wade, to relate what he knew about the burning of the Oliver barns.[48]

Wade Sparks said and subsequently testified in court that Joe Banty and his wife, Elvira Gregory, gave him and Dana Gregory fifty dollars each to burn the barns of John and Will Oliver. The Gregorys believed John Oliver had initially reported their still, and they blamed his father, Will (William Howell Oliver), for allowing the officers to haul the confiscated still to the railroad station with his wagon and mules. Wade gave all the details of how they carried out their assignment, noting that Dana Gregory struck the match to set both barns on fire. Dana and Wade had followed the Olivers home from school that night, firing their barn and then walking across the fields to Grandfather Oliver's barn.[49]

About a week later, a little boy named Henry Burchfield, who lived with his grandparents, Uncle Ike and Aunt Kansas Tipton, appeared at Uncle Bud (James E.) Gregory's store to purchase a plug of apple chewing tobacco and a pair of cotton socks. All the cove residents knew in intimate detail the habits of their neighbors, and Uncle Bud's suspicions were immediately aroused by these purchases. He knew Ike grew his own tobacco and never used any other kind. He also knew that the year around Ike wore only wool socks knitted by his wife. Uncle Bud passed this information on to Dave Sparks. As a consequence, officers and some of the Sparks men went that night to Uncle Ike's house and found Joe Banty and Dana Gregory hiding there in the attic. The Gregorys were arrested on a warrant for shooting the Sparks boys and were taken to jail in Maryville.[50]

On October 19, 1922, a jury convicted Dana of burning John Oliver's barn, and found Joe and Elvira Gregory guilty as accessories before the fact. All three Gregorys were sentenced to imprisonment in the penitentiary "for a period of not less than two years nor more than twenty-one." On October 26, the Blount County Circuit Court judge, Sam Brown, reversed this conviction and sentence on the ground that they were based wholly upon the uncorroborated testimony of Wade Sparks, an admitted accomplice.[51]

Both John and Asa Sparks recovered from the shooting. On June 24, 1922, Joe Banty and Dana Gregory were convicted of felonious assault with the intent to commit first degree murder against John Sparks; on June 29 both Gregorys were convicted of felonious assault with the intent to commit second degree murder on Asa Sparks. Sentenced to from three to twenty years in the penitentiary, the Gregorys appealed to the state Supreme Court in both cases. In its September 1923 term the Tennessee Supreme Court in Knoxville affirmed both convictions and directed that the Gregorys, then out on bond, be taken immediately to begin serving their term in the penitentiary.[52]

At this point, John Mitchell, a Maryville druggist with strong political connections, interceded on behalf of the Gregorys with Governor Austin Peay. Many years earlier, Joe Banty Gregory had served on the jury which acquitted Mitchell of killing his father-in-law. Joe Banty had long had the reputation of making the finest whiskey in the Great Smokies; in the intervening years Mitchell had become one of his best customers. In any event, Governor Peay pardoned the Gregorys in time for both men to be back home in Cades Cove by Christmas, 1923.[53] It was later rumored that some of Joe Banty's finest whiskey found its way into the governor's mansion in Nashville shortly thereafter.

Despite all the bitterness over the barn burnings, when Joe Banty Gregory died in 1933, his family requested John Oliver to conduct his funeral. That Oliver agreed to do so, and managed this funeral in a way pleasing to the Gregorys, indicates that the old community ties, while severely strained, were never quite broken. Elvira Gregory died ten years later when the home where she was living in Knox County was destroyed by fire.[54]

In comparison to conflicts in other parts of Appalachia, the Sparks-Gregory shootings seem to scarcely merit designation as a feud. Family honor, a disrupted economy, and temporarily taking the law into one's own hands were all ingredients shared in common with Kentucky feudists. But in Cades Cove the violence was limited in both scope and duration, and the protagonists resorted to the formal legal process—the sheriff and the Blount County Circuit Court—as a final resort. No killing occurred, and violence did not beget a long bloody chain reaction of vengeance as so often happened in the mountains of eastern Kentucky.[55] Compared to the total population of Blount County, cove citizens in the 1920s were not frequently before the circuit court for misdemeanors or felonies other than for those offenses associated with illicit distilling.

The broader significance of this saga of the barn burnings lies in the fact that the conflict was ultimately resolved or adjudicated in the appropriate court of law. Even in the tumultuous times following prohibition, lawlessness occasionally flared out but did not finally triumph in Cades Cove. Likewise, progressive reforms, such as the very successful consolidated school, continued to prosper throughout the 1920s, overshadowed but not extinguished by the struggle over prohibition.

The first decades of the twentieth century witnessed the heights of progressive prosperity and the depth of community dissension and anguish over illicit distilling in Cades Cove. In both progressive reforms and his fight against the moonshiners, John Oliver, "Cades Cove's leading citizen," in the words of Justice William O. Douglas, "served its people as no one else, bringing them enlightenment and guidance in raising their standard of living."[56] Ahead loomed the worst crisis in the cove's history, and it is not surprising that caught up in the maelstrom of the birth of the Great Smoky Mountains National Park, the cove people would once again turn to John Oliver for leadership and moral direction.

Death by Eminent Domain

On a hot September afternoon in 1929 John Oliver found himself once again engaged in legal battle before the Blount County Circuit Court. Even unfriendly spectators in the old courthouse in Maryville, however, grudgingly conceded Oliver's audacity and courage in fighting a seemingly hopeless battle against impossible odds. Arraigned against him were the full force of the federal government, the state of Tennessee, and widespread public disapproval throughout East Tennessee. He was challenging the right of the state to seize his farm by eminent domain, but in so doing he threatened the larger progress of the entire movement to establish the Great Smoky Mountains National Park.

To Carlos C. Campbell, leader in the park movement and later chronicler of its history, Oliver had created "one of the most troublesome and lengthy cases" confronting the Park Commission, a case "out of all proportion" to the small size – 337.5 acres – of the farm. "It had been expected," Campbell asserts, that because of his education and standing within the community "Oliver would be a local leader in the park work."[1] Instead Oliver fought a bitter battle in the courts for more than six years, including three appeals before the Tennessee Supreme Court.

Ironically Oliver shared the same progressive values as the Knoxville boosters who initially proposed and fought to establish a national park in the Great Smokies. These men – Colonel David C. Chapman, J. Wylie Brownlee, Cowan Rodgers, Willis P. Davis, and Carlos C. Campbell – were all prominent business or civic leaders in Knoxville during the 1920s. Most were members of the Knoxville Chamber of Commerce; Campbell himself was its manager.[2]

Although some of these businessmen had a genuine concern for conservation, it is undeniably evident that from the beginning of the park movement their primary motive was profit. Even the most cursory glance at the correspondence of these men or at the Knoxville newspapers at the time shows that they expected an unprecedented financial bonanza for Knoxville and the surrounding region to result from the establishment of a national park. This expectation of enormous profit was repeated countless times in the propaganda used to solicit private donations to the park fund. So vital did the park seem to the city's economic future that on March 31, 1926, Knoxville's city council took the unprecedented step of voting to pay one-third of the purchase price for the Little River Lumber tract, the first large segment of park land acquired.[3]

Knoxville's motivation may also be gauged by the lengthy debate over whether the new park should be a national park or a national forest. Colonel Chapman, who quickly became the park movement's leader and most prominent spokesman, pointed out in 1925 that no commercial or financial benefits would accrue if a national forest were established in the Great Smokies. Two such national forests were already located in East Tennessee, he argued, but neither had brought "advertising" or "prestige." Only a national park, Chapman maintained, would bring "nationwide" attention and commerce to Knoxville.[4]

Like their Knoxville counterparts, many cove citizens hoped that the 1920s would bring a new era of prosperity and growth to their community. The long-anticipated railroad never reached the cove, but a new road (the present route) was completed in 1922. This route to Townsend was far superior to older roads and for the first time made Cades Cove easily accessible by motor vehicles. The cove's century-old struggle for better transportation seemed now finally to be solved in the automobile era. Such access not only made marketing crops easier but promised the advent of an entirely new tourist industry to exploit Cades Cove's unparalleled natural beauty. "Cades Cove will be the chief summer resort of the South," one optimistic cove resident went so far as to predict in July 1921.[5]

Commercial development began in earnest July 11, 1925, with the opening of Gregorys Cave, complete with an electric power plant. Other cove families took advantage of the influx of tourists by offering summer board and lodgings. In 1924, John Oliver began renting tourist cabins and offering his services as a guide to hikers who wanted to see the mountains, particularly such spots as Gregory Bald, Thunderhead, and the Spence Field. By 1928, when Oliver constructed a large and commodious lodge, he had developed a large clientele from the Midwest and New England. Descriptions of this lodge and of other Cades Cove tourist accommodations appeared in national magazines. Oliver's Lodge attracted Mellinger Henry, a noted folklorist, as well as numerous local civic and school groups from Maryville and Knoxville.[6]

Profits and development from such tourism were regarded as yet another aspect of progressivism by many of the cove people. Like the park boosters in Knoxville, they saw personal profit through new businesses as a desirable goal not at odds with earlier civic and educational objectives. John Oliver and many others therefore welcomed the idea of a national park to preserve and advertise their surrounding mountains. Oliver, an ardent conservationist, had long deplored periodic fires that often raged out of control in the Great Smokies. He believed a national park would be a means of stopping such fires and of halting the wholesale destruction of forests and subsequent erosion by the Little River Lumber Company.[7]

Although it is evident that park promoters intended to include Cades Cove within park boundaries almost from the beginning of the movement, they launched an elaborate campaign to assure cove citizens that their homes and farms would never be molested. Carlos Campbell befriended Oliver, using his tourist cabins to show prospective park supporters the beauty of the cove and surrounding mountains. Warning might have been taken from the fact that every major group shown the Great Smokies, from national and state legislators to John D. Rockefeller Jr., were taken to Cades Cove. But Campbell and others on the Park Commission reiterated over and over their promises that private homes would not be taken over by the proposed park.[8] This campaign was extremely successful and lasted well into 1927, when the state passed the final park bill.

A letter from Campbell to Oliver on March 24, 1927, indicates that both men were still on extremely cordial terms. Campbell and other

Tyson Issues Statement.

Senator L. D. Tyson today issued a statement to allay the fears of those residing in the area to be included in the Great Smokies park that their homes may be taken from them. Nothing of the kind will happen, the senator said. His statement follows:

"I have noticed reports to the effect that the people within the boundary which is proposed to be taken in for the Great Smoky Mountain park are somewhat disturbed over the situation, feeling that they may be compelled to sell their land and to move out of the area within the boundary and be put to other inconvenience thereby.

"The bill which has been introduced for this proposed park in the senate and house carries no authority whatever to move anyone, and there is no authority whatever for buying any land or of doing anything in regard to the land except to receive it as a donation. No person within the boundary limits so far as any authority is contained in this bill, is compelled to move or in any way to be disturbed nor their land taken over under this bill.

"I do not understand how such a rumor could have gotten out.

Matter for States Alone.

"Of course, I do not know what the states of Tennessee and North Carolina will do in the future; as congress has nothing whatever to do with that, but congress can pass no bill whatever that can in any way take away the land of any citizen. Under the bill, land can only be received by donation, and the United States does nothing whatever until a minimum amount of land designated in the bill is donated and turned over to the United States for park purposes."

Knoxville Journal, May 9, 1926.

"The eviction of the mountain people after they had been promised they could remain during their lifetime was a shocking breach of faith on the part of this legalized agency of the state of Tennessee, the park commission" (T.H. Alexander in the *Nashville Tennessean*, September 1, 1932). *Oliver Family Collection.*

Chamber of Commerce members had just returned from a weekend visit to Oliver's home. Enclosed were clippings from the *Knoxville News-Sentinel* describing the cove's beauty by another guest, Edward Meeman, editor of that paper. Campbell also enclosed a booklet of the Great Smoky Mountains Hiking Club, which included a description, he pointed out, of the Oliver home.[9]

From the point of view of cove people who later tried to resist the seizure of their homes by eminent domain, this period between 1923 and 1927 of being lulled into a false sense of security proved to be their worst mistake. Oliver was culpable to some degree for accepting these reassuring promises. The problem was that he, as an old progressive, understood and shared the same values as these Knoxville boosters. The point of divergence was their willingness to use what would appear in retrospect to cove citizens to have been blatant deceit to take Cades Cove as part of the park — a deceit which Oliver recognized far too late.

With the passage in April 1927, by the Tennessee General Assembly of a bill to appropriate $1,500,000 for buying park lands, the battle to save Cades Cove was already lost. This bill specifically gave the newly created Park Commission the power to seize homes within the proposed boundaries by right of eminent domain. Concerted political pressure from cove citizens before 1927 might well have altered the outcome. Such pressure was successfully applied by citizens of Sevier County in 1927 to leave key portions of that county out of the proposed park boundaries.[10]

Cove citizens were also beguiled by a barrage of public statements by their political leaders throughout 1926. In May, Senator Lawrence D. Tyson issued "a statement to allay the fears of those residing in the area to be included in the Great Smokies park that their homes may be taken from them." Tyson went on to assure the public that no person within the boundary limits of the park "is compelled to move or in any way to be disturbed nor their land taken over under the bill." He concluded that such seizure of mountain farms was so preposterous he could "not understand how such a rumor could have gotten out."[11]

Tyson's statement was widely printed in local papers and greatly reassured cove residents. Tennessee governor Austin Peay also publicly assured owners of land within the park that "they need have no alarm."

At Elkmont in 1926 Governor Peay met with three or four hundred concerned citizens and repeated assurances that their farms would never be seized by eminent domain for park purposes. "As long as I am a member of the Park Commission," Peay argued, "I wish to assure these people that there will be no condemnation of their homes." Such evictions "for the pleasure and profit of the rest of the state," he continued, "would be a blot upon the state that the barbarism of the Huns could not match!"[12]

A reporter for *Progressive Labor* was in the crowd at Elkmont and recorded both Governor Peay's promises and the reaction of the mountain people to these assurances. In April 1927 a lengthy editorial in that journal bitterly condemned state officials and the Park Commission for blatantly lying to these people about the seizure of their homes. However worthy and desirable the establishment of a national park in the Great Smokies might be for the commercial advancement of Knoxville, the editorial concluded, the price being asked of "unsuspecting" mountaineers was far too high.[13]

The boundary line of the proposed park before the passage of the final law by the Tennessee legislature creating the Great Smoky Mountains National Park in April 1927 included many large and well-established communities: Townsend, Walland, Sunshine, Elkmont, Pigeon Forge, Miller's Cove, Tuckaleechee Cove, and Wear's Valley. Public protest over forced inclusion within the park of these communities was too powerful to be ignored. As a consequence, these areas were all excluded from the final bill. Unfortunately, because of its smaller population and geographic position within the mountains, Cades Cove was not omitted.[14] So after passage of the Tennessee Act, the cove community stood alone as the only major settled area within the new park. No one in the cove realized yet, however, that promises by Senator Tyson and Governor Peay that they should remain undisturbed in their homes were no longer valid.

After the Rockefeller donation of $5,000,000 to the park campaign was announced in March 1928, the reaction of the cove people to increased efforts by the Park Commission to buy their farms was mixed. Some willingly sold their land, but most of the people viewed the prospect of removal with dread and apprehension. A pervasive feeling of helplessness in light of the coercive power of eminent domain seemed to preclude any effective community opposition. Who could withstand the power of the state or federal government? In June 1928, two cove residents, Mrs. R.D. Burchfield and G. Walter Gregory, wrote long personal letters to John D. Rockefeller Jr. begging him to intercede on their behalf with the Park Commission to leave Cades Cove out of the park. But these appeals and others of similar nature to other representatives were now uniformly ignored.[15]

John Oliver had finally realized by the middle of 1927 that the Park Commission intended to take all of the cove. He and other cove residents like Mrs. Burchfield and Walter Gregory began writing impassioned and desperate letters of protest to various state and national politicians. The major problem confronting the cove people at this point was the continued public denial by the Park Commission that Cades Cove would definitely be included in the new park. Local newspapers reflected this confusion. "It is understood," noted the *Maryville Times* in November 1928, "that there is some question about the government taking over property in Cades Cove." Even when the Blount County court clerk, George D. Roberts, wrote directly to Colonel Chapman about this rumor, Chapman replied that no final decision had been made about Cades Cove. In December the Park Commission was examining additional sections of the Chilhowee mountains "with the purpose of considering recommending that some sections now omitted from the boundary be substituted for parts of Cades Cove."[16]

No one was more deeply aware of the terrible fear and anguish within the community, particularly among the elderly, than John Oliver. Daily he counseled with his neighbors in the role of friend, pastor, and adviser. It was extremely difficult to articulate to outsiders the importance of place in the lives of ordinary cove people. The very existence of their community was now threatened, a threat even more serious than the continuing raids by North Carolina guerrillas in 1864. But the enemy now, ironically for this Union stronghold, was their own beloved federal government! For the first time in anyone's experience, loyalty to the cove community was directly at odds with loyalty to the United States. "Our ancestors fought in the American Revolution," one cove citizen wrote plaintively, "must Cades Cove now submit to Kaiserism?" Appeals for help from cove citizens often enumerated the cove men who had fought in all the nation's wars since the first John Oliver's service in the War of 1812, but such appeals fell on deaf ears.[17]

On behalf of the community paralyzed by confusion and fear, Oliver decided to fight the Park Commission through the courts. In the summer of 1929, his son Wayne rode a horse around the cove securing pledges to hire a lawyer from those interested in testing their rights under the law. At this juncture many were leaning toward the idea of accepting what the Park Commission offered, but some made or pledged a contribution. The lawyer chosen, Russell R. Kramer, was an extremely capable attorney. A graduate of the University of Michigan School of Law, Kramer had been practicing in Maryville since 1913.[18]

In July 1929, the legal battle for Cades Cove began when the Park Commission brought a condemnation suit in the Blount County Circuit Court against Oliver to acquire his property—three tracts of land containing a total of 337.5 acres. At the outset of what became a lengthy and complex court battle, both sides realized the stakes were far greater than Oliver's small farm. If Oliver could win, the rest of the cove farmers might also successfully resist seizure of their homes by eminent domain. Because of the serious constitutional questions raised in this case, the Park Commission delayed starting condemnation proceedings on other tracts until the outcome.[19]

Oliver's defense involved numerous technical challenges to the 1927 Act of the Tennessee legislature establishing the Great Smoky Mountains National Park. One such challenge asserted that an unfair burden was placed on the defendant because this Act "authorized condemnation of their property while exempting the property of others" within the park boundary. Other challenges involved the legality of reducing the size and tax base of Blount County by removing her entire sixteenth civil district.[20]

The critical issue, however, was whether one sovereignty, the state of Tennessee, could exercise the power of eminent domain to secure land for the public use of another sovereignty, the federal government. Judge Pat Quinn agreed with Oliver's counsel that the state could not exercise such power in this instance and dismissed the state's suit in August 1930. But upon appeal, the Tennessee Supreme Court in February 1931 rejected Judge Quinn's decision and sent the case back to the

Blount County Circuit Court for further proceedings. The Supreme Court held that the public necessity justifying exercise of the power of eminent domain need not "be exclusively the necessity of the particular sovereignty seeking to condemn."[21]

Following this Supreme Court decision, a jury of view was appointed August 8, 1931, to examine Oliver's property and after considering further evidence from the condemnor and the land owner, to fix the damages occasioned to the owner by the appropriation of his property. This jury of view fixed the value of Oliver's property at $10,650 on August 27, 1931. Oliver through his attorney again appealed the case to the Tennessee Supreme Court, raising in essence the same constitutional questions. In July 1932, the Supreme Court held that questions of law decided upon appeal are settled and cannot be re-examined upon a subsequent appeal of the same case. Since the court was bound by its former judgment that the state had a right to take Oliver's property, the case was remanded a second time to the Blount County Circuit Court.[22]

This second opinion in July 1932 settled finally the basic constitutional question about the state's right to exercise the power of eminent domain to acquire property in Cades Cove for the park. Thereafter the Park Commission could expedite acquisition of cove farms without the threat of any legal impediment. By 1932, the cove people therefore realized that the last hope or possibility of saving their community from destruction had evaporated.

In spite of legal defeat on every point, Oliver continued the battle. His appeal from the jury of view's assessment of $10,650 was granted by the trial judge, and a new trial began before a full jury of twelve to determine the fair value of his property. In June of 1934, this jury fixed the value of Oliver's farm at $17,000. Earlier in 1933, the state had appealed Oliver's right to this second trial, but in January 1934 the Supreme Court confirmed Judge Quinn's decision allowing such a trial. On May 9, 1935, the Tennessee Court of Appeals in Knoxville affirmed the judgment of the trial court, adding interest of $807.51.[23] Oliver had lost the war to save Cades Cove, but even his critics were forced to concede his courage and tenacity throughout these long and complicated legal proceedings during the worst years of the Great Depression.

In the meantime, the Park Commission had accelerated the forced sale of homes and farms throughout the cove. In 1928, the cove population was approximately 600 people or 110 families. By the end of 1929, the Park Commission had purchased 52 farms, approximately one half of the total number. Many of these families who sold their land before 1930, however, did not leave immediately. The 1930 census listed 424 people still living in the cove.[24]

In return for payment of less than the real value of their farms, many families were given leases or special permission to continue living on their property. These promises, given as early as 1926, would later cause serious problems and bitter misunderstanding because the Park Commission had no legal authority to grant such leases or to bind the National Park Service later to such prior commitments. Expediency dictated this policy, nevertheless, because such leases could later be repudiated. In the meantime, leasing made it much easier to obtain farms from reluctant cove citizens and allowed the Park Commission to purchase most of the property at reduced rates.[25]

By 1933, 75 farms totaling 8,164.96 acres had been purchased for $340,071.52. The average cove farm was 108.87 acres; 89 percent of these farms were under 200 acres in size. Prices varied widely; the average price per acre on farms sold before 1934 was $41.65. Two or three agents appraised each farm; 34 owners offered their own estimate of the value of their property. The final price paid by the commission averaged approximately 75 percent of the owner's estimate.[26] Again, fair value is a relative judgment almost impossible to determine in retrospect, particularly in cases where most owners did not want to sell in the first place. Also, farm prices had been steadily dropping in Blount County throughout the 1920s.

By 1936, according to A. Randolph Shields, a total of 11,273 acres had been purchased from resident cove owners for a sum of $442,950, or about $39 per acre. Ironically, an absentee corporate land owner, the Morton Butler Lumber Company, received more money than the total paid cove farmers — $483,500 for 25,243.75 acres of mountainous land between Cades Cove and Gregory Bald.[27]

The real tragedy for the cove people was that they were forced to sell and move during the midst of the Great Depression. Many owned substantial homes, some equipped with running water and electricity furnished by a Delco battery system. The economy throughout Blount

County and East Tennessee was collapsing by 1930. Unemployment was rising at a catastrophic rate; a more hostile or unwelcome environment for newcomers could scarcely be imagined. Not only were most cove families unable to re-create their prosperous farms, but in their new homes they were now scattered and isolated from their former neighbors and friends. In this their greatest hour of need, they could no longer rely upon a supportive traditional community for assistance. Isolation from family and friends was particularly hard on the elderly. Finally, many banks to which cove people entrusted money from their farms collapsed in 1932–33. Especially devastating was the failure of First National Bank in Maryville in January 1933.[28]

Bad though the sufferings of these mainstream cove farmers were, their problems pale in comparison to the dire predicament in which former cove tenants found themselves in 1931. No clear estimate of the number of these tenants is available, but from twenty-five to thirty families seems a not unreasonable figure. Such tenants owned no property but farmed land belonging to others for a share of the crop. The harshness of tenancy or sharecropping had always been mitigated in Cades Cove by the fact that most rented land from relatives or friends who felt some personal obligation for their well-being. Now these families, often with numerous children, were thrust out of the cove into a hostile environment with absolutely no personal resources and practically no prospect of any employment.[29]

Also difficult to measure were the fears and anxiety among elderly cove people, most of whom had lived their entire lives there. William Howell Oliver, seventy-four years old in 1931, particularly dreaded selling their churches and cemeteries to the Park Commission. It seemed "like selling our dead," he lamented. By 1932, persistent rumors that part of Cades Cove would be turned into a lake further terrified elderly residents, since such a lake would necessitate relocation of many of their family graves. The lake proposal was given serious consideration by the Park Commission because it would, in Colonel Chapman's words, greatly enhance the "recreational" attraction of the park to tourists. By 1934, however, this untenable scheme had been dropped.[30]

Typical of the plight of many elderly cove residents was the anguish of Uncle Noah Burchfield, one of the community's most beloved patriarchs. This gentle old man refused in 1932 to even sign a petition against the park takeover. He told the agents for the Park Commission he would sell at whatever they considered a fair price. Evidently this naive faith was sadly misplaced because the final commission offer, $9,000, was less than their own minimum estimate of $11,620. Uncle Noah grieved to see all his former neighbors' homes razed to the ground as soon as they became vacant. He also deplored the fact that so much of the cove was returning to its primordial wilderness state. Once carefully cultivated fields, the pride and triumph of generations of cove farmers, were now rapidly growing up. He died in 1934 at the age of eighty-five, after having lost what he had received for his home in a bank failure.[31]

In December 1935 the twenty-one remaining families living in the cove received notice that they must vacate their property by January 1, 1936. Although some twelve families would eventually be allowed to continue living on a yearly lease in the cove, the departing families were bitter about broken promises. Even those families permitted to remain were bitter about the destruction of their community. One such leaseholder, Kermit Caughron, recalled in 1984 that the seizure of their land and homes "sent a lot of people in their 60's and 70's to their graves." The land remained, Caughron argued, but in the death of the community he "lost a way of life and much of his freedom."[32]

Civic functions of the sixteenth civil district, which Cades Cove comprised, were surprisingly slow in dying. Although most of the population had left by 1934, elections for various local officials, such as constables and justices of the peace, continued throughout 1936. In that year pupils were combined into a single school, the Cable School, in the western end of the cove. The last session at this site was in 1943–1944. After Oliver retired as rural mail carrier in 1936, Murray Boring took over the route until it was discontinued in 1940. The post office of Cades Cove was closed October 31, 1947, after 114 years of continuous service.[33]

The Primitive Baptist church, the oldest in the cove, was unwilling to disband and maintained its membership into the 1960s. This congregation fought through the courts and in 1940 secured the right to maintain their church property and cemetery by yearly lease for a nominal sum. The other churches, the Missionary Baptist, the Southern Methodist, and the Northern Methodist, disbanded as their members were scattered. The building of the Northern Methodist church, called Hopewell, gradually deteriorated to the point that it fell into ruins and was removed by the Park Service. When in the mid-thirties a nearby Civilian Conservation Corps camp removed the old bell from the belfry of the Southern Methodist church, John Oliver vigorously protested in a letter to President Roosevelt. A presidential order resulted, returning the bell to its rightful place.[34]

On Christmas Day, 1937, John Oliver moved the last of his household goods from his home in the cove. It was a bitterly cold day, and traces of snow were falling intermittently. Without its human inhabitants, the cove already seemed alien. Most of the homes had been destroyed, leaving no trace of their former occupants, and much of the land was reverting to its wilderness state. Yet, in his mind, there were many people whose spirits remained. The ghosts of the original John and Lucretia Oliver, Uncle Peter and Aunt Catherine Cable, Daniel Foute and Dr. Calvin Post, Russell Gregory, Daniel Lawson, Elijah and Mary Jane Oliver, Uncle Noah Burchfield, and a host of other memorable cove citizens traveled with him. They represented to Oliver the richest inheritance and finest examples of the cove's existence as an organized community since 1818. As long as their memory remained alive, John Oliver reasoned to himself, the community of Cades Cove would never die.

Epilogue

Today the Great Smoky Mountains National Park is the most popular park in the nation, attracting 9.3 million visitors in 1985. Cades Cove is one of the greatest attractions of this park, preserving there, as the National Park Service maintains, an authentic living museum of native Southern Appalachian culture in the extant cabins and remaining structures. What is perhaps most intriguing to the cove's visitors, however, are the traces of forgotten homesteads, betrayed each spring by jonquils, roses, and hyacinths appearing in profusion unexpectedly in the middle of open meadows.

By 1935 it was apparent to the Park Service that its policy of allowing the cove to return to its wilderness state was a serious mistake. Cades Cove's great beauty and charm had always been the contrast of its carefully cultivated fields and farms surrounded by high mountains. A wilderness cove, indistinguishable from the forests of its bordering wilderness, presented little of interest or scenic beauty to the tourist.

A solution to the problem of what to do with Cades Cove, now that it was depopulated, appeared in a 1935 letter from Waldo G. Leland, permanent secretary of the American Council of Learned Societies, to Arno B. Cammerer, director of the National Park Service. Leland strongly urged that some effort be made to both record and preserve the extant native culture and lifestyle of the Great Smokies before the advent of millions of tourists erased this last remaining vestige of Southern Appalachia.

Two lengthy studies for the National Park Service by Charles S. Grossman and Hans Huth followed which carefully defined this culture and the best means of preserving it. Here was yet another incident characteristic of a pattern of America's approach to Southern Appalachia so lucidly examined in Henry D. Shapiro's *Appalachia On Our Mind*. Having fairly rid the cove of its bothersome native inhabitants, the National Park Service sought national authorities to define and reproduce their native culture so recently expired.

The results of these studies would have been completely satisfying to both Mary Noailles Murfree and Horace Kephart because most of their enduring stereotypes were clearly reflected in the final product. All modern structures, particularly numerous homes of frame construction, were obliterated. The single guiding principle was that anything which might remotely suggest progress or advancement beyond the most primitive stages should be destroyed. A sort of pioneer primitivism alone survived in the cove structures left standing.

It was as though, having destroyed the community of Cades Cove by eminent domain, the community's corpse was now to be mutilated beyond recognition. If the history of the cove had any meaning, it was simply that the people followed regional and national patterns of development. Cove residents witnessed many periods of progressive development in both the nineteenth and twentieth centuries. They were neither the picturesque, superhuman, and romanticized figures of Mary Noailles Murfree nor the wretched backward creatures living in depravity and degradation as represented by Horace Kephart. Rather, they were in the final analysis representative of the broad mainstream of nineteenth- and twentieth-century American culture and society from whence they came: ordinary, decent citizens who often reacted collectively — and within their limitations, courageously and responsibly — to the enormous economic fluctuation, social change, and political disruption surrounding their lives in the last two centuries within the American commonwealth.

In the peaceful cemetery of the old Primitive Baptist church lie the first and last John Oliver — the founding settler and his great-grandson — some sixty feet apart. Within these four generations of Olivers the community of Cades Cove was born, flourished for a season, and died. Nothing can rob them now of their beloved cove or cherished community. To these sleeping patriarchs, the whole cove has become itself a larger graveyard for the community, since only their ghosts remember in minute detail the place names and lore of its streams and meadows, forgotten orchards and abandoned homesteads. With the passage of time, the collective consciousness of their community has dimmed to extinction, but among their descendants its afterglow still illumines Cades Cove.

Notes

1. Settlement and Early History

1. From the Oliver family history, "Sketches of the Olivers," written between 1931 and 1934 by a grandson of the first John Oliver, William Howell Oliver, who was born in Cades Cove, May 16, 1857, and died there September 13, 1940. In manuscript form, this 151-page history, in the author's possession, represents the oldest and, with certain critical limitations, the most complete narrative source on Cades Cove. Because of its importance and frequent use, it is hereafter cited as W.H. Oliver, Sketches. Oliver's account of Junuluska at Horseshoe Bend is corroborated by other historians. Actually the Cherokees under Junuluska later used these same canoes to counterattack the Creeks in support of Jackson. Grace Steele Woodward, *The Cherokees* (Norman, 1963), 132.

2. W.H. Oliver, Sketches, 3–5.

3. The massacre of eleven members of John Kirk's family occurred in May 1788 on Little River in Blount County. The Cherokee later charged that Kirk had settled on their land illegally. John Haywood, *The Civil and Political History of the State of Tennessee* (Knoxville, 1823), 194; Randolph C. Downes, "Cherokee-American Relations in the Upper Tennessee Valley, 1776–1791," East Tennessee Historical Society's *Publications*, No. 8 (1936), 47 (hereafter cited as ETHS *Publications*).

4. Will of Samuel Tipton, August 23, 1822, Carter County Wills and Inventories, 1797–1847, pp. 107–12, Carter County Courthouse, Elizabethton, Tenn. On page 112, Tipton mentions "a tract of land twenty acres including John Oliver's improvement in Carter County," which was probably the homestead Oliver rented before he moved to Cades Cove in 1818. It is not unlikely that he worked in Samuel Tipton's forge, which is mentioned on the same page.

5. George Andrews, The Adjutant General, War Department, Washing-

ton, D.C., to John W. Oliver, June 13, 1914; A.D. Hiller, Executive Assistant to the Administrator, Veterans Administration, Washington, D.C., to W. Wayne Oliver, January 16, 1937, Oliver Family Collection. For the only published list of the soldiers in Colonel Ewen Allison's Regiment, East Tennessee Militia, War of 1812, see Penelope Johnson Allen, comp., *Tennessee Soldiers in the War of 1812: Regiments of Col. Allcorn and Col. Allison* (Chattanooga, 1947), 50.

6. W.H. Oliver, Sketches, 3.

7. Marriage bond, John Oliver and Lucretia Frazier, April 22, 1812, Marriage Records, Carter County Courthouse, Elizabethton, Tenn.; A.D. Hiller to W.W. Oliver, January 16, 1937; W.H. Oliver, Sketches, 4–5.

8. *Knoxville Register*, Nov. 17, 1849.

9. Manuscript history of Cades Cove entitled "Fifty Years in Cades Cove" by John W. Oliver, son of William Howell Oliver. The three manuscript books written between 1938 and 1946 are a synthesis of much of the information John W. Oliver collected earlier. They are hereafter cited J.W. Oliver, Cades Cove, with appropriate volume and page numbers.

10. Although Oliver received two tracts of bounty land for his services in the War of 1812, they came too late to do him any good in 1818. The first, warrant No. 31577, for 80 acres under the act of 1850, was sold June 15, 1852, to Jacob Halderman; the second, warrant No. 46352, for 80 acres under the act of 1855, was sold May 21, 1858, to Noah N. Kaufman. Commissioner of the General Land Office, United States Department of the Interior, Washington, D.C.

11. J.W. Oliver, Cades Cove, I, 8.

12. W.H. Oliver, Sketches, 10.

13. Interview on March 23, 1973, with Bertha Dunn, Townsend, Tenn., a great-granddaughter of Peter Snider, who lived in the Tuckaleechee Cove and was an early trader with the Cherokees. See also Inez Burns, "Settlement and Early History of the Coves of Blount County, Tennessee," ETHS *Publications*, No. 24 (1952), 47.

14. North Carolina Grant No. 172, registered April 18, 1794, Eastern District, Book 7, p. 263; Book 9, p. 155. Tennessee State Archives, Nashville.

15. *Petitions*, Box 24; Register of East Tennessee, Book "O", p. 538, Tennessee State Archives, Nashville. This deed is also recorded in Blount County records in Deed Book 3, p. 3, Blount County Courthouse, Maryville, Tenn. Hereafter cited as Blount Deeds, Wills.

16. The Oliver family's account of Chief Kade is corroborated by the papers of Peter Snider. The story that Cades Cove was named after Chief Abraham's wife, Kate, is spurious, but has unfortunately been so often repeated in the historical literature of the period that it is now almost accepted as fact. The earliest correct published account of Chief Kade is given in Robert Lindsay Mason, *The Lure of the Great Smokies* (Boston, 1927), 11.

17. Paul M. Fink, "Smoky Mountains History as Told in Place-Names," ETHS *Publications*, No. 6 (1934), 5; J.G.M. Ramsey, *Annals of Tennessee* (Charleston, S.C., 1853), 156.

18. James Mooney, comp., "Myths of the Cherokee," Bureau of American Ethnology, *Nineteenth Annual Report* (2 vols. Washington, D.C., 1900), I, 11–12, 538; Samuel Cole Williams, ed., *Lieut. Henry Timberlake's Memoirs, 1756–1765* (Johnson City, Tenn., 1927), 69. Timberlake at this point was visiting Chilhowey (Chilhowee), a Cherokee town that he indicates on his own map to be just southwest of Cades Cove. Timberlake's map also delineates the Chilhowee Mountains and outlines the course of Abram's Creek, which drains Cades Cove. See Paul M. Fink, "Early Explorers in the Great Smokies," ETHS *Publications*, No. 5 (1933), 57–58.

19. Burns, "Settlement and Early History," 44; Haywood, *Civil and Political History*, 40–41.

20. William E. Myer, comp., "Indian Trails of the Southeast," Bureau of American Ethnology, *Forty-Second Annual Report* (Washington, D.C., 1928), 772. Myer's description of the major Cherokee trails and their exact location in reference to present towns and landmarks is the most complete published record. See also Fink, "Early Explorers," 56, and Burns, "Settlement and Early History," 45.

21. William R. Garrett and Albert V. Goodpasture, *History of Tennessee* (Nashville, 1903), 135 and map. For a more complete discussion of Calhoun's Treaty, see Stanley J. Folmsbee, Robert E. Corlew, and Enoch L. Mitchell, *History of Tennessee* (2 vols. New York, 1960), I, 273, 287–88. Calhoun's Treaty ceded three tracts of land not included in former treaties. Two of these were in Tennessee, including the Hiwassee District in which Cades Cove is located. Actually, the treaty gave a respite from immediate pressure for removal of the Cherokees to the West, since a provision offering individual Indians citizenship and a square mile of land was renewed from a former treaty. So the Indians were not immediately removed from the Hiwassee District in 1819, as is erroneously stated by A. Randolph Shields, "Cades Cove in the Great Smoky Mountains National Park," in Robert M. McBride, ed., *More Landmarks of Tennessee History* (Nashville, 1969), 32.

22. W.H. Oliver, Sketches, 6.

23. Interview with John W. Oliver, July 18, 1963.

24. W.H. Oliver, Sketches, 6; J.W. Oliver, Cades Cove, I, 13–14.

25. Philip B. King and Arthur Stupka, "The Great Smoky Mountains, Their Geology and Natural History," *Scientific Monthly*, LXXI (July 1950), 31; Charles W. Wilson, Jr., "The Great Smoky Thrust Fault in the Vicinity of Tuckaleechee, Wear, and Cades Coves, Blount and Sevier Counties, Tennessee," *Tennessee Academy of Science Journal*, X (Jan. 1935), 58–59; Fred H. Rittgers, A Geographical Survey of Blount County, Tennessee (master's thesis, Univ. of Tennessee, Knoxville, 1941), 44–57; William W. Burchfiel, Jr., The Unaka

Mountains of Tennessee and North Carolina (master's thesis, Univ. of Tennesse, Knoxville, 1941), 15–17.

26. James M. Safford, *Geology of Tennessee* (Nashville, 1869), 52, 226; C.H. Gordon, "Notes on the Geology of the Cove Areas of East Tennessee," *Science*, LI (May 1920), 492; Robert B. Neuman, "Notes on the Geology of Cades Cove, Great Smoky Mountains National Park, Tennessee," *Tennessee Academy of Science Journal*, XXII (July 1947), 167–68.

27. W.H. Oliver, Sketches, 10–11; J.W. Oliver, Cades Cove, I, 14.

28. J.W. Oliver, Cades Cove, I, 7.

29. Blount Deeds, Book 2, pp. 480–81; Tennessee Grant No. 3397, February 3, 1827, to John Oliver by Absolom C. Renfro, General Enterer, Entry Taker's Office of the Hiwassee District, for forty acres, in Blount County, seventh range, east of the meridian, second fractional township, the south half of lot No. 24 for eighty acres. Original grant in Oliver Family Collection.

30. A careful correlation between the inhabitants in Cades Cove enumerated by the 1830 census and Blount Deeds, 1820–1830 shows that less than 10 percent had registered their deeds. Many families reported their land holdings to the captain of their local militia for tax purposes, but most of these early Blount County tax lists have unfortunately been destroyed. Manuscript Returns, Fifth Census of the United States, 1830, Population Schedule, Blount County, Tennessee, microfilm roll no. 178 (National Archives; hereafter cited as 1830 Census, Population, Blount County).

31. Dr. Abraham Jobe, of Elizabethton, Tenn., Autobiography or Memoirs (written between 1849 and 1905). A complete typed copy is in the Tennessee State Library, Nashville. The original manuscript is in the possession of Mrs. Harlow (Sophie Hunter) Dixon, Durham, N.C. Hereafter cited Jobe, Autobiography. Dr. Jobe received his medical degree from Transylvania University in Lexington, Ky., in March 1849. His autobiography spans most of the nineteenth century, from his childhood in Cades Cove through his harrowing experiences during the Civil War. Joshua Jobe's purchase from William Tipton of 426 acres in Cades Cove on December 3, 1821, is recorded in Blount Deeds, Book 2, p. 324.

32. Ibid., 7.

33. Ibid., 15–16.

34. Blount Deeds, Books 2, 3, 4, 5 (1821–1836); Blount Wills, Book 1, p. 197; Burns, "Settlement and Early History," 59.

35. Jobe, Autobiography, 11–14.

36. Burns, "Settlement and Early History," 60; J.W. Oliver, Cades Cove, I, 10–13; Jobe, Autobiography, 15–16.

37. J.W. Oliver, Cades Cove, I, 23–25.

38. Jobe, Autobiography, 20; J.W. Oliver, Cades Cove, I, 10; Burns, "Settlement and Early History," 62. Former residents frequently maintained an ac-

tive correspondence with their friends and relatives back in Cades Cove, and were often outspoken about the disadvantages as well as the advantages of their Western lands. For an excellent example, see Jacob and Ann Tipton, Newton County, Missouri, to John and Isaac Tipton, Cades Cove, August 16, 1847, Oliver Family Collection.

39. J.W. Oliver, Cades Cove, II, 15–18.

40. Blount Deeds, Book 5, pp. 345–46; Book 2, pp. 480–81, 503–504, 324.

41. William B. Tipton, Newton County, Missouri, to John Tipton, Cades Cove, August 16, 1847; Oliver Family Collection; Inez Burns, *History of Blount County, Tennessee* (Maryville, Tenn., 1957), 275.

42. Interview with John W. Oliver, Aug. 14, 1963. The importance of place traditions connected with landmarks is succinctly discussed by Richard M. Dorson, *American Folklore and the Historian* (Chicago, 1971), 155. See also Ronald L. Baker, "The Role of Folk Legends in Place-Name Research," *Journal of American Folklore*, LXXXV (Oct.-Dec. 1972), 367–73.

43. J.P. Lesley, *Iron Manufacturer's Guide* (Philadelphia, 1859), 202. Lesley states in 1859 that the Cades Cove Bloomery Forge was located ten miles south of the Amerine Forge, and was abandoned in 1847. Signs of coaling and excavation are still visible there today. See Burns, *Blount County*, 60.

44. Interview with John W. Oliver, July 18, 1963; Mooney, "Myths of the Cherokee," 264–65.

45. Nathaniel C. Browder, *The Cherokee Indians and Those Who Came After* (Hayesville, N.C., 1973), 56.

2. The Impact of the Wilderness

1. Isaac P. Martin, *A Minister in the Tennessee Valley: Sixty-Seven Years* (Nashville, 1954), 65.

2. Nathalia Wright, "Montvale Springs under the Proprietorship of Sterling Lanier, 1857–1863," ETHS *Publications*, No. 19 (1947), 54–59; Mason, *Lure of the Great Smokies*, 11; *Knoxville Whig*, Aug. 27, Feb. 5, 1853, Jan. 3, 1857. William G. Brownlow, editor of the *Knoxville Whig* from the time of his removal from Jonesboro to Knoxville in 1849 until the Civil War, was "without question the most regular and ardent patron" of Montvale Springs. From this resort he visited the surrounding mountains and coves, and wrote frequent and glowing accounts of the area in his newspaper.

3. Otis K. Rice, *The Allegheny Frontier: West Virginia Beginnings, 1730–1830* (Lexington, 1970), 376–79.

4. Folmsbee et al., *Tennessee*, II, 97, 129. That Tennessee agriculture remained depressed through most of the period between 1865 and 1900 is illustrated by the fact that in 1890 the average value of farm lands per acre in the

state was still 93 cents below the 1860 level, and the total value of Tennessee's farm products in 1890 was 36 percent below that of 1870. U.S. Department of Commerce, Bureau of the Census, *Twelfth Census of the United States, 1900: Agriculture*, Part I, 694–95, 703. These census statistics reveal not only a drastic drop in Tennessee's farm property and products after 1860, but also a decline between 1870 and 1890.

5. W.H. Oliver, Sketches, 19–20; J.W. Oliver, Cades Cove, I, 5–6; Burns, *Blount County*, 276; 1880 Census, Population, Blount County.

6. Arthur Stupka, *Great Smoky Mountains National Park* (Washington, D.C., 1960), 1–15.

7. Frank W. Woods, Natural Replacement of Chestnut by Other Species in the Great Smoky Mountains (doctoral diss., Univ. of Tennessee, Knoxville, 1957), 2–4; Paul Edward Barnett, A Comparative Study of Phenolics in Chestnut (*Castanea*), and Their Relationships with Resistance to *Endothia parasitica* (doctoral diss., Univ. of Tennessee, Knoxville, 1972), 116–20; Stupka, *Great Smoky Mountains*, 23–36. Chestnut was widely used in early America for kitchen utensils, bowls, boxes, and ware that had hard usage. Mary Earle Gould, *Early American Wooden Ware and Other Kitchen Utensils* (Rutland, Vt., 1962), 27.

8. Amanda Ulm, "Remember the Chestnut," *Annual Report of the Smithsonian Institution, 1948* (Washington, D.C., 1948), 377–82.

9. H.B. Ayres and W.W. Ashe, "The Southern Appalachian Forests," *U.S. Geological Survey Professional Paper No. 37* (Washington, D.C., 1905), 177–81.

10. W.H. Oliver, Sketches, 51–58; J.W. Oliver, Cades Cove, I, 24.

11. Commenting on agriculture in the Little Tennessee River basin, Ayres and Ashe stated in 1905 that "all of the land available for tillage has been cleared," and that outside of a few alluvial bottoms and fertile coves, this area contained "some of the most rugged land in the Southern Appalachians," completely unsuitable for cultivation. Ayres and Ashe, "Southern Appalachian Forests," 180.

12. W.H. Oliver, Sketches, 33.

13. Ibid., 26; J.W. Oliver, Cades Cove, II, 8–9.

14. Mason, *Lure of the Great Smokies*, 141–57; J.W. Oliver, Cades Cove, II, 9.

15. Interview with John W. Oliver, July 19, 1963; W.H. Oliver, Sketches, 22–23.

16. Mason, *Lure of the Great Smokies*, 148–59.

17. W.H. Oliver, Sketches, 24–27. Cades Cove was the scene of more guerrilla raids than any other area of Blount County, probably because of its accessibility to North Carolina. Burns, *Blount County*, 65.

18. W.H. Oliver, Sketches, 24–27.

19. Ibid., 34–35, 54.

20. Interview with John W. Oliver, July 19, 1963.

21. Blount Minutes, 1834–1840 *passim*. John Preston Arthur related that hunters often sought wolves for their bounty in western North Carolina. They would follow the gaunt mother wolf to her den and kill her litter, which usually numbered six to ten pups. For each scalp, the hunter received $2.50, regardless of the animal's size. By killing only the pups and allowing the mother wolves to escape, they assured another year's litter. John Preston Arthur, *Western North Carolina: A History* (Raleigh, 1914), 523.

22. W.H. Oliver, Sketches, 39; John C. Gunn, *Gunn's Domestic Medicine* (Knoxville, 1830, rpt., facsimile, 1986). The enormous popularity of this work is reflected in its numerous editions: second edition, 1834, Madisonville, Tenn.; third edition, 1839, Pumpkintown, Tenn. These subsequent editions were altered very little, and Gunn's publisher claimed in the preface of his new book (1857) that 100,000 copies of the older work had been printed in a short time. In 1857 Gunn greatly enlarged and revised the older work into *Gunn's New Domestic Physician*, containing 1,046 pages. This second enlarged work received wide critical acclaim. John C. Gunn, *Gunn's New Domestic Physician* (3rd ed., Cincinnati, 1860), i, 1047–48.

23. William O. Douglas, "The People of Cades Cove," *National Geographic,* CXXII (July 1962), 85; Sydney and Marjorie Barstow Greenbie, *Gold of Ophir: The China Trade in the Making of America* (New York, 1937), 32–37, 84–86, 151.

24. F.A. Michaux, *Travels to the Westward of the Allegany Mountains to the States of Ohio, Kentucky, and Tennessee in the Year 1802*, trans. from the French (London, 1805), 71–72.

25. Ibid.; Gunn, *Domestic Medicine* (1830), 369.

26. Gunn, *New Domestic Physician* (1860), 796; Douglas, "People of Cades Cove," 85.

27. The trapping of animals and exporting of fur skins to Europe comprised most of the fur business in the United States until 1900. By the 1830s, cow hides had largely replaced deerskins in the domestic tannery industry. Victor R. Fuchs, *The Economics of the Fur Industry* (New York, 1957), 4; Verner W. Crane, *The Southern Frontier, 1670–1732* (Ann Arbor, 1929), 111; Paul Christler Phillips, *The Fur Trade* (2 vols., Norman, 1961), II, 78–80.

28. The two best summaries of the problem are V.C. Gilbert, Jr., Vegetation of the Grassy Balds of the Great Smoky Mountains National Park (master's thesis, Univ. of Tennessee, Knoxville, 1954), and A.F. Mark, An Ecological Study of the Grass Balds of the Southern Appalachian Mountains (doctoral diss., Duke Univ., Durham, N.C., 1958).

29. Gilbert, Vegetation of the Grassy Balds, 15–16, 22–23; Mary Ellen Bruhn, Vegetational Succession on Three Grassy Balds of the Great Smoky Mountains (master's thesis, Univ. of Tennessee, Knoxville, 1964), 40–51.

30. Diary of Samuel McCammon, 1846-1854 (McClung Collection, Lawson McGhee Library, Knoxville, *passim.*

31. Ibid.; Gilbert, Vegetation of the Grassy Balds, 22.

32. W.H. Oliver, Sketches, 21-23; Burns, *Blount County*, 64-65.

33. Douglas, "People of Cades Cove," 86-89; W.H. Oliver, Sketches, 19-20.

34. 1850 Census, Population, Blount County; 1860 Census, Population, Blount County; W.H. Oliver, Sketches, 33-34; Ayres and Ashe, "Southern Appalachian Forests," 177.

35. A. Randolph Shields, "Cades Cove in the Great Smoky Mountains National Park," *Tennessee Historical Quarterly*, XXIV (Summer 1965), 116.

36. Henry H. Glassie, Southern Mountain Houses: A Study in American Folk Culture (master's thesis, State Univ. of New York at Oneonta, 1965), 145-59. The LeQuire cabin is no longer extant, but an excellent photograph of it is found in Joseph S. Hall, *Smoky Mountain Folks and Their Lore* (Asheville, 1960), 71.

37. Glassie, Southern Mountain Houses, 209; J.W. Oliver, Cades Cove, I, 25. Pennsylvania Germans were called Pennsylvania-Dutch, a corruption of the German "deutsch." Henry Glassie, *Pattern in the Material Folk Culture of the Eastern United States* (Philadelphia, 1968), 36.

38. Glassie, Southern Mountain Houses, 169-76.

39. *East Tennessean*, July 17, 1857; J.W. Oliver, Cades Cove, I, 23. Manuscript entitled Robert Burchfield and Tiptons Relating to Cades Cove by John W. Oliver, written in 1947. This book contains 41 pages and is in the author's possession. It is hereafter cited as J.W. Oliver, Burchfield and Tiptons.

40. Numerous passes to Koxville and bills of sale from Knoxville and Maryville merchants are in the Oliver Papers in possession of Judge W. Wayne Oliver, Maryville, Tenn. These passes from the Office of the Provost Marshal General of East Tennessee were issued to Elijah Oliver as receipts that he had furnished proof of loyalty, and range from June 7, 1861 to January 11, 1865.

41. J.W. Oliver, Cades Cove, I, 25.

42. Jobe, Autobiography, 7.

43. Interview with John Oliver, July 18, 1963.

44. Ibid.; W.H. Oliver, Sketches, 23-37.

45. Interview with John W. Oliver, July 18, 1963.

46. Jobe, Autobiography, 19.

47. Miscellaneous Account Book No. 1, pp. 126-27. This book containing numerous scraps of cove history was written by John W. Oliver and is in the Oliver Family Collection.

48. J.W. Oliver, Cades Cove, II, 9-10.

49. Ibid., 11-12.

50. Ibid., 11.

51. Olga Jones Edwards and Izora Waters Frizzell, *The "Connection" in East Tennessee* (Washington College, Tenn., 1969), 239.

3. The Market Economy

1. Stanley J. Folmsbee, *Sectionalism and Internal Improvements in Tennessee, 1796–1845* (Knoxville, 1939), 1–19; Henry H. Gauding, A History of Water Transportation in East Tennessee Prior to the Civil War (master's thesis, Univ. of Tennessee, Knoxville, 1933), 101; Riley O. Biggs, The Development of Railroad Transportation in East Tennessee During the Reconstruction Period (master's thesis, Univ. of Tennessee, Knoxville, 1934), 118–37. It is Bigg's thesis that East Tennesseans used their temporary control of the state government after the Civil War to obtain enormous loans to finance local railroad construction and enjoyed privileges not shared by other sections of the state.

2. Burchfiel, The Unaka Mountains, 2, 118–22; Lewis Cecil Gray, *History of Agriculture in the Southern United States to 1860* (2 vols., Washington, D.C., 1933), II, 754, 773, 816, 840, 882–83; Hugh T. Lefler, *History of North Carolina* (2 vols., New York, 1956), I, 303; Arthur, *Western North Carolina*, 230.

3. Ora Blackmun, *Western North Carolina: Its Mountains and Its People to 1880* (Boone, N.C., 1977), 226–28; Folmsbee, *Sectionalism*, 86; *Knoxville Register*, March 12, 1828. Dr. Ramsey, an acute observer of the economic development of East Tennessee, early recognized the area's need for better transportation facilities. For the best analysis of Ramsey's role in attempting to obtain better transportation facilities, see David Lawson Eubanks, Dr. J.G.M. Ramsey of East Tennessee: A Career of Public Service (doctoral diss., Univ. of Tennessee, Knoxville, 1965), 94–141.

4. George C. Martin, Jr., The Effect of Physiography on the Trade Routes of East Tennessee (master's thesis, Univ. of Tennessee, Knoxville, 1932), 100–103.

5. Eubanks, Dr. J.G.M. Ramsey, 94–141; Daniel J. Boorstin, *The Americans: The National Experience* (New York, 1965), 296–97.

6. Burns, *Blount County*, 41, 65, 79, 80, 85, 119, 173, 174, 210, 242, 244, 276, 280; Blount Deeds, 1826–1860, *passim*; Elvie Eagleton Skipper and Ruth Gove, eds., "'Stray Thoughts': The Civil-War Diary of Ethie M. Foute Eagleton," Part I, ETHS *Publications*, No. 40 (1968), 130.

7. J.W. Oliver, Cades Cove, I, 23–25; Margaret Elisabeth Gamble, The Heritage and Folk Music of Cades Cove, Tennessee (master's thesis, Univ. of Southern California, 1947), 43.

8. Interview with John W. Oliver, July 19, 1963.

9. J.W. Oliver, Cades Cove, I, 23–24.

10. Ayres and Ashe, "Southern Appalachian Forests," 176.

11. W.H. Oliver, Sketches, 1–4; Frank Merritt, Selected Aspects of Early Carter County History, 1760–1861 (master's thesis, Univ. of Tennessee, Knoxville, 1950), 60.

12. Jobe, Autobiography, 18; interview with Bertha Dunn, granddaughter

of George Snider, son of Peter Snider. Townsend, Tenn., Dec. 8, 1973; George Snider's Store Account Book, 1867–73, in possession of the author. Snider operated the first store in Tuckaleechee Cove. Burns, "Settlement and Early History," 54.

13. Blount Deeds, 1820–1850, *passim*.

14. Blount Deeds, 1821–1836, *passim*; Burns, "Settlement and Early History," 59.

15. 1850 Census, Agriculture, Blount County.

16. 1860 Census, Agriculture, Blount County; 1850 Census, Population, Blount County; 1860 Census, Population, Blount County; Ben T. Lanham, Jr., Type-Of-Farming Regions, and Factors Influencing Type-Of-Farming Regions in Tennessee (master's thesis, Univ. of Tennessee, Knoxville, 1938), 61.

17. 1880 Census, Agriculture, Blount County.

18. Ibid.; 1850 Census, Agriculture, Blount County.

19. Blount Deeds, 1821–1860, *passim*.

20. Ayres and Ashe, "Southern Appalachian Forests," 176.

21. Most of the Tiptons sold their property in the 1840s and moved to Missouri. Often they were able to find someone in the cove to act as their agent in selling their cove property, but the number of farms suddenly placed on the market during this period lowered the price of land. Blount Deeds, 1840–1849, *passim*; Burns, *Blount County*, 275; J.W. Oliver, Cades Cove, I, 10, 21–22.

22. Blount Deeds, 1830–1860, *passim*; Burns, "Settlement and Early History," 62. At the time of his death in 1865 Foute still owned 20,000 acres in the cove.

23. W.H. Oliver, Sketches, 10; *East Tennessean*, July 17, 1857; Blount Deeds, 1861–65, *passim*. An ardent Confederate, Foute used Confederate money in his exchanges throughout the war. This is probably one reason he died in poverty in 1865. Burns, *Blount County*, 65. There is also evidence that state bonds were used earlier in the century, which might have inflated prices. One such transaction in 1847 mentioned "$12,000 to be paid in South or North Carolina money and in trade." Thomas Davis to D.D. Foute, January 14, 1847, Blount Deeds, Book V, p. 138.

24. Blount Deeds, 1821–1890, *passim*. Examples are William Tipton to Martha Hart, 80 acres "for love and affection," April 2, 1825, Blount Deeds, Book 2, p. 497; Thomas Carver Sr. to Alfred Burton Carver, son of Reuben Carver, 52 acres, February 6, 1836, Blount Deeds, Book 3, p. 190; William Tipton to David B. Tipton, 140 acres, May 25, 1837, Blount Deeds, Book M, p. 300.

25. Ibid. Foute traded a town lot in 1830 for two saddles, which gives some idea of relative land values and the scarcity of specie. Skipper and Gove, "'Stray Thoughts,'" Part I, 130.

26. Blount Minutes, 1866; Blount County Chancery Court, Report on the

Daniel D. Foute Estate Settlement, 1866. The Chancery Court settled the estate of Foute as an insolvent estate, selling his extensive holdings in three public land auctions.

27. Ayres and Ashe, "Southern Appalachian Forests," 177.

28. 1860 Census, Population, Blount County; 1870 Census, Population, Blount County.

29. 1880 Census, Population, Blount County; 1880 Census, Agriculture, Blount County; 1850 Census, Population, Blount County; J.W. Oliver, Cades Cove, III, 2–18. Most of the older cove families — the Olivers, Cables, Shields, Burchfields, Tiptons, and Gregorys — had intermarried by 1880. See also Edwards and Frizzell, The "Connection," 243–53.

30. 1880 Census, Agriculture, Blount County; W.H. Oliver, Sketches, 79–80. See also an article by J.W. Oliver entitled "Cades Cove" in the Maryville Times, Sept. 15, 1932.

31. J.W. Oliver, Cades Cove, I, 15–18.

32. Interview with John W. Oliver, July 19, 1963.

33. 1870 Census, Population, Blount County; 1880 Census, Population, Blount County; 1850 Census, Population, Blount County.

34. J.W. Oliver's Carrier's Route Directory, 1904, in possession of author. For a discussion of families who emigrated farther west during the more prosperous years, 1905–1914, see Edwards and Frizzell, The "Connection," i–iii.

35. 1850 Census, Agriculture, Blount County; 1860 Census, Agriculture, Blount County; 1880 Census, Agriculture, Blount County.

36. Ibid.

37. W.H. Oliver, Sketches, 35–37.

38. For comparative data on livestock in other East Tennessee counties, see Blanche Henry Clark, The Tennessee Yeoman, 1840–1860 (Nashville, 1942), 193. 1850 Census, Agriculture, Blount County; 1860 Census, Agriculture, Blount County; 1880 Census, Agriculture, Blount County; Gray, Agriculture, II, 840–41, 883.

39. 1850 Census, Agriculture, Blount County; 1860 Census, Agriculture, Blount County; 1880 Census, Agriculture, Blount County.

40. U.S. Department of Commerce, Bureau of the Census, Twelfth Census of the United States, 1900: Agriculture, Part I, 694–95, 703. The agricultural depression was accentuated by the great postwar depression that began in 1873. Lanham, Type-Of-Farming Regions, 60. See also Blount Deeds, 1860–1880, passim.

41. J.W. Oliver, Cades Cove, I, 6.

42. 1860 Census, Agriculture, Blount County; 1880 Census, Agriculture, Blount County.

43. Maryville Index, Sept. 18, 1878; Shields, "Cades Cove," 107; Burns, Blount County, 243, 276.

44. J.W. Oliver, Cades Cove, I, 4–5.

45. 1850 Census, Population, Blount County; 1860 Census, Population, Blount County; 1870 Census, Population, Blount County; 1880 Census, Population, Blount County; W.H. Oliver, Sketches, 18–29.

46. 1880 Census, Agriculture, Blount County; Burns, *Blount County*, 229–31. Although the Shields Mill and the Cable Mill produced lumber for local use, it was not until the Little River Lumber Company went into operation in 1901 and the Little River Railroad built extensions onto Eldorado Creek and Laurel Creek in the Cades Cove section that commercial sawmilling began seriously to deplete forests around the cove to supply a national market. See also Ayres and Ashe, "Southern Appalachian Forests," 176.

47. *Knoxville Journal*, Aug. 17, 1960.

48. J.W. Oliver, Cades Cove, I, 25–26; 1860 Census, Population, Blount County.

49. 1850 Census, Population, Blount County; 1860 Census, Population, Blount County.

50. Dr. Anderson believed that mineral wealth from the mountains could be used to support "thousands of missionaries, and to establish on the coast of Africa a republic of civilized and Christianized people of color." Isaac Anderson to [?], January 7, 1847, quoted in John J. Robinson, *Memoir of Rev. Isaac Anderson, D.D.* (Knoxville, 1860), 155.

51. Jobe, Autobiography, 19–20; Edwards and Frizzell, *The "Connection,"* 239; *East Tennessean*, July 17, 1857.

52. J.W. Oliver, Cades Cove, III, 1–2.

53. Shields, "Cades Cove," 108; J.W. Oliver, Cades Cove, II, 1–3. Frederick married Mary (Polly) Oliver, the oldest daughter of John and Lucretia Oliver. J.W. Oliver, Cades Cove, I, 15.

54. J.W. Oliver, Cades Cove, II, 1–3.

55. Ibid., 2.

56. Ibid.; George Snider's Store Account Book, *passim.*

57. Blount Deeds, 1821–1830, *passim*; Burns, *Blount County*, 276. Although Foute's forge is the only one recorded in Cades Cove, curious references in the deeds indicate that other forges were in operation there during the 1830s. One such deed mentions repaying a loan "at Shields own house in Cades Cove on which land is a forge." Robert Shields to Hugh Bogle, May 29, 1834, Blount Deeds, Book 5, p. 240. Possibly these forges were much smaller ones used primarily for blacksmithing. For the best description of the bloomery forge and its operation, see Arthur, *Western North Carolina*, 277–79.

58. J.W. Oliver, Cades Cove, I, 25; Shields, "Cades Cove," 107. Evidence of searches for other minerals is found in numerous leases to land in the cove during the 1850s. One example states clearly that "the lease is for the purpose of investigating for minerals, I to have one-half of whatever is taken out." William Rorex to B.O. Brabson and A.M. Wallace, January 1, 1854, Blount Deeds, Book X, p. 649.

59. Myer, "Indian Trails," 772; Burns, "Settlement and Early History," 45.

60. W.H. Oliver, Sketches, 5.

61. Interview with John W. Oliver, Aug. 7, 1963.

62. Burns, *Blount County*, 80; Blount Deeds, 1840–1860, *passim*; Tennessee General Assembly, *Private Acts*, 1851–52, Ch. CCLXI. Hereafter cited *Tenn. Acts*, with appropriate year and chapter.

63. Burns, *Blount County*, 41; Shields, "Cades Cove," 107; Arthur, *Western North Carolina*, 230.

64. Robinson, *Memoir*, 153; Arthur, *Western North Carolina*, 241; *Maryville Times*, Sept. 13, 1926.

65. Miscellaneous Notes on Cades Cove, pp. 8–10, written June 1, 1948, by John W. Oliver, in author's possession. Hereafter cited J.W. Oliver, Notes, with appropriate page numbers. 1850 Census, Agriculture, Blount County; 1860 Census, Agriculture, Blount County; 1880 Census, Agriculture, Blount County.

66. Shields, "Cades Cove," 105; J.W. Oliver, Notes, 14–15.

67. Blount Deeds, 1826–1860, *passim*.

68. Burns, *Blount County*, 65.

69. From an unpublished Family History compiled and written by Dr. Calvin Post's granddaughter, Jessie Eugenia Turner, Chattanooga, Tenn. Hereafter cited as Jessie Eugenia Turner, Family History.

70. Interview with Jonnie Post, a great-granddaughter of Dr. Post, April 9, 1975. Miss Post has in her home in Maryville, Tenn., an extensive collection of Dr. Post's correspondence, reports, notebooks, and photographs, which she kindly allowed me to inspect. Born March 21, 1803, in Elmira, New York, Dr. Post was of Dutch extraction, the son of James and Alyea Hathorne Post. During the 1850s, he acquired several tracts of land of 5,000 and 10,000 acres each in the mountains surrounding the cove. Blount Deeds, 1850–1860, *passim*.

71. Dr. Calvin Post's Notebook, 1849–1851, in possession of Jonnie Post, Maryville, Tenn. Hereafter cited as Post's Notebook. Post was a close friend of Dr. Isaac Anderson, whose only son married Mrs. Post's sister. Both men shared a broad interest in the mineral wealth of the cove and surrounding mountains, and often took leases on large amounts of land there. Blount Deeds, 1849–1860, *passim*.

72. Post's Notebook, 1850.

73. Shields, "Cades Cove," 105; J.W. Oliver, Cades Cove, II, 26.

74. Lanham, Type-Of-Farming Regions, 61–62; Clark, *Tennessee Yeoman*, 34–161; Snider's Store Account Book, *passim*.

4. Religion and the Churches

1. W.H. Oliver, Sketches, 6–7. Quotations from manuscript sources continue to be given with no changes in the original spelling or orthography. The

conversion experience described here had long been a necessary requirement for church membership in practically all Protestant denominations. The theological assumptions underlying this experience are nowhere more lucidly analyzed than in Perry Miller, *The New England Mind: The Seventeenth Century* (New York, 1939), 365–97. See also Alan Simpson, *Puritanism in Old and New England* (Chicago, 1955), 2–6, 24–25, 35–36, and Darrett B. Rutman, *American Puritanism: Faith and Practice* (Philadelphia, 1970), 15–16, 20, 26–27, 99–106.

2. Elmer T. Clark, ed., *The Journal and Letters of Francis Asbury* (3 vols., London, 1958), II, 125.

3. Ibid., I, 709, II, 287; Walter B. Posey, *Methodism in the Old Southwest* (Tuscaloosa, Ala., 1933), 12–15. See also Allen James Ledford, Methodism in Tennessee, 1783–1866 (master's thesis, Univ. of Tennessee, Knoxville, 1941), 34–36. The best contemporary description of the drunkenness, vice, gambling, brutal fights, and antagonism to itinerant preachers is found in W.P. Strickland, ed., *Autobiography of Peter Cartwright, the Backwoods Preacher* (New York, 1856), 45–83.

4. William Warren Sweet, *The Rise of Methodism in the West* (New York, 1920), 58–70; Clark, *Asbury's Journal*, I, 632. Similar areas of North Carolina suffered a decline in organized religion from the close of the Revolution until after 1810. Lefler, *History of North Carolina*, I, 431.

5. Minutes of the Miller's Cove Baptist Church, Book II, March 5, 1825. A typescript copy of these records, which date from 1812, is in the McClung Collection, Lawson McGhee Library, Knoxville.

6. Ibid., *passim.*

7. Ibid., November 3, 1826; W.H. Oliver, Sketches, 7.

8. Cades Cove Baptist Church Book, 1827–1905, in possession of Ray Taylor, Maryville, Tenn. The church changed its name to Primitive Baptist in 1841. Hereafter cited Primitive Baptist Minutes.

9. Ibid., June 19, 1829.

10. Ibid., *passim*; W.H. Oliver, Sketches, 7–8, 52–144.

11. W.H. Oliver, Sketches 7–8, 60–61, 107–108; Lawrence Edwards, History of the Baptists of Tennessee with Particular Attention to the Primitive Baptists of East Tennessee (master's thesis, Univ. of Tennessee, Knoxville, 1941), 4. See also J.B. Moody, *The Distinguishing Doctrines of Baptists* (Nashville, 1901), 85–140.

12. The best analysis of Baptists in East Tennessee is Edwards, Primitive Baptists, 15–106, which makes the most complete use of unpublished church and association minutes, often overlooked by other scholars. Other standard monographs include B.F. Riley, *Baptists of the South in States East of the Mississippi* (Philadelphia, 1898); S.W. Tindell, *The Baptists of Tennessee* (2 vols., Kingsport, Tenn., 1930); Walter Brownlow Posey, *Religious Strife on the South-*

ern Frontier (Baton Rouge, 1965), and O.W. Taylor, *Early Tennessee Baptists, 1768–1832* (Nashville, 1957).

13. W.H. Oliver, Sketches, 107–108.

14. Ibid., 8.

15. Ibid., 11–17. Evidence of this consensus mechanism occurs repeatedly throughout the century; every decision was voted on by the congregation, which reserved the right to reverse its former decisions at any time. Primitive Baptist Minutes, *passim*.

16. W.H. Oliver, Sketches, 7–8; Primitive Baptist Minutes, *passim*.

17. Ibid.

18. J.H. Grime, *History of Middle Tennessee Baptists* (Nashville, 1902), 548; Robert Douthat Meade, *Patrick Henry: Patriot in the Making* (Philadelphia, 1957), 245–62; William Wert Henry, *Patrick Henry, Life, Correspondence and Speeches* (3 vols., New York, 1891), I, 117–19, II, 202–205.

19. W.H. Oliver, Sketches, 72–75; Primitive Baptist Minutes, *passim*; Edwards, Primitive Baptists, 8.

20. Primitive Baptist Minutes, *passim*; Edwards, Primitive Baptists, 8.

21. *Minutes of the Ninety-Third Anniversary of the Tennessee Association of Primitive Baptist* (1894), 9. Hereafter cited *Primitive Baptist Association Minutes* with appropriate year.

22. Primitive Baptist Minutes, 1827–1832, *passim*; Burns, "Settlement and Early History," 60.

23. These ministers were Thomas Hill, Richard Wood, George Snider, Dukes Kimbrough, James Taylor, William Billue, Joseph Lambert, Noah Haggard, Billy Hollaway, Augustine Bowers, and Elijah Rogers. Primitive Baptist Minutes, 1827–1835, *passim*; Burns, *Blount County*, 118–24. Brief biographies of these ministers are given in Miller's Cove Primitive Baptist Church: Committee's Report on Origin and History, written November 18, 1951, by John W. Oliver, John Ogle, and Hoyle Taylor. A copy is in the author's possession and is hereafter cited Report on Miller's Cove Primitive Baptist Church.

24. Primitive Baptist Minutes, 1833–1845, *passim*.

25. Oliver's presbytery included Jackson B.J. Brickey, William Brickey, Giles Dunn, Levi Adams, Absalom A. Abbott, and David McDaniel. Primitive Baptist Minutes, 1845–1882, *passim*; W.H. Oliver, Sketches, 73–75.

26. Primitive Baptist Minutes, 1880–1900, *passim*; Burns, *Blount County*, 123.

27. Primitive Baptist Minutes, *passim*.

28. Ibid. Miscellaneous church letters dating from 1834 throughout the century in author's possession. Many Cades Cove church letters are found in the manuscript collections of other area churches. An excellent example is a letter found among the Stock Creek Baptist church records which reads as follows: "We the Primitive Baptist church of Christ in Cades Cove now in session send-

eth greeting to her beloved sister Stock Creek Church our Sister in the Lord we wish you to send us our beloved Brother Ace Delosur to take the pastoral care of our church done in Church Conference the third Saturday of October 1854 Peter Cable Clerk." Copy in author's possession.

29. Primitive Baptist Minutes, *passim.*

30. Ibid.

31. Ibid.

32. Ibid.

33. Ibid.

34. Ibid. "There are gross crimes which a single member commits against the whole church, such as outlaw violating crimes, swearing, public drunkness, stealing, robbing, murder, and such like, this is not individual violation, as the other, but this outlaw, open transgression affects the whole cause of Christ and Christianity. This calls for immediate action of the church. The violator is to be notified to come before the whole body and publicly make confession of his or her faults, and in this way to take off the disgrace he or she has brought on the cause of the whole church and if he refused to do this the church is to exclude him or her from their fellowship to save the body. Amputation is necessary. Whereupon if he repents and confesses his sins, and acknowledges that the church done right, he may be received back into fellowship again." W.H. Oliver, Sketches, 145–46.

35. *Primitive Baptist Association Minutes* (1881), 1; Blount County Census, Population, 1880.

36. Primitive Baptist Minutes, *passim*; Skipper and Gove, " 'Stray Thoughts,' " Part I, 129–31.

37. Perry Miller maintains that in the eighteenth century the basic frame of reference of Protestant theology was shared in varying degrees by all Americans, regardless of geographical dispersion or sectarian preference. Perry Miller, "From the Covenant to the Revival," in James W. Smith and A. Leland Jamison, eds., *Religion in American Life: The Shaping of American Religion* (4 vols., Princeton, N.J., 1961), I, 322–50. Whether this generalization holds for new frontier areas in the nineteenth century is questionable, but the compact nature of society in Cades Cove made it highly improbable that most of the residents had not been exposed to some form of evangelizing at one time or another. J.W. Oliver, Cades Cove, I, 10–13.

38. An excellent example of their control over the larger community is the continuing pressure by the Primitives to end distilling and sales of whiskey; they succeeded in keeping distilleries out of the cove proper throughout the century. Yet distilling continued to be a highly profitable occupation, particularly after the Civil War. Primitive Baptist Minutes, *passim*; Gamble, Heritage and Folk Music, 67–68; Burns, *Blount County,* 243.

39. William Tipton to John Oliver and Peter Cable, October 1836, Blount Deeds, Book M, p. 178; J.W. Oliver, Notes, 7.

40. Edwards, Primitive Baptists, 56–70.

41. Primitive Baptist Minutes, September 15, 1838.

42. *Minutes of the Tennessee Association of United Baptists*, Report on Cades Cove Baptist Church, May 11, 1839, in the Baptist Archives, Nashville. This report was made before the Cades Cove church formally separated from the old Tennessee Association in 1841 and assumed the name "Primitive." Later both groups contended that they were the legitimate heirs of the older association. See Edwards, Primitive Baptists, 72–73; Report on Miller's Cove Primitive Baptist Church, 4.

43. Minutes of the Ellejoy Baptist Church, August to October 4, 1839, photostatic copy in the McClung Collection, Lawson McGhee Library, Knoxville.

44. Primitive Baptist Minutes, May 15, 1841; Burns, *Blount County*, 123.

45. Edwards, Primitive Baptists, 56–70; Primitive Baptist Minutes, *passim* W.H. Oliver, Sketches, 87–94. Dr. Jobe recalled going to school during the 1820s to William Davis, first clerk of the church. Jobe, Autobiography, 15–16.

46. Primitive Baptist Minutes, *passim*; W.H. Oliver, Sketches, 8–9. A polemic widely circulated in the cove after 1910 which expressed the theological objections of the Primitive Baptists to missions was Thomas E. Watson, *Foreign Missions Exposed* (Atlanta, 1910). Watson argued that missionaries were "agents of American commercialism," and represented "cultural imperialism."

47. Primitive Baptist Minutes, June, 1865.

48. Ibid.; W.H. Oliver, Sketches, 21–38. The influence of the American sectarian church within the community is analyzed by Sidney Mead as the principle of "voluntaryism," which means "that a powerful selective factor is at work in the choice of denominational leaders, since such leaders finally gain and hold support and power in the group through persuasion and popular appeal to the constituency . . . each group has a kind of massive and stubborn stability, inertia, and momentum of its own, deeply rooted and broadly based in the voluntary consent and commitment of the individuals composing it. Here is the real basis for the tremendous vitality of these denominations. This is likely to become evident in periods of internal stress or of threat to the existence of the group from the outside. . . ." Sidney E. Mead, "Denominationalism: The Shape of Protestantism in America," *Church History* XXIII (Dec. 1954), 300.

49. Primitive Baptist Minutes, *passim*; Blount Deeds, 1830–1860, *passim*; Burns, *Blount County*, 58–59; 1850 Census, Population, Blount County; 1860 Census, Population, Blount County; *East Tennessean*, July 17, 1857.

50. Primitive Baptist Minutes, *passim*; W.H. Oliver, Sketches, 21–38.

51. W.H. Oliver, Sketches, 21–38.

52. Ibid.; J.W. Oliver, Cades Cove, II, 13–15.

53. Primitive Baptist Minutes, *passim*; W.H. Oliver, Sketches, 21–38.

54. W.H. Oliver, Sketches, 21–38; J.W. Oliver, Cades Cove, II, 13–15.

Inez Burns discusses the reaction of the people in the coves of Blount County to the threat of formal invasion. Burns, *Blount County*, 60.

55. This period of comparative calm within the church extended to 1870. Primitive Baptist Minutes, 1860–1870, *passim*.

56. Ibid., 1870–1880, *passim*. For a discussion of the Two-Seed doctrine among Primitive Baptists in the larger area of East Tennessee, see Edwards, Primitive Baptists, 81–89.

57. Expulsions for adhering to the Two-Seed doctrine are numerous after 1875. Primitive Baptist Minutes, 1875–1900, *passim*. In rejecting this doctrine, the Cades Cove church appears to have been an exception to regional Primitive Baptists, who increasingly accepted the absolute predestinarian position. O.K. Armstrong and Marjorie M. Armstrong, *The Indomitable Baptists: A Narrative of Their Role in Shaping American History* (New York, 1967), 157–59. In 1914, W.H. Oliver of the Cades Cove church led a withdrawal from the old Tennessee Association of Primitive Baptist over the question of Two-Seedism, taking seven churches with him to set up a rival association. Why the Cades Cove church took such a strong position in contrast to other area churches is puzzling, since Two-Seedism appeared stronger among the more isolated churches in the South as a general rule. Edwards, Primitive Baptists, 98–99; *Primitive Baptist Association Minutes* (1914).

58. Primitive Baptist Minutes, April 26, 1890. There were not enough secret orders in the cove to occasion the reaction of Primitive Baptists in more populous areas. For a discussion of the secret order controversy, see Edwards, Primitive Baptists, 90–99. The thirteenth article of faith of the Tennessee Association of Primitive Baptist stated explicitly that "we believe the Church of Jesus Christ should have no organic connection with any society or institution of man not authorized in God's Word." *Primitive Baptist Association Minutes* (1889), 4.

59. Eight churches with a total membership of 313 belonged in 1879; by 1900, 13 churches with 787 members had joined. *Primitive Baptist Association Minutes*, 1879–1900, *passim*. Article II of the association constitution states that the association cannot "infringe on any of the internal rights of any church in the Union." Typescript copy of the constitution in author's possession.

60. Primitive Baptist Minutes, *passim*. Union meetings were reciprocal; each church membership attended the meetings of all the others. Dates of these union meetings at various churches were printed in the association minutes. *Primitive Baptist Association Minutes*, 1879–1900, *passim*.

61. W.H. Oliver, Sketches, 97–108. As one scholar states, "social issues over which Baptists were most concerned were those which had some moral or religious implication for the individual or some significance for the denomination. Baptists continued to be oriented toward the individual and his *spiritual* needs." Rufus B. Spain, *At Ease in Zion: Social History of the Southern Baptists, 1865–1900* (Nashville, 1961), 213.

62. Johnson Adams served as pastor of the group and Green Hill was chosen clerk. Robert Burchfield was clerk from 1846 to 1858; J.Y. Burchfield served from 1859 until 1862; Nathan Burchfield from 1867 to 1870; John P. Cable from 1871 until 1890, and Homer Lemon's term extended through 1900. Prominent preachers included John Wallace, James Russell, William Adams, and Andy Greer during the 1850s. Between 1874 and 1879, J.M. Saults, William Lowe, and William Boring officiated as pastors. In 1890 T.J. Caldhoun was called as pastor, and served with W.T. Campbell, G.B. Rice, W.H. Hodges, and Butler Tipton into the twentieth century. History of the Missionary Baptist Church in Cades Cove, written in 1920 by J.W.H. Myers. Copy in author's possession. This brief sketch is the only extant record of the Missionary Baptists in the cove during the nineteenth century.

63. Ibid.

64. Jobe, Autobiography, 8; Posey, Methodism in the Old Southwest, 11–15. Eakin was sent to the Holston Circuit in 1811. "One of the most remarkable men in his time," he "penetrated the hills and hollows, byways and hedges even into the Smoky and Chilhowee mountains." Burns, Blount County, 111.

65. James F. Deaver to Henry Seebow and others, September 7, 1840, Blount Deeds, Book U, p. 98; Sketches of the Methodist Church in Cades Cove, written in 1962 by John W. Oliver, in author's possession.

66. Ibid., 4; Martin, Minister in the Tennessee Valley, 66.

67. Ibid.

68. Shields, "Cades Cove," 108. There is no evidence of the bitter conflict between the Methodist Episcopal Church, South, and the Northern Methodist Episcopal church analyzed in William W. Sweet, The Methodist Episcopal Church and the Civil War (Cincinnati, 1912), 96–110. See also Ledford, Methodism in Tennessee, 103–118; Horace Eugene Orr, The Tennessee Churches and Slavery (master's thesis, Univ. of Tennessee, Knoxville, 1924), 124–52.

5. The Civil War

1. John C. Inscoe, "Mountain Masters: Slaveholding in Western North Carolina," North Carolina Historical Review, LXI (April 1984), 163–72.

2. Asa Earl Martin, "The Anti-Slavery Societies of Tennessee," Tennessee Historical Magazine, I (Dec. 1915), 264, 271–73; Hamer, Tennessee, I, 469; Burns, Blount County, 39, 58–59, 161. James Jones, a Blount Quaker, was president of the Manumission Society of Tennessee for many years and expressed his views frequently in Benjamin Lundy's Genius of Universal Emancipation.

3. W. Freeman Galpin, ed., "Letters of an East Tennessee Abolitionist," ETHS Publications, No. 3 (1931), 146.

4. Emancipator, March 16, 1838, p. 178. Another Maryville abolitionist, R.G. Williams, stated in a letter to the Emancipator, February 24, 1838, that

"notwithstanding the strict laws of Tennessee, we meet through the country and discuss the merits of abolition and colonization; the former is ably defended by Rev. T.S. Kendall, pastor of the Seceder Church in this county, and several others." In 1833 William Goodell began to publish in New York the *Emancipator,* which the following year became the American Anti-Slavery Society's official publication. Gerald Sorin, *The New York Abolitionists: A Case Study of Political Radicalism* (Westport, Conn., 1971), 59.

5. "Dr. Isaac Anderson had more to do with fixing the stand taken than any other person. He was teaching the young men who went out into the country as leaders, and through his teachings, the doctrines of loyalty to the Union and the old flag, and opposition to slavery were absorbed into their natures, and, through their influence, were reproduced in others until they permeated all the citizenship of East Tennessee." Will A. McTeer, *History of New Providence Presbyterian Church, Maryville, Tennessee, 1786–1921* (Maryville, 1921), 43–44; Robinson, *Memoir,* 124, 174–75; Jessie Eugenia Turner, Family History.

6. Dr. Calvin Post's many reports and correspondence in possession of Jonnie Post, Maryville, Tenn., hereafter cited Post Papers. Among his correspondence are several abolitionist tracts which were allegedly sent to the *New York Evening Post.* Examination of the *Evening Post* between 1850 and 1860 was inconclusive, since the authorship of such contributions is frequently not given. Under the editorship of William Cullen Bryant and William Leggett, the *Post* took an uncompromising stand against slavery and offered a sympathetic forum to abolitionist writers throughout this period. Allan Nevins, *The Evening Post: A Century of Journalism* (New York, 1922), 145–48.

7. Blount Deeds, 1830–1860, *passim,* show frequent traffic in the slave trade by Foute, none of which occurred in Cades Cove. Robert Burchfield sold his slaves when he left Yancey County, North Carolina, to move to the cove in 1834. J.W. Oliver, Cades Cove, II, 4–6, citing Burchfield's bill of sale for his household effects. An extensive examination of the cove deeds and land transactions between 1820 and 1860 gives no evidence of slaves' being bought or sold, in contrast to the frequent mention of such traffic in other areas of Blount County. Cooper, 50 years old, listed North Carolina as his place of birth; his wife, Ellen (25), listed Tennessee. The children, Elizabeth (8), Dorchus (6), Martha (2), and Danuel (8 months), were all born in Tennessee. 1850 Census, Population, Blount County; *East Tennessean,* July 17, 1857.

8. 1860 Census, *Population,* 459–61; 1860 Census, *Agriculture,* 133; Marguerite Bartlett Hamer, The Presidential Campaign of 1860 in Tennessee," ETHS *Publications,* No. 3 (1931), 20–21; *Nashville Banner,* Aug. 18, 1860.

9. James W. Fertig, *The Secession and Reconstruction of Tennessee* (Chicago, 1898), 20; J.S. Hurlburt, *History of the Rebellion in Bradley County, East Tennessee* (Indianapolis, 1866), 33; *Memphis Daily Appeal,* June 20, 1861; Oliver P. Temple, *East Tennessee and the Civil War* (Cincinnati, 1899), 186, 191, 199; James W. Patton, *Unionism and Reconstruction in Tennessee, 1860–*

1869 (Chapel Hill, 1934), 11; Stanley F. Horn, ed., *Tennessee's War, 1861–1865* (Nashville, 1965), 18. Both Secessionists and Unionists conducted vigorous rallies in Blount County; Horace Maynard spoke for two and a half hours at Ellejoy in May 1861 to a crowd of six or seven hundred. "The right spirit prevailed there," reported the *Knoxville Whig,* May 25, 1861, "and curses loud and bitter were heaped upon the unconstitutional and corrupt acts of the legislature." For the best analysis of the sectional division over secession, see Mary Emily Robertson, *The Attitude of Tennesseans Toward the Union, 1847–1861* (New York, 1961), 11–63.

10. Burns, *Blount County,* 59–60; Temple, *East Tennessee,* 388–411; Beatrice L. Garrett, Confederate Government and the Unionists of East Tennessee (master's thesis, Univ. of Tennessee, Knoxville, 1932), 52–64; Horn, *Tennessee's War,* 33. Thomas A.R. Nelson, a prominent Union speaker, was met in "strongly Unionist Blount County" two miles out of Maryville, "by an escort of perhaps three hundred horsemen." Thomas B. Alexander, *Thomas A. R. Nelson of East Tennessee* (Nashville, 1956), 78; Frank P. Smith, Military History of East Tennessee, 1861–1865 (master's thesis, Univ. of Tennessee, Knoxville, 1936), 8–41.

11. Jesse Burt, "East Tennessee, Lincoln, and Sherman," ETHS *Publications,* No. 34 (1962), 3–25; Harold S. Fink, "The East Tennessee Campaign and the Battle of Knoxville in 1863," ETHS *Publications,* No. 29 (1957), 79–117; James B. Campbell, "East Tennessee During the Federal Occupation, 1863–1865," ETHS *Publications,* No. 19 (1947), 64–80; Horn, *Tennessee's War,* 34; Burns, *Blount County,* 62; Thomas W. Humes, *The Loyal Mountaineers of Tennessee* (Knoxville, 1888), 138–249.

12. Hurlburt, *Rebellion in Bradley County,* 29.

13. Burns, *Blount County,* 65. See Chapter 4 for an analysis of the overlapping of religious and political attitudes during the Civil War. Oliver had also benefited materially from his service in the War of 1812; he received 80 acres of bounty land on Warrant No. 31577, March 10, 1851, and an additional 80 acres on Warrant No. 46352, December 5, 1857. Photostatic copies of these grants from the General Land Office, Department of the Interior, in author's possession.

14. Mary Bird, Catoosa County, Georgia, to Jacob Bird, Cades Cove, August 23, 1863, in author's possession. The relationship of the Tennessee and Georgia Birds is given in Edwards and Frizzell, *The "Connection,"* 142–48.

15. Of the 21 Union volunteers, 5 sickened and died in the army; one, George W. Shields, was wounded by a cannon ball. The 12 Confederate volunteers survived the conflict, although one of them, Theadore Pearson, was killed by ambush after the close of the war. J.W. Oliver, Cades Cove, II, 26–27. The class division in the cove closely follows patterns of allegiance in the larger area of East Tennessee, where Confederates were usually "of wealthy and aristocratic classes living in or near towns," while the Unionists "came

from the yeomanry of the rural and mountainous regions." Campbell, "East Tennessee," 65.

16. Burns, *Blount County*, 33; J.W. Oliver, Cades Cove, II, 28. A typical notice, dated July 20, 1841, directed Major J.C. Murphy to proceed "to open and hold an election at the usual muster grounds in Cades Cove for the purpose of electing one captain, one first lieutenant, and one ensign for above company attendant by me." Original document in author's possession.

17. J.W. Oliver, Cades Cove, II, 32; Burns, *Blount County*, 41-42, 65.

18. J.W. Oliver, Cades Cove, II, 32; Burns, *Blount County*, 62. No other contemporary manuscripts give such a sense of hiatus, or political disruption caused by the complete breakdown of civil order in the cove as these justice of the peace dockets. Foute's docket dates from 1856 to 1922; Lemons' docket dates from 1851 to 1929. Many of the earlier pages in both dockets have unfortunately been torn out. Both documents in author's possession.

19. Absolom C. Renfro was the first postmaster, serving until 1836, when he was replaced by Daniel H. Emmet. Foute served from 1843 until the close of the Civil War, not from 1837 until 1847 as is erroneously stated in Skipper and Gove, " 'Stray Thoughts,' " Part I, 131. Allen M. Ross, Director, Industrial Records Division, National Archives, to John W. Oliver, July 14, 1948; J.W. Oliver, Cades Cove, II, 29.

20. Post Papers, *passim*.

21. Will A. McTeer, "Among Loyal Mountaineers," in *Miscellaneous Pamphlets on the Civil War*, 1, an undated volume in Special Collections, Univ. of Tennessee Library, Knoxville. A prominent Blount County lawyer, local historian, judge, and state legislator, Major McTeer served in the Union army. Burns, *Blount County*, 213; Arthur, *Western North Carolina*, 609.

22. Daniel Ellis, *Thrilling Adventures of Daniel Ellis* (New York, 1867), 407; Arthur, *Western North Carolina*, 600-604; Burns, *Blount County*, 65.

23. J.W. Oliver, Cades Cove, I, 25-26; II, 27.

24. Quotations from manuscripts continue to be given without change in the original spelling or orthography. W.H. Oliver, Sketches, 21-25.

25. Ibid., 34-35. Elijah Oliver's Civil War passes and loyalty oaths in possession of Judge W. Wayne Oliver, Maryville, Tenn.

26. Campbell, "East Tennessee," 70; *Report to the Contributors to the Pennsylvania Relief Association for East Tennessee by a Commision Sent by the Executive Committee to Visit that Region and Forward Supplies to the Loyal and Suffering Inhabitants* (Philadelphia, 1864), 18; Brownlow's *Knoxville Whig and Rebel Ventilator*, March 5, 1864; Humes, *Loyal Mountaineers*, 316-33.

27. J.W. Oliver, Cades Cove, II, 15.

28. Primitive Baptist Minutes, June 1865. The strongly pro-Union position of the Primitive Baptist Church is analyzed in Chapter 4.

29. J.W. Oliver, Cades Cove, II, 14-15.

30. Ibid., 15.

31. Ibid., 15–18. Captain Ghormley's raiders were active in several other coves, particularly in Tuckaleechee Cove, where his horse was shot from under him by a member of the fifteenth district home guard, Abriam Greenberry Dunn, the author's great-grandfather. Burns, *Blount County*, 65.

32. The details of Russell's death were given to J.W. Oliver by Noah Burchfield, a grandson, who was 15 years old at the time and assisted in preparing the body for burial. J.W. Oliver, Cades Cove, II, 16.

33. W.B. Hesseltine, "The Underground Railroad From Confederate Prisons to East Tennessee," ETHS *Publications*, No. 2 (1930), 55–59; Paul A. Whelan, Unconventional Warfare in East Tennessee, 1861–1865 (master's thesis, Univ. of Tennessee, Knoxville, 1963), 114–51; Arnold Ritt, The Escape of Federal Prisoners Through East Tennessee, 1861–1865 (master's thesis, Univ. of Tennessee, Knoxville, 1965), 17–54.

34. Excerpt from typed manuscript of Major Charles G. Davis, copy in Special Collections, Univ. of Tennessee Library, Knoxville. The original is property of his grandson, Eliot Davis, Grand Marais, Minn. For a discussion of various routes out of the prison camps at Columbia, S.C., see Whelan, Unconventional Warfare, 124–40, and W.H. Shelton, "A Hard Road to Travel Out of Dixie," *Century*, XVIII (Oct. 1890), 931–49.

35. Ibid.

36. Ethie traveled back and forth to Cades Cove throughout the war. Her son, Exile, was born there at "Paradise Lost" on April 22, 1863. Skipper and Gove, "'Stray Thoughts,'" Part II, 118.

37. J.W. Oliver, Cades Cove, II, 8–9; Gamble, Heritage and Folk Music, 49; Blount Deeds, 1840–1860, *passim*; Agreement between Reuben Tipton and Daniel D. Foute, September 17, 1841, and Agreement between Jacob Tipton and Daniel D. Foute, September 5, 1845, mentioning an exchange of land for wagons, gearage, and horses, in author's possession.

38. Skipper and Gove, "'Stray Thoughts,'" Part II, 116–28; Wright, "Montvale Springs," 61.

39. In August 1864, Ethie Eagleton's husband, George, a Presbyterian minister, was lured from his home and brutally beaten. Skipper and Gove, "'Stray Thoughts,'" Part II, 119. Brownlow denounced Ethie as a "she-devil, the wife of a rebel preacher," who "had come in advance of him to spy out the land." Brownlow's *Knoxville Whig and Rebel Ventilator*, March 15, 1865; Burns, *Blount County*, 65. Ethie "heard that everything Pa had was taken from him, poor old man to be deprived of the comforts of life in his old age. . . ." Skipper and Gove, "'Stray Thoughts,'" Part II, 123.

40. W.H. Oliver, Sketches, 16–35; J.W. Oliver, Cades Cove, II, 30–32.

41. Burns, *Blount County*, 276. For the postwar effects of guerrilla warfare, see Whelan, Unconventional Warfare, 148–49; 1850 Census, Population,

Blount County; 1880 Census, Population, Blount County. For an excellent analysis of guerrilla warfare in western North Carolina, see Phillip S. Paludan, *Victims: A True Story of the Civil War* (Knoxville, 1981).

6. The Folk Culture

1. Folmsbee et al., *Tennessee*, II, 97–149. Parson Brownlow's Radical Republican regime exacerbated existing political differences and retarded the state's postwar economic recovery. Thomas B. Alexander, *Political Reconstruction in Tennessee* (Nashville, 1950), 69–245; Fertig, *Secession and Reconstruction*, 61–108; Verton M. Queener, "A Decade of East Tennessee Republicanism, 1867–1876," ETHS *Publications*, No. 14 (1942), 59–85.

2. According to one scholar, "the present relationship between folklore and anthropology could almost be defined as one of mutual contempt." Norbert F. Riedl, "Folklore and the Study of Material Aspects of Folk Culture," *Journal of American Folklore*, LXXIX (1966), 557–63.

3. This definition follows the lines of American anthropologists, "who have insisted on treating culture as a whole or in its entirety." German anthropologists, conversely, define folk culture "as being the unconscious, unreflective, traditional part of culture, distinct from the totality of man's learned behavior." Ibid., 558–59. See also Robert Redfield, "The Folk Society," *American Journal of Sociology*, LII (1947), 293–308, and Richard M. Dorson, "Current Folklore Theories," *Current Anthropology*, IV (1963), 93–112.

4. Dorson's criticisms of various approaches to folk culture apply particularly well to early writers such as Robert Lindsay Mason and Horace Kephart who visited Cades Cove and attempted to analyze the people and mountain culture there. Dorson, *American Folklore*, 8, 15–48.

5. 1840 Census, Population, Blount County; 1850 Census, Population, Blount County.

6. J.W. Oliver, Cades Cove, I, 5–7.

7. A classic enumeration of early stereotypes regarding Southern Appalachia was written by a former president of Maryville College, Samuel Tyndale Wilson, *The Southern Mountaineers* (New York, 1914), 11–78. Other writers who visited Cades Cove and perpetuated existing stereotypes of the mountain people and their culture are Mason, *Lure of the Great Smokies*, 22–209; Horace Kephart, *Our Southern Highlanders* (New York, 1922; rpt., facsimile, Knoxville, 1976), 286–452; John C. Campbell, *The Southern Highlander and His Homeland* (New York, 1921), 72–151; and Laura Thornborough, *The Great Smoky Mountains* (New York, 1937; rev. ed. Knoxville, 1962), 8–18.

8. Mason, *Lure of the Great Smokies*, 57–61. Wilson believed that these "mountaineers of the near future will help the nation win many battles for temperance and other social reforms." "Take courage," he exhorted his weary

readers, "you who in many states are fighting your apparently death-struggle battles against an organized and wealthy saloon-power upheld by depraved Americans and by many as yet un-Americanized though naturalized foreign immigrants! If you will but listen, you may hear the 'tramp, tramp, tramp, the boys are marching' of Americans from the free hills, coming to share with you the contest and to join with you in the victory that awaits our common cause. Be assured that these stalwart recruits from 'the land of the mountains and the glen' will stay in the fight to the finish." Wilson, *Southern Mountaineers*, 190.

9. These names are taken from the 1830, 1840, and 1850 Census, Population, Blount County, but the French and German origins of most of these families has been established by genealogists. See Edwards and Frizzell, *The "Connection,"* 1–3, for a discussion of the Myers and Headrick families. Actually, the census records show many names which appear to be non-English, e.g., Manol, Nugon, Nossun, Nupell, Swany, Cuttan, Schlessell, Deasmon, and Rustil, all from the 1850 Census, Population, Blount County.

10. James W. Wright, *Great Smoky Mountains National Park* (Knoxville, 1929), 57.

11. 1830 Census, Population, Blount County; 1840 Census, Population, Blount County; 1850 Census, Population, Blount County; 1860 Census, Population, Blount County.

12. Interview with John W. Oliver, Nov. 4, 1963.

13. Ibid., Kephart, *Our Southern Highlanders*, 238–307; Campbell, *Southern Highlander*, 123–51.

14. Ibid.; Blount Deeds, 1830–1880, *passim*.

15. Interview with John W. Oliver, Sept. 5, 1963.

16. Ibid.

17. Ibid. The binding force of their common culture and sense of community often made removal from the cove difficult for postwar residents, although early writers failed completely to comprehend this situation. Wilson, for example, lists inertia, attachment to the mountains, love of independence, lack of ambition, nostalgia, timidity, poverty, and lack of precedent as the basic reasons why Southern mountaineers refused to emigrate from their homes. Wilson, *Southern Mountaineers*, 62–63.

18. For a plethora of excellent examples and illustration of their use in specific contexts, see Joseph S. Hall, *Sayings From Old Smoky* (Asheville, N.C., 1972), 1–149.

19. Ibid. Wilson did perceive differences among the mountain people, although he made three classifications based on these differences that were completely erroneous. Wilson, *Southern Mountaineers*, 19–25. Mason made the mistake of representing men whom the community considered notorious outlaws as "typical mountaineers." Mason, *Lure of the Great Smokies*, 106–261. Unfortunately many of the stereotypes and misconceptions of writers such as

Mason and Horace Kephart have been uncritically perpetuated by modern authors such as Michael Frome, *Strangers in High Places* (New York, 1966; rev. ed. Knoxville, 1980), 57–69, 145–60.

20. "At the 'old field schools' as they were called, we had no recess, as it is now called. It was study from morning till noon, then an hour for play time, and study from one oclock till turning out time. And teachers received less than half the tuition now paid. . . . Under Butler Tipton, William Davis, Arindatis Martin and others, who taught in Cades Cove and Tuckeleache Cove, the students advanced rapidly. My memory was good, and I made fine progress at these schools." Jobe, Autobiography, 15–16.

21. Gamble, Heritage and Folk Music, 54–55. Five members listed as school directors for the sixteenth civil district of Blount County in 1869 were John Oliver, Will Lawson, Calvin Post, A.B. Burchfield, and J.B. Gregory. Burns, *Blount County*, 173, 320; N.H. Sparks and William A. Feezell, School Directors, 16th Civil District, Blounty County, Tennessee, to Elijah Oliver, Clerk and Treasurer, January 16, 1874. Original in possession of Judge W. Wayne Oliver, Maryville, Tenn.

22. Primitive Baptist Minutes, 1830–1880 *passim.* In 1870, 101 children between the ages of 6 and 13 had attended school within the year; 21 children in this age group had not. Out of 138 adults, 21 years old or older, 50 indicated they could not read, and 80 that they could not write. 1870 Census, Population, Blount County; J.W. Oliver, Cades Cove, I, 7–8; W.H. Oliver, Sketches, 27–52.

23. Interview with John W. Oliver, Oct. 13, 1963. These various folk narratives were repeated to the author innumerable times in his own childhood by elderly former residents of the cove; the fact that they were part of a shared culture makes specific citations difficult, since every member of the community was familiar with them, and the same story was often heard from different sources.

24. The phantom cat was a favorite motif and reoccurs in countless variations in such tall tales primarily intended for children. Ibid.

25. Ibid.; Douglas, "People of Cades Cove," 90.

26. Mellinger, E. Henry, *Folk-Songs from the Southern Highlands* (New York, 1938), 18.

27. Interview with John W. Oliver, Oct. 13, 1963.

28. Davis Manuscript, December 3, 1864; W.H. Oliver, Sketches, 1–3. Spelling and orthography continue to be given as in the original manuscript.

29. Dorson, *American Folklore,* 17–77.

30. Henry's articles and headnotes to ballads are found in the following issues of the *New Jersey Journal of Education*: Feb. 1926, p. 5; March 1926, p. 6; Sept. 1926, p. 20; Feb. 1927, p. 7; June 1927, p. 9; Dec. 1927, p. 11; March 1928, p. 13; Feb. 1929, p. 10; March 1929, p. 12; April 1929, p. 10; May 1929, p. 9; Sept. 1929, p. 9; Nov.–Dec. 1929, p. 10; Jan. 1930, p. 10; March 1930,

p. 8; Oct. 1930, p. 4; Nov.–Dec. 1930, p. 6; Jan.–Feb. 1931, p. 15. Henry, *Folksongs from the Southern Highlands*, 1–449; Mellinger E. Henry, *Songs Sung in the Southern Appalachians* (London, 1934), 1–253.

31. Henry, *Folksongs from the Southern Highlands*, 19–21.

32. Gamble, Heritage and Folk Music, 1–207.

33. Ibid., 63, 68, 109–15; J.W. Oliver, Cades Cove, I, 17.

34. Gamble, Heritage and Folk Music, 58, 112.

35. Joseph S. Hall, *The Phonetics of Great Smoky Mountain Speech* (New York, 1942), 4. See also Kephart, *Our Southern Highlanders*, 350–98.

36. M. Jean Jones, The Regional English of the Former Inhabitants of Cades Cove in the Great Smoky Mountains (doctoral diss., Univ. of Tennessee, Knoxville, 1973), 33.

37. Hall, *Phonetics*, 1–4; Josiah Combs, "The Language of the Southern Highlander," *PMLA*, 46 (1931), 1302–22; Charles Carpenter, "Variations in the Southern Mountain Dialect," *American Speech*, 8 (1933), 22–25; Gordon Wood, *Vocabulary Change: A Study of Variation in Regional Words in Eight of the Southern States* (Carbondale, Ill., 1971).

38. Hall, *Sayings*, 1.

39. Jones, Regional English, iii–iv, 93.

40. Joseph S. Hall, *Smoky Mountain Folks and Their Lore* (Asheville, 1960), 54.

41. George F. Mellen, "First Tennessee Novel," *Knoxville Sentinel*, Nov. 26, 1910; Charles W. Todd, *Woodville; Or Anchoret Reclaimed* (Knoxville, 1832), in Wright, American Fiction, v. 1, 1774–1850, No. 2600, Research Publications Microfilm, Reel T-5.

42. George F. Mellen, "First Tennessee Novel," *Knoxville Sentinel*, Nov. 26, 1910; John E. Alexander, *A Brief History of the Synod of Tennessee, From 1817–1887* (Philadelphia, 1890), 135.

43. *Peterson Magazine*, LIII (1868), 237; Sidney Lanier, *Tiger-Lilies* (New York, 1867), 57–58.

44. Lanier, *Tiger-Lilies*, 5.

45. Wright, *Great Smoky Mountains National Park*, 57; Mason, *Lure of the Great Smokies*, 11. The 'Squire was probably Daniel Lawson, one of the justices of the peace in the 1880s, who also was a comparatively wealthy and hospitable man. The other justice of peace during this period was Nathan H. Sparks. J.W. Oliver, Cades Cove, II, 26. Early critics speculated that internal evidence placed "The 'Harnt' that Walks Chilhowee" on Chilhowee Mountain in Blount County, Tennessee. Miss Murfree did not visit Montvale Springs until fall 1885, but one critic argues that the internal evidence of "The 'Harnt'" proves that she was in the Smokies before June 1882, when she announced the story ready for publication. It is highly probable, therefore, that Miss Murfree's extended visit to Cades Cove occurred before 1882. Mary Noailles Murfree, *In the Tennessee Mountains* (Boston, 1894; facsimile ed., Knoxville, 1970),

304, 307, 310, 316, 318; Nathalia Wright, "A Note on the Setting of Mary Noailles Murfree's 'The "Harnt" That Walks Chilhowee,'" *Modern Language Notes*
LXII (April 1947), 272.

46. Charles Egbert Craddock, *The Raid of the Guerilla* (Philadelphia, 1912),
7–8; Charles Egbert Craddock, *In the Clouds* (Boston, 1886), 1; Charles Egbert
Craddock, *The Prophet of the Great Smoky Mountains* (Boston, 1885), 1, 6,
209. Even the most cursory reading of Murfree's short stories indicates that
she had a thorough knowledge of Cades Cove and its environs.

47. Edd Winfield Parks, *Charles Egbert Craddock* (Chapel Hill, 1941), 195.

48. Hall, *Phonetics*, 3.

49. Nathalia Wright, Introduction, Mary Noailles Murfree (Charles Egbert
Craddock), *In the Tennessee Mountains* (rpt., facsimile, in *Tennesseana Editions*, ed. Nathalia Wright, Knoxville, 1970), xxxiii; Frank Waldo, "Among
the Southern Appalachians," *New England Magazine*, XXIV (May 1901), 241.

50. William Allen White, "Fiction of the Eighties and Nineties," in John
Macy, ed., *American Writers on American Literature* (New York, 1931), 395;
Eva Malone Byrd, The Life and Writings of Mary Noailles Murfree (master's
thesis, Univ. of Tennessee, Knoxville, 1937), 201–39. For a review of contemporary criticism of Mary Murfree's works, see Mary Sue Mooney, An Intimate Study of Mary Noailles Murfree, Charles Egbert Craddock (master's
thesis, George Peabody College for Teachers, Nashville, 1928), 133–305.

51. Robert Love Taylor, Jr., Mainstreams of Mountain Thought: Attitudes
of Selected Figures in the Heart of the Appalachian South, 1877–1903 (doctoral diss., Univ. of Tennessee, Knoxville, 1971), 60–105; Charles Egbert Craddock, *The Despot of Broomsedge Cove* (Boston, 1889), 1.

52. Richard Cary, *Mary N. Murfree* (in *Twayne's United States Authors
Series*, ed. Sylvia E. Bowman, New York, 1967), 174.

53. Durwood Dunn, "Mary Noailles Murfree: A Reappraisal," *Appalachian Journal*, VI (Spring, 1979), 196–204.

7. Family Life and Social Customs

1. 1900 Census, Population, Blount County.

2. Symptomatic of their intense knowledge of all members of the community was the ability of most cove residents to also list lengthy genealogies of distant neighbors who were not related to them. Genealogy was evidently a highly
developed form of oral communication. For examples see J.W. Oliver,
Cades Cove, III, 3–10.

3. 1900 Census, Population, Blount County.

4. Ibid.

5. Blount Deeds, Book, 64, p. 212; Book 62, p. 149. I have examined all
of the deeds for Cades Cove between 1890 and 1920. Countless instances occur

of land given for personal reasons. One such example is the sale of one-fifth interest in 50 acres in 1908 from E.A. White an wife M.E. White to Mrs. M.A. Cable for "$1.00 and the further consideration of care given to the mother of the said E.A. White during her last sickness." Book 67, p. 234.

6. Blount Deeds, Book 56, p. 134; Book 64, p. 213; Book 70, p. 164.

7. "It is further agreed that if the second party sells he shall sell to one of my sons or grandsons," Blount Deeds, Book 65, p. 364; Book 70, p. 196.

8. Compiled from 1900 Census, Population, Blount County. One writer after visiting this section of Southern Appalachia during this period claimed that "mountain women marry early, many of them at fourteen or fifteen. . . ." "Extremely early marriages are tolerated," he asserted, "as among all primitive people." Horace Kephart, *Our Southern Highlanders*, 297, 332.

9. 1900 Census, Population, Blount County.

10. Ibid.

11. Blount Deeds, Books 48–55, *passim*.

12. Blount Wills, Book 2, pp. 147–49.

13. A. Randolph Shields, *The Cades Cove Story* (Gatlinburg, 1977), 18–37.

14. R.D. Burchfield's Store Account Book, 1915–1922, Oliver Family Collection.

15. J.W. Oliver, Cades Cove, I, 5–6.

16. Ibid., 4–5. A very similar account of the family gathered around the fireplace at night while children were given Bible lessons and taught to sing hymns is given by J.W. Oliver's father. W.H. Oliver, Sketches, 44–46.

17. J.W. Oliver, Cades Cove, II, 2–3. Aunt Becky's lifestyle was described by Vic Weals in the *Knoxville Journal*, August 17, 1960. She died in 1944. Shields, "Cades Cove in the Great Smoky Mountains National Park," 107.

18. One cove resident still had in his possession in 1950 a flax hackle made by Peter Cable in the early part of the nineteenth century. "It consists of a piece of oak timber about 18 inches long by about 5 inches wide and about 1 inch thick with steel spikes about 6 inches long and as sharp as needles driven through it probably one inch apart." A difficult tool to make, this flax hackle was forged by hand and used to cut flax stalks and in separating the fiber from lint. J.W. Oliver, Cades Cove, I, 25.

19. I am indebted for these compilations from all the cove cemeteries to Karen S. Koehn, Cades Cove: Population Study, a seminar paper prepared June 7, 1977, for Dr. Joyce Bishop, Dept. of Anthropology, Univ. of Tennessee, Knoxville.

20. Ibid.

21. Interview May 12, 1979, with Lucille Oliver Dunn, a niece of George Oliver and granddaughter of W.H. Oliver.

22. *Maryville Times*, June 14, 1907; interview with J.W. Oliver, *Maryville Daily Times*, April 3, 1949. See also an interview with former cove resident John McCaulley, *Knoxville Journal*, Aug. 17, 1960.

23. W.H. Oliver, Sketches, 79; *Maryville Times*, Jan. 11, 1907.

24. Detailed descriptions of Primitive Baptist services and revivals are contained in W.H. Oliver, Sketches, 28-76.

25. In 1901 the other eleven churches in the Tennessee Association were Beech Grove, Bird's Creek, Grassy Gap, Green Brier, Hopewell, Law's Chapel, Miller's Cove, Mt. Pleasant, Mt. Zion, Tuckaleechee, and Wear's Valley. Dates and places of union meetings are contained in the annual *Minutes of the Tennessee Association of Primitive Baptists.* An almost complete collection of these minutes for the twentieth century is in the Oliver Family Collection.

26. Primitive Baptist Minutes, 1913-1941, *passim.* See also W.H. Oliver, Sketches, 145-47.

27. Shields, *Cades Cove Story,* 35-37.

28. M.L. Swan, *The New Harp of Columbia* (Nashville, 1867; rpt., facsimile, Knoxville, 1978).

29. Gamble, Heritage and Folk Music, 57-58.

30. Ibid., 58-59.

31. Shields, *Cades Cove Story,* 47-48.

32. Interview with John W. Oliver, June 19, 1961.

33. Interview with Lucille Oliver Dunn, Dec. 8, 1978.

34. Ibid.; Shields, *Cades Cove Story,* 41-43; interview with John McCaulley in the *Knoxville Journal,* Aug. 12, 1960; Gamble, Heritage and Folk Music, 64.

35. One elderly cove resident was "wonderfully alarmed" in 1931 at the prospect of "selling our dead" to the National Park and seriously considered having his family disinterred and buried in another location. "Our dead are so close to our hearts," he lamented, "we cannot and do not want to give them up!" W.H. Oliver, Sketches, 41.

36. Ibid., 143-46.

37. Ibid.

38. The best record of the community's awareness of adultery and fornication is contained in the often brutally explicit records of the Primitive Baptist church. Reinstatement and full acceptance back into the congregation followed a public confession and repentance; most persons thus accused were willing to follow the prescribed course of action. It is significant that no one ever denied charges of adultery or fornication in these records. Primitive Baptist Minutes, 1913-1941, *passim.*

39. A Primitive Baptist member reported drinking any form of alcohol was almost automatically "excluded from fellowship." Ibid.

40. Gamble, Heritage and Folk Music, 68.

41. J.W. Oliver, Cades Cove, I, 23-24, II, 9-10.

42. Shields, *Cades Cove Story,* 76.

43. W.H. Oliver, Sketches, 75-81.

44. No published or written account exists about the true nature of this unique subcommunity. The following analysis of Chestnut Flats comes from a series of discussions with John W. Oliver between 1959 and 1962. Interviews with other

members of the cove community living in 1900 reveal an identical description of life there, but no one wished to be quoted or associated in any way with the flats as late as 1979. Oliver was a rural mailman from 1904 until the community was dispersed in the 1930s. Since he was also a Primitive Baptist minister, flats women often stopped him on his delivery route and asked him to hold a brief service over the graves of their babies. At such times they confided to him the distressing circumstances of their lives and their attitudes of hopelessness and desperate resignation to their fate.

45. Ibid.; Shields, *Cades Cove Story*, 7, 78–81, 84–85. Sam Burchfield was a brother of Wils, discussed in Chapter 2. J.W. Oliver said that Robert Shields first settled in Chestnut Flats in the 1830s but later moved down into the cove near the center on the south side. For many years before the Civil War, the place in the flats later settled by Powell was known as the Shields place. Since the Shields were always one of the cove's most respectable families, there is no indication that Chestnut Flats had any hint of its later notoriety before the Civil War. J.W. Oliver, Cades Cove, III, 1.

46. *Maryville Index*, Sept. 18, 1878.

47. "On September 26, John Harvey Burchfield was killed at his home in the mountains near George Powell's. Theodore Rose and Will Burchfield, son of Sam, of the Flats, went to Harvey B's home and raised a quarrel over some old grudge when Rose pulled a revolver and shot once. Harvey then took Rose's pistol away from him, but Will B. who was standing near, gave Rose his revolver with which he finished the job. Drs. Blankenship and Martin of this place reached there the next evening and found Burchfield shot in three places, once through the upper part of the lung, a little below the heart, and in his right arm, with a 38 caliber revolver. He died the next morning at 1 o'clock. A wife and three small children are left in destitute circumstances without any means of support. Both Rose and Will Burchfield had been drinking and were quarrelsome when they arrived at the home of Harvey Burchfield." *Maryville Times*, Oct. 4, 1893.

48. *Maryville Times*, June 10, 1899. This Sam Burchfield was not the original Sam who moved to the flats in 1866 with his wife Mary Ann (Polly) Shuler. This latter Sam ("Smoke") shot and killed "Chicken Eater" John Tipton in August 1901. Convicted and sentenced for this crime, "Smoke" Sam became ill in prison and was sent home, where he died in 1904. Shields, *Cades Cove Story*, 78. The Burchfields in the cove were descended from Robert Burchfield; the flats Burchfields were descended from Robert's brother, Nathan, whose sons were Wils, Nathan, Sam ("Smoke"), Zeke, and a daughter, Ann, who married George W. Powell Sr. J.W. Oliver, Burchfield and Tiptons Related to Cades Cove, 2–6.

49. Interview with John W. Oliver, Dec. 7, 1961.

50. Interview with Lucille Oliver Dunn, July 9, 1979. Peddlers were single merchants who carried all their stock with them; "drummers" were wholesale agents who visited the cove stores with sample supplies and took large orders.

51. A photograph of George W. Powell's home taken in the 1920s illustrates graphically this retrogression. On the back of this photograph, J.W. Oliver wrote of Chestnut Flats: "its history can never be written."

52. John W. Oliver wrote in 1932 that "many false and malicious stories have been told and written about the mountain people. Men representing themselves to be great authors, have spent a few weeks or months among the mountain people, feasting on their hospitality and then gone away and written books about their customs, manner of life, etc., which is as far from the truth as day is from night. For instance, they have taken up some outlaw and pictured him as a very bad character, and set him up as typical of all the mountain people. Such is the general tone of *The Lure of the Great Smokies* written by Robert L. Mason. Mr. Mason has completely overlooked one hundred years of Christian citizenship among the mountain people." *Maryville Times*, Sept. 15, 1932.

53. Mason, *Lure of the Great Smokies*, 197–200. Ann Powell's date of birth is given as 1834 in the 1900 Census, Population, Blount County.

54. J.W. Oliver, unpublished article, written in 1928, Oliver Family Collection.

8. Government, Law, and Politics

1. Kephart, *Our Southern Highlanders*, 387. Two Cades Cove justice of the peace dockets, the first volume dating from 1851 to 1929 and the second dating from 1856 to 1922, are in the author's possession and are hereafter cited Cades Cove JP Docket, with appropriate volume and page.

2. Burns, *Blount County*, 41, 197–99.

3. Return J. Meigs and William F. Cooper, *Code of Tennessee Enacted By the General Assembly of 1857–58* (Nashville, 1858), 741–53.

4. Ibid., 754–56; Burns, *Blount County*, 32, 198.

5. Burns, *Blount County*, 32–33; Meigs and Cooper, *Code of Tennessee*, 754–59; Lee S. Greene and Robert S. Avery, *Government in Tennessee* (Knoxville, 1962), 334–36.

6. Blount Deeds, 1830–1924, *passim*. John Oliver's application for bounty land in 1857 was prepared by Daniel D. Foute, justice of the peace in the cove between 1856 and 1862. This application is in File of John Oliver, Private, Capt. Adam Winsell's Co., Col. Ewen Allison's Regiment, East Tennessee Militia, War of 1812, National Archives.

7. J.W. Oliver, Cades Cove, II, 32; Burns, *Blount County*, 216, 330–31.

8. *Maryville Record*, July 29, 1904.

9. George Roulstone, comp., *Laws of the State of Tennessee, 1792–1801* (Knoxville, 1803), 155; Edward Scott, comp., *Laws of the State of Tennessee including Those of North Carolina Now in Force in This State from the year 1715 to the Year 1820, inclusive* (2 vols. Knoxville, 1821), I, 533, 559; Burns, *Blount County*, 42, 276; J.W. Oliver, Cades Cove, II, 28.

10. Burns, *Blount County,* 204; *Maryville Times,* Feb. 8, March 29, 1907.

11. *Maryville Times,* Feb. 10, 1886; tax receipts for Elijah Oliver, 1861–1905, and W.H. Oliver, 1899–1914, in Oliver Family Collection.

12. *Maryville Enterprise,* Feb. 18, 1918; Feb. 16, 1915; *Maryville Times,* May 18, 1906; Elijah Oliver's tax receipts in Oliver Family Collection.

13. All of the official records, correspondence and affidavits cited are in the File of John Oliver, Private, Capt. Adam Winsell's Co., Col. Ewen Allison's Regiment, East Tennessee Militia, War of 1812, National Archives. The original act of Congress authorizing pensions for service in the War of 1812 was passed on February 14, 1871. Lucretia was called "Lurena" in most of this correspondence.

14. Records of the Postmaster General, National Archives; J.W. Oliver, Cades Cove, II, 29–31.

15. Cades Cove JP Dockets, I and II, *passim.*

16. Tuckaleechee Cove Justice of the Peace Docket, 1880–1901, *passim.* William Hurst Dunn was the justice of the peace; his docket is in the author's possession.

17. Blount Circuit Court Minutes, Book A, pp. 542–46.

18. Ibid., Book 1, p. 602.

19. Ibid., Book 1, p. 637.

20. Ibid., Book 2, p. 2.

21. Ibid., Book 2, p. 50.

22. Blount Chancery Court Minutes, Book 2, pp. 341, 128.

23. Ibid., Book 4, pp. 126–27.

24. Ibid., Book 3, pp. 504–505.

25. Ibid., Book 6, pp. 303–304.

26. Ibid., Book 5, pp. 354–55.

27. Ibid., Book 5, pp. 613–20; *Maryville Record,* June 3, 1904; W.H. Oliver, Sketches, 79.

28. J.W. Oliver, Cades Cove, I, 26; *Maryville Times,* March 3, May 5, Oct. 6, 1886; Oct. 5, 1887; May 11, 1892; Jan. 3, Oct. 3, 1894; June 7, 1902; July 15, 1904; May 18, 1906; March 15, April 26, 1907.

29. *Maryville Times,* April 7, May 27, 1886.

30. Gordon B. McKinney, *Southern Mountain Republicans, 1865–1900: Politics and the Appalachian Community* (Chapel Hill, 1978), 20–24, 132–36, 143–49.

31. This analysis is based on local, state, and national manuscript election returns for the sixteenth civil district of Blount County, Tennessee between 1867 and 1924 in the Tennessee State Library and Archives, hereafter cited Blount Returns with appropriate year.

32. *Maryville Index,* Dec. 4, 1878; *Maryville Times,* Jan. 12, 1906.

33. Blount Returns, November 5, 1912; *Maryville Times,* Aug. 9, 1886.

34. Blount Returns, Second Congressional District, 1868–1924; *Maryville Index,* Nov. 13, 1878; *Blount County Democrat,* Nov. 23, 1882; *Maryville Times,* Nov. 3, 1886; Nov. 12, 1890; Nov. 16, 1892; Nov. 14, 1894; Nov. 19, 1898; Nov. 15, 1902; Nov. 18, 1904.

35. *Blount County Democrat*, April 29, 1882; *Maryville Times*, May 5, 1886; May 10, 1893; Aug. 9, 1902; Sept. 26, 1894; Nov. 5, 1896.

36. *Maryville Times*, Nov. 12, 1890; Nov. 16, 1892; Roger L. Hart, *Redeemers, Bourbons & Populists: Tennessee 1870–1896* (Baton Rouge, 1975), 122–50.

37. 1900 List of Voters, Sixteenth Civil District, Blount County, in the Tennessee State Library and Archives; 1900 Census, Population, Blount County.

38. Ibid.

39. *Maryville Times*, May 27, 1886; *Maryville Enterprise*, Nov. 26, 1909.

9. Progressivism and Prohibition

1. Unpublished article by John W. Oliver, written June 1, 1948, p. 1; Obituary of James R. Oliver (grandson of the first John Oliver, first cousin of William Howell Oliver), written in 1952 by J.W. Oliver, 3–4.

2. W. Wayne Oliver, Memoirs of Judge William Wayne Oliver, 16, unpublished typescript, written in 1983, in author's possession; *Maryville Times*, August 1, 1903; Feb. 20, 1904.

3. Interview with Lucille Oliver Dunn, March 22, 1978.

4. Ibid.

5. J.W. Oliver, 1948 unpublished article, 1; Primitive Baptist Minutes, 1901–1916.

6. *Maryville Times*, July 16, 1909.

7. *Maryville Enterprise*, Aug. 24, 1915; March 21, 1916; *Maryville Times*, Sept. 29, 1915.

8. J.W. Oliver, 1948 unpublished article, 3.

9. *Maryville Times*, March 29, 1907; Aug. 23, 1915.

10. 1890 Census, Population, Blount County; 1910 Census, Population, Blount County.

11. *Maryville Times*, Aug. 1, 1903; Feb. 20, 1904; Feb. 9, Sept. 28, Nov. 9, 1906; March 15, 1907; July 16, 1909; April 28, 1911; April 17, 1914; *Maryville Enterprise*, Jan. 7, 28, March 11, 1910; Jan. 19, March 9, Oct. 20, 1911.

12. *Maryville Times*, May 24, 1907; *Maryville Enterprise*, May 21, 1910.

13. *Maryville Enterprise*, April 28, 1911; Jan. 19, 1912.

14. *Maryville Times*, March 29, 1907.

15. *Maryville Record*, June 3, 1904; *Maryville Times*, April 26, 1907; *Maryville Enterprise*, March 21, 1916.

16. Shields, *Cades Cove Story*, 8–9; *Maryville Record*, June 3, 1904; *Maryville Times*, Jan. 18, March 8, 1907; *Maryville Enterprise*, Jan. 8, 1909.

17. *Maryville Times*, March 8, 1907.

18. W.W. Oliver, Memoirs, 34.

19. *Maryville Enterprise*, June 4, 1914; *Maryville Times*, Aug. 23, Nov. 11, 1915.

20. W.W. Oliver, Memoirs, 33; *Maryville Enterprise*, April 6, 1915; Black Joe's Account Book, 1917, Oliver Family Collection.

21. W.W. Oliver, Memoirs, 33–34; *Maryville Times*, Jan. 18, March 29, 1907; *Maryville Enterprise*, March 5, 1909.

22. W.W. Oliver, Memoirs, 34–35; *Maryville Times*, Feb. 3, 1911.

23. W.W. Oliver, Memoirs, 22–23, 33, 51.

24. Ibid., 40–42; *Maryville Times*, March 8, 1907; Aug. 6, 1914.

25. Douglas, "People of Cades Cove," 84–85.

26. W.W. Oliver, Memoirs, 33.

27. Ibid., 35–37; Douglas, "People of Cades Cove," 79.

28. *Maryville Enterprise*, March 9, 1911.

29. *Maryville Times*, Aug. 26, 1915.

30. *Maryville Enterprise*, Aug. 24, 1915; March 21, 1916.

31. W.W. Oliver, Memoirs, 106–123.

32. *Maryville Enterprise*, April 27, 1915.

33. Ibid., June 13, 1918.

34. Ibid., June 4, 1914.

35. *Maryville Times*, March 8, 1907.

36. *Maryville Enterprise*, Jan. 22, 1914; Feb. 15, 1917.

37. Ibid., May 11, 1915.

38. Gamble, Heritage and Folk Music, 68–69; *Maryville Enterprise*, Feb. 2, 9, July 27, 1921.

39. Interview with Lucille Oliver Dunn, March 22, 1978.

40. W.W. Oliver, Memoirs, 80–81.

41. Interview with Lucille Oliver Dunn, March 25, 1978.

42. Ibid., Oct. 20, 1979.

43. Ibid.; *Maryville Enterprise*, Dec. 14, 1921.

44. Interview with W. Wayne Oliver, May 29, 1979; W.H. Oliver, Sketches, 80.

45. W. H. Oliver, Sketches, 81; interview with Lucille Oliver Dunn, Oct. 20, 1979.

46. Interview with W. Wayne Oliver, May 29, 1979.

47. W.W. Oliver, Memoirs, 83–84; *Joe Gregory and Dana Gregory v. The State*, Tennessee Supreme Court, 1922, Box 976, Tennessee State Archives.

48. Interview with W. Wayne Oliver, May 29, 1979.

49. Interview with Lucille Oliver Dunn, Oct. 20, 1979.

50. W.W. Oliver, Memoirs, 84–85; *Maryville Enterprise*, Dec. 28, 1921.

51. Blount Circuit Court Civil and Criminal Minutes, Book 13, pp. 103–104, 136.

52. W.W. Oliver, Memoirs, 87; Blount Circuit Court Civil and Criminal Minutes, Book 13, pp. 47, 64, 69–72.

53. Interview with W. Wayne Oliver, May 29, 1979.

54. W.W. Oliver, Memoirs, 87.

55. James G. Klotter, "Feuds in Appalachia: An Overview," *Filson Club History Quarterly*, LVI (July 1982), 290–317.

56. Douglas, "People of Cades Cove," 92.

10. Death by Eminent Domain

1. Carlos C. Campbell, *Birth of a National Park in the Great Smoky Mountains* (Knoxville, 1960), 98.

2. Ibid., 12–24.

3. John Thomas Whaley, A Timely Idea At An Ideal Time: Knoxville's Role in Establishing The Great Smoky Mountains National Park (master's thesis, Univ. of Tennessee, Knoxville, 1984), 54–55, 100; *Knoxville Journal*, Jan. 6, March 23, April 2, 4, 1926; *Knoxville News*, March 16, 1926; *Knoxville Sentinel*, March 7, 1926; *Maryville Times*, March 26, 1928.

4. Campbell, *Birth*, 55–58; *Knoxville Journal and Tribune*, Feb. 1, 1925; Wright, *National Park*, 13–15.

5. W.W. Oliver, Memoirs, 79; *Maryville Times*, July 25, 1921; *Knoxville Sentinel*, Sept. 12, 1926.

6. *Maryville Times*, July 9, 1925; Feb. 6, March 6, 1930; July 25, 1931; July 28, 1932; Mellinger E. Henry, "Life in The Great Smoky Park," *New Jersey Journal of Education* (Oct. 1930), 4–5

7. Interview with Lucille Oliver Dunn, March 23, 1979.

8. Campbell, *Birth*, 28, 32, 40, 52, 63; Wright, *National Park*, 25; *Maryville Times*, April 18, Dec. 15, 1927; *Knoxville Sentinel*, May 2, 1926; *Knoxville Journal*, April 23, 24, May 9, 1926.

9. Carlos C. Campbell to John Oliver, March 24, 1927, Oliver Family Collection.

10. *Tenn. Acts*, 1927, Ch. 54; *Knoxville Journal*, April 23, 1927.

11. *Knoxville Journal*, April 23, May 9, 1926; *Knoxville Sentinel*, May 2, 1926.

12. *Maryville Times*, April 18, Dec. 15, 1927; Wright, *National Park*, 29; Testimony of Colonel David C. Chapman, 1939, Great Smoky Mountains National Park Records, Gatlinburg, Tenn.

13. *Progressive Labor*, April 21, 1927, quoted in Wright, *National Park*, 30.

14. *Maryville Times*, April 18, 28, 1927; *Knoxville Journal*, April 23, 1927; Campbell, *Birth*, 53; Wright, *National Park*, 61.

15. *Maryville Times*, March 8, 1928; G. Walter Gregory to John D. Rockefeller, Jr., June 18, 1928, Park Records; Mrs. R.D. Burchfield to John D. Rockefeller, Jr., June 22, 1928, Eugene Clyde Brooks Papers, North Carolina State Archives, Raleigh.

16. *Maryville Times*, June 30, Dec. 15, 1927; Nov. 1, Dec. 3, 1928; George

D. Roberts to David C. Chapman, Nov. 19, 1928; David C. Chapman to George D. Roberts, Dec. 8, 1928, Park Records. "It now seems Cades Cove will be eliminated from the park area." *Maryville Enterprise*, Dec. 12, 1928.

17. *Maryville Times*, June 26, 1924; June 30, Dec. 15, 1927; Wright, *National Park*, 57.

18. Burns, *Blount County*, 215; W.W. Oliver, Memoirs, 90–91.

19. Blount Circuit Court Civil Minutes, Book 3, pp. 519, 526; David C. Chapman to Edward E. Barthell, June 2, 1931; David C. Chapman to Arno B. Cammerer, June 19, 1934, Park Records.

20. Blount Circuit Court Civil Minutes, Book 4, pp. 335–41.

21. Ibid.; *State* v. *Oliver*, Supreme Court of Tennessee, Feb. 7, 1931, Vol. 162 *Tennessee Reports* (9 Smith), 100–21.

22. Blount Circuit Court Civil Minutes, Book 5, pp. 50–51; *State* v. *Oliver*, Supreme Court of Tennessee, July 5, 1932, Vol. 164 *Tennessee Reports* (11 Smith), 555–61.

23. Blount Circuit Court Civil Minutes, Book 5, p. 577; *State* v. *Oliver*, Supreme Court of Tennessee, January 16, 1934, Vol. 167 *Tennessee Reports* (3 Beeler) 155–60; W.W. Oliver, Memoirs, 91–95.

24. Park Commission Land Sales File, Park Records; 1930 Census, Population, Blount County.

25. *Maryville Times*, March 15, 1928; *Knoxville Sentinel*, May 2, 1926; *Knoxville Journal*, April 23, 1926; David C. Chapman to Arno B. Cammerer, July 13, 1927, Park Records; *Maryville-Alcoa Daily Times*, Feb. 24, 1984.

26. Park Commission Land Sales File, Park Records.

27. Shields, *Cades Cove Story*, 9, 109; Campbell, *Birth*, 117–18; Frome, *Strangers in High Places*, 172, 196.

28. Park Commission Land Sales File, Park Records; *Maryville-Alcoa Daily Times*, Feb. 24, 1984; *Maryville Times*, Jan. 9, 1933.

29. Interview with John W. Oliver, Dec. 13, 1962; David C. Chapman to J.R. Eakin, July 26, 1933, Park Records.

30. W.H. Oliver, Sketches, 41; *Nashville Tennessean*, Sept. 1, 1932; Arno B. Cammerer to David C. Chapman, Jan. 8, 1934; David C. Chapman to R.P. White, Nov. 13, 1934; David C. Chapman to Wilbur A. Nelson, Dec. 2, 1935; Robert P. White to David C. Chapman, Nov. 14, 1934, Park Records.

31. Mr. and Mrs. Willie Myers to David C. Chapman, Nov. 7, 1932; Park Commission Land Sales File, Park Records; *Maryville Times*, Feb. 11, 1935; Gamble, Heritage and Folk Music, 72.

32. *Maryville Times*, Dec. 5, 1935; *Maryville-Alcoa Daily Times*, Feb. 24, 1984; J.R. Eakin to Jack Anthony, Dec. 2, 1935; Special Use Permit, Great Smoky Mountains National Park to Jack Anthony of Cades Cove, Tennessee, Jan. 1, 1935, Oliver Family Collection.

33. *Maryville Times*, March 23, July 23, Aug. 10, 1936; *Maryville-Alcoa Daily Times*, Feb. 24, 1984.

34. *United States* v. *John W. Oliver, Tyra Shields, and James Cooper, Trustees of the Cades Cove Primitive Baptist Church,* U.S. District Court for Eastern District of Tennessee, Northern Division, No. 83–Civil, 1940; Great Smoky Mountains National Park, Lease to Primitive Baptist Church of Cades Cove, December 4, 1939, Oliver Family Collection; *Maryville-Alcoa Daily Times,* Feb. 24, 1984.

Bibliography

Manuscript Collections

Brooks, Eugene Clyde. Papers. North Carolina State Archives, Raleigh.
Davis, Charles G. Army Life and Prison Experiences of Major Charles G. Davis. Unpublished typed manuscript, no date, in the possession of his grandson, Eliot Davis, Grand Marais, Minn. Xerox copy also in Special Collections, Univ. of Tennessee Library, Knoxville.
Great Smoky Mountains National Park Records. Gatlinburg, Tenn.
Jobe, Abraham. Autobiography or Memoirs. Unpublished manuscript, written between 1849 and 1905, in the possession of Mrs. Harlow (Sophie Hunter) Dixon, Durham, N.C. Typed copy also in the Tennessee State Library, Nashville.
McCammon, Samuel. Diary. Unpublished manuscript, written between 1846 and 1854, McClung Collection, Lawson McGhee Library, Knoxville.
Oliver Family Collection. In author's possession.
Post Family Papers and Notebooks. In possession of Jonnie Post, Maryville, Tenn.
Snider Family Collection. In author's possession.
Turner, Jessie Eugenia. Family History. Unpublished manuscript in the possession of Jessie Eugenia Turner, Chattanooga, Tenn.

Manuscript Documents

Blount County Chancery Court Records. Blount County Courthouse, Maryville, Tenn.
Blount County Circuit Court Civil and Criminal Minutes. Blount County Courthouse, Maryville, Tenn.

Blount County Court Minutes. Blount County Courthouse, Maryville, Tenn.

Blount County Deed Books. Blount County Courthouse, Maryville, Tenn.

Blount County Entry Taker's Book. Blounty County Courthouse, Maryville, Tenn.

Blount County Marriage Records. Blount County Courthouse, Maryville, Tenn.

Blount County Manuscript Election Returns, 1867–1930. Tennessee State Archives, Nashville.

Blount County Wills and Inventories. Blount County Courthouse, Maryville, Tenn.

Cades Cove Baptist Church Book, 1827–1905. In the possession of Ray Taylor, Maryville, Tenn.

Carter County Court Minutes. Carter County Courthouse, Elizabethton, Tenn.

Carter County Deed Books. Carter County Courthouse, Elizabethton, Tenn.

Carter County Marriage Records. Carter County Courthouse, Elizabethton, Tenn.

Carter County Wills and Inventories. Carter County Courthouse, Elizabethton, Tenn.

Minutes of the Ellejoy Baptist Church. McClung Collection, Lawson McGhee Library, Knoxville.

Minutes of the Miller's Cove Baptist Church, 1812–1900. Typescript copy in the McClung Collection, Lawson McGhee Library, Knoxville.

North Carolina Grants to Land in Tennessee. Tennessee State Archives, Nashville.

Register of East Tennessee. Tennessee State Archives, Nashville.

U.S. Bureau of the Census. Fifth Census of the United States (1830), Population, Blount County, Tennessee.

――――. Sixth Census of the United States (1840), Population, Blount County, Tennessee.

――――. Seventh Census of the United States (1850), Agriculture, Blount County, Tennessee.

――――. Seventh Census of the United States (1850), Population, Blount County, Tennessee.

――――. Eighth Census of the United States (1860), Agriculture, Blount County, Tennessee.

――――. Eighth Census of the United States (1860), Population, Blount County, Tennessee.

――――. Ninth Census of the United States (1870), Population, Blount County, Tennessee.

――――. Tenth Census of the United States (1860), Agriculture, Blount County, Tennessee.

――――. Tenth Census of the United States (1880), Population, Blount County, Tennessee.

――――. Eleventh Census of the United States (1890), Population, Blount County, Tennessee.

————. Twelfth Census of the United States (1900), Population, Blount County, Tennessee.

Printed Documents

Acts of the State of Tennessee, 1851–1927. Nashville, 1852–1928.
Minutes of the Tennessee Association of Primitive Baptist, 1879–1900. Copies in author's possession.
Minutes of the Tennessee Association of United Baptists. Baptist Archives, Nashville.
Petitions. Tennessee State Archives, Nashville.
Tennessee General Assembly, Joint Legislative Committee. *Report on the Great Smoky Mountains and Other Areas for a National or State Park.* Nashville, 1925.
U.S. Bureau of the Census. *Seventh Census of the United States: 1850.* Washington, D.C., 1853.
————. *Eighth Census of the United States: 1860.* Washington, D.C., 1864.
————. *Ninth Census of the United States: 1870.* Washington, D.C., 1872.
————. *Tenth Census of the United States: 1880.* Washington, D.C., 1883.
————. *Eleventh Census of the United States: 1890.* Washington, D.C., 1895.
————. *Twelfth Census of the United States: 1900.* Washington, D.C., 1901–1902.
————. *Thirteenth Census of the United States: 1910.* Washington, D.C., 1912–14.
————. *Fourteenth Census of the United States: 1920.* Washington, D.C., 1921–23.
————. *Fifteenth Census of the United States: 1930.* Washington, D.C., 1932–33.

Newspapers

Brownlow's *Knoxville Whig and Rebel Ventilator,* 1864–1865.
East Tennessean, 1856–1858.
Emancipator, 1838.
Knoxville Journal, 1926–1960.
Knoxville News, 1926.
Knoxville News-Sentinel, 1960.
Knoxville Register, 1828–1849.
Knoxville Sentinel, 1926.
Knoxville Whig, 1850–1861.

Maryville Enterprise, 1909–1928.
Maryville Index, 1878.
Maryville Record, 1904.
Maryville Times-Maryville-Alcoa Daily Times, 1899–1984.
Memphis Daily Appeal, 1861.
Nashville Tennessean, 1932.
New York Evening Post, 1850–1860.

Books

Abrahams, Roger D., and George Foss. *Anglo-American Folksong Style*. Englewood Cliffs, N.J., 1968.
Alexander, Thomas B. *Political Reconstruction in Tennessee*. Nashville, 1950.
———. *Thomas A. R. Nelson of East Tennessee*. Nashville, 1956.
Allen, Penelope Johnson, trans. *Tennessee Soldiers in the War of 1812: Regiments of Col. Allcorn and Col. Allison*. Chattanooga, 1947.
American State Papers, Military Affairs. 7 vols. Washington, D.C., 1832–1861.
Arensberg, Conrad M., and Solon T. Kimball. *Culture and Community*. New York, 1956.
Armstrong, O.K., and Marjorie M. Armstrong. *The Indomitable Baptists: A Narrative of Their Role in Shaping American History*. New York, 1967.
Arthur, John Preston. *Western North Carolina: A History*. Raleigh, 1914.
Bergeron, Paul H. *Antebellum Politics in Tennessee*. Lexington, Ky., 1982.
Billington, Ray Allen. *Frederick Jackson Turner: Historian, Scholar, Teacher*. New York, 1973.
Blackmun, Ora. *Western North Carolina: Its Mountains and Its People to 1800*. Boone, N.C., 1977.
Boorstin, Daniel J. *The Americans: The National Experience*. New York, 1965.
Bowman, Elizabeth S. *Land of High Horizons*. Kingsport, Tenn., 1938.
Browder, Nathaniel C. *The Cherokee Indians and Those Who Came After*. Hayesville, N.C., 1973.
Burns, Inez E. *History of Blount County, Tennessee, From War Trail to Landing Strip, 1795–1955*. Nashville, 1957.
Callahan, North. *Smoky Mountain Country*. New York, 1952.
Campbell, Carlos C. *Birth of a National Park in the Great Smoky Mountains*. Knoxville, 1960.
Campbell, John C. *The Southern Highlander and His Homeland*. New York, 1921.
Clark, Blanche Henry. *The Tennessee Yeoman, 1840–1860*. Nashville, 1942.
Clark, Elmer T., ed. *The Journal and Letters of Francis Asbury*. 3 vols. London, 1958.

Crane, Verner W. *The Southern Frontier, 1670–1732*. Ann Arbor, Mich., 1929.

Dolan, J.R. *The Yankee Peddlers of Early America*. New York, 1964.

Dorson, Richard M. *American Folklore and the Historian*. Chicago, 1971.

———. *Folklore: Selected Essays*. Bloomington, Ind., 1972.

Driver, Carl S. *John Sevier, Pioneer of the Old Southwest*. Chapel Hill, N.C., 1932.

Dundes, Alan, ed. *The Study of Folklore*. Englewood Cliffs, N.J., 1965.

Eaton, Allen H. *Handicrafts of the Southern Highlands*. New York, 1937.

Edwards, Olga Jones, and Izora Waters Frizzell. *The "Connection" in East Tennessee*. Washington College, Tenn., 1969.

Eller, Ronald D. *Miners, Millhands, and Mountaineers: Industrialization of the Appalachian South, 1880–1930*. Knoxville, 1982.

Ellis, Daniel. *Thrilling Adventures of Daniel Ellis*. New York, 1867.

Fertig, James W. *The Secession and Reconstruction of Tennessee*. Chicago, 1898.

Folmsbee, Stanley J. *Sectionalism and Internal Improvements in Tennessee, 1796–1845*. Knoxville, 1939.

Folmsbee, Stanley J., Robert E. Corlew, and Enoch L. Mitchell. *History of Tennessee*. 2 vols. New York, 1960.

Frome, Michael. *Strangers in High Places*. New York, 1966; rev. ed. Knoxville, 1980.

Fuchs, Victor R. *The Economics of the Fur Industry*. New York, 1957.

Garrett, William R., and Albert V. Goodpasture. *History of Tennessee*. Nashville, 1903.

Glassie, Henry. *Pattern in the Material Folk Culture of the Eastern United States*. Philadelphia, 1968.

Gould, Mary Earle. *Early American Wooden Ware and Other Kitchen Utensils*. Rutland, Vt., 1962.

Gray, Lewis Cecil. *History of Agriculture in the Southern United States to 1860*. 2 vols. Washington, D.C., 1933.

Greenbie, Sydney, and Marjorie Barstow. *Gold of Ophir: The China Trade in the Making of America*. New York, 1937.

Greene, Lee S., and Robert S. Avery. *Government in Tennessee*. Knoxville, 1962.

Grime, J. H. *History of Middle Tennessee Baptists*. Nashville, 1902.

Gunn, John C. *Gunn's Domestic Medicine*. Knoxville, 1830; rpt., facsimile, 1986.

———. *Gunn's New Domestic Physician*. 3rd ed., Cincinnati, 1860.

Hall, Joseph S. *Sayings From Old Smoky*. Asheville, N.C., 1972.

———. *Smoky Mountain Folks and Their Lore*. Asheville, N.C., 1960.

———. *The Phonetics of Great Smoky Mountain Speech*. New York, 1942.

Hamer, Philip M. *Tennessee: A History: 1673–1932*. 4 vols. New York, 1933.

Hardacre, Val. *Woodland Nuggetts of Gold: The Story of American Ginseng Cultivation*. New York, 1968.

Hart, Roger L. *Redeemers, Bourbons & Populists: Tennessee 1870–1896*. Baton Rouge, 1975.

Haywood, John. *The Civil and Political History of the State of Tennessee.* Knoxville, 1823.

Henry, Mellinger E. *Folk-Songs from the Southern Highlands.* New York, 1938.

———. *Songs Sung in the Southern Appalachians.* London, 1934.

Horn, Stanley F., ed. *Tennessee's War, 1861–1869.* Nashville, 1965.

Humes, Thomas W. *The Loyal Mountaineers of Tennessee.* Knoxville, 1888.

Hurlburt, J.S. *History of the Rebellion in Bradley County, East Tennessee.* Indianapolis, 1866.

Isaac, Paul E. *Prohibition and Politics: Turbulent Decades in Tennessee, 1885–1920.* Knoxville, 1965.

Kephart, Horace. *Our Southern Highlanders.* New York, 1913; rpt., facsimile, Knoxville, 1976.

Kurath, Hans. *A Word Geography of the Eastern United States.* Ann Arbor, 1949.

Lefler, Hugh T. *History of North Carolina.* 2 vols. New York, 1956.

Lesley, J.P. *Iron Manufacturer's Guide.* Philadelphia, 1859.

McBride, Robert M., ed. *More Landmarks of Tennessee History.* Nashville, 1969.

McKinney, Gordon B. *Southern Mountain Republicans, 1865–1900: Politics and the Appalachian Community.* Chapel Hill, 1978.

McTeer, Will A. *History of New Providence Presbyterian Church, Maryville, Tennessee, 1786–1921.* Maryville, 1921.

Martin, Isaac P. *A Minister in the Tennessee Valley: Sixty-Seven Years.* Nashville, 1954.

Mason, Robert Lindsay. *The Lure of the Great Smokies.* Boston, 1927.

Massengill, Samuel Evans. *The Massengills, Massengales, and Variants, 1492–1931.* Bristol, Tenn., 1931.

Masterson, William H. *William Blount.* Baton Route, 1954.

Michaux, F.A. *Travels to the Westward of the Allegany Mountains to the States of Ohio, Kentucky, and Tennessee in the Year 1802.* Trans. from the French. London, 1805.

Moody, J.B. *The Distinguishing Doctrines of Baptists.* Nashville, 1901.

Nash, Roderick. *Wilderness and the American Mind.* New Haven, 1967.

Paludan, Phillip S. *Victims: A True Story of the Civil War.* Knoxville, 1981.

Patton, James W. *Unionism and Reconstruction in Tennessee, 1860–1869.* Chapel Hill, 1934.

Posey, Walter B. *Methodism in the Old Southwest.* Tuscaloosa, 1933.

———. *Religious Strife on the Southern Frontier.* Baton Rouge, 1965.

Prucha, Francis Paul. *American Indian Policy in the Formative Years: The Indian Trade and Intercourse Acts, 1790–1834.* Cambridge, 1962.

Ramsey, J.G.M. *Annals of Tennessee.* Charleston, S.C., 1853.

Rice, Otis K. *The Allegheny Frontier: West Virginia Beginnings, 1730–1830*. Lexington, Ky., 1970.

Riley, B.F. *Baptists of the South in States East of the Mississippi*. Philadelphia, 1898.

Robertson, Mary Emily. *The Attitude of Tennesseans Toward the Union, 1847–1861*. New York, 1961.

Robinson, John J. *Memoir of Rev. Isaac Anderson, D.D.* Knoxville, 1860.

Safford, James M. *Geology of Tennessee*. Nashville, 1869.

Shapiro, Henry D. *Appalachia On Our Mind: The Southern Mountains and Mountaineers in the American Consciousness, 1870–1920*. Chapel Hill, 1978.

Shields, A. Randolph. *The Cades Cove Story*. Gatlinburg, Tenn., 1977.

———. *The Families of Cades Cove, 1821–1936*. Maryville, Tenn., 1981.

Smith, James W., and A. Leland Jamison, eds. *Religion in American Life: The Shaping of American Religion*. 4 vols. Princeton, N.J., 1961.

Spain, Rufus B. *At Ease in Zion: Social History of the Southern Baptists, 1865–1900*. Nashville, 1961.

Stupka, Arthur. *Great Smoky Mountains National Park*. Washington, D.C., 1960.

Swan M.L. *The New Harp of Columbia*. Nashville, 1867; rpt., facsimile, Knoxville, 1978.

Sweet, William W. *The Methodist Episcopal Church and the Civil War*. Cincinnati, 1912.

Sweet, William Warren. *The Rise of Methodism in the West*. New York, 1920.

Taylor, O.W. *Early Tennessee Baptists, 1768–1832*. Nashville, 1957.

Temple, Oliver P. *East Tennessee and the Civil War*. Cincinnati, 1899.

Thornborough, Laura. *The Great Smoky Mountains*. New York, 1937; rev. ed., Knoxville, 1962.

Tindell, W.W. *The Baptist of Tennessee*. 2 vols. Kingsport, Tenn., 1930.

Turner, Frederick Jackson. *The Frontier in American History*. New York, 1920.

Watson, Thomas E. *Foreign Missions Exposed*. Atlanta, 1910.

Whittle, W.O. *Movement of Population From the Smoky Mountains Area*. Knoxville, 1934.

Williams, Samuel Cole. *History of the Lost State of Franklin*. Johnson City, Tenn., 1924.

———, ed. *Lieut. Henry Timberlake's Memoirs, 1756–1765*. Johnson City, Tenn., 1927.

Wilson, Samuel Tyndale. *The Southern Mountaineers*. New York, 1914.

Wood, Gordon. *Vocabulary Change: A Study of Variation in Regional Words in Eight of the Southern States*. Carbondale, 1971.

Woodward, Grace Steele. *The Cherokees*. Norman, 1963.

Wright, James B. *Great Smoky Mountains National Park*. Knoxville, 1929.

Articles

Ayres, H.B., and W.W. Ashe. "The Southern Appalachian Forests," *U.S. Geological Survey Professional Paper No. 37*, Washington, D.C., 1905, pp. 177–81.

Baker, Ronald L. "The Role of Folk Legends in Place-Name Research," *Journal of American Folklore*, LXXXV (Oct.–Dec. 1972), 367–73.

Buchanan, Ronald H. "Geography and Folk Life," *Folk Life*, I (1963), 5–15.

Burns, Inez. "Settlement and Early History of the Coves of Blount County, Tennessee," East Tennessee Historical Society's *Publications*, No. 24 (1952), 44–67.

Burt, Jesse. "East Tennessee, Lincoln, and Sherman," East Tennessee Historical Society's *Publications*, No. 34 (1962), 3–25.

Campbell, James B. "East Tennessee During the Federal Occupation, 1863–1865," East Tennessee Historical Society's *Publications*, No. 19 (1947), 64–80.

Carpenter, Charles. "Variations in the Southern Mountain Dialect," *American Speech*, VIII (1933), 22–25.

Combs, Josiah. "The Language of the Southern Highlander," *PMLA*, XLVI (1931), 1302–22.

Dorson, Richard M. "Current Folklore Theories," *Current Anthropology*, IV (1963), 93–112.

Dunn, Durwood. "Mary Noailles Murfree: A Reappraisal," *Appalachian Journal*, VI (Spring 1979), 196–204.

Douglas, William O. "The People of Cades Cove," *National Geographic*, CXXII (July 1962), 60–95.

Fink, Harold S. "The East Tennessee Campaign and the Battle of Knoxville in 1863," East Tennessee Historical Society's *Publications*, No. 29 (1957), 79–117.

Fink, Paul M. "Early Explorers in the Great Smokies," East Tennessee Historical Society's *Publications*, No. 5 (1933), 55–68.

———. "Smoky Mountain History as Told in Place-Names," East Tennessee Historical Society's *Publications*, No. 6 (1934), 3–11.

Galpin, W. Freeman, ed. "Letters of an East Tennessee Abolitionist," East Tennessee Historical Society's *Publications*, No. 3 (1931), 134–49.

Gordon, C.H. "Notes on the Geology of the Cove Areas of East Tennessee," *Science*, LI (May 1920), 492–93.

Hamer, Marguerite Bartlett. "The Presidential Campaign of 1860 in Tennessee," East Tennessee Historical Society's *Publications*, No. 3 (1931), 3–22.

Hesseltine, W.B. "The Underground Railroad From Confederate Prisons to East Tennessee," East Tennessee Historical Society's *Publications*, No. 2 (1930), 55–69.

Hough, Walter. "James Mooney," in Allen Johnson and Dumas Malone, eds.,

Dictionary of American Biography. 20 vols., 2 supplements, and index. New York, 1928–1958.

Inscoe, John C. "Mountain Masters: Slaveholding in Western North Carolina," *North Carolina Historical Review,* LXI (April 1984), 143–73.

Jacobs, Wilbur R. "The Tip of an Iceberg: Pre-Columbian Indian Demography and Some Implications for Revisionism," *William and Mary Quarterly,* XXXI (Jan. 1974), 123–32.

King, Philip, and Arthur Stupka. "The Great Smoky Mountains, Their Geology and Natural History," *Scientific Monthly,* LXXI (July 1950), 31–43.

Klotter, James C., "Feuds in Appalachia: An Overview," *Filson Club History Quarterly,* LVI (July 1982), 290–317.

McTeer, Will A. "Among Loyal Mountaineers," in *Miscellaneous Pamphlets on the Civil War.* Undated volume in Special Collections, Univ. of Tennessee Library, Knoxville.

Martin, Asa Earl. "The Anti-Slavery Societies of Tennessee," *Tennessee Historical Magazine,* I (Dec. 1915), 261–81.

Mead, Sidney E. "Denominationalism: The Shape of Protestantism in America," *Church History,* XXIII (Dec. 1954), 291–320.

Mooney, James, comp. "Myths of the Cherokee," Bureau of American Ethnology, *Nineteenth Annual Report,* 2 vols., Washington, D.C., 1900, I, 11–548.

Myer, William E., comp. "Indian Trails of the Southeast," Bureau of American Ethnology, *Forty-Second Annual Report,* Washington, D.C., 1928, 727–857.

Neuman, Robert B. "Notes on the Geology of Cades Cove, Great Smoky Mountains National Park, Tennessee," *Tennessee Academy of Science Journal,* XXII (July 1947), 167–72.

Queener, Verton M. "A Decade of East Tennessee Republicanism, 1867–1876," East Tennessee Historical Society's *Publications,* No. 14 (1942), 59–85.

Riedl, Norbert F. "Folklore and the Study of Material Aspects of Folk Culture," *Journal of American Folklore,* LXXIX (1966), 557–63.

Shelton, W.H. "A Hard Road to Travel Out of Dixie," *Century,* XVIII (Oct. 1890), 931–49.

Shields, A. Randolph. "Cades Cove in the Great Smoky Mountains National Park," *Tennessee Historical Quarterly,* XXIV (Summer 1965), 103–20.

Skipper, Elvie Eagleton, and Ruth Gove, eds. "'Stray Thoughts': The Civil-War Diary of Ethie M. Foute Eagleton," Part I, East Tennessee Historical Society's *Publications,* No. 40 (1968), 128–37; Part II, East Tennessee Historical Society's *Publications,* No. 41 (1969), 116–28.

Ulm, Amanda. "Remember the Chestnut," *Annual Report of the Smithsonian Institution, 1948.* Washington, D.C., 1948, pp. 377–82.

Wilson, Charles W., Jr. "The Great Smoky Thrust Fault in the Vicinity of Tuckaleechee, Wear, and Cades Cove, Blount and Sevier Counties, Tennessee," *Tennessee Academy of Science Journal,* X (Jan. 1935), 57–63.

Wright, Nathalia. "Montvale Springs under the Proprietorship of Sterling Lanier, 1857–1863," East Tennessee Historical Society's *Publications,* No. 19
  (1947), 48–63.

Unpublished Theses and Dissertations

Barnett, Paul Edward. A Comparative Study of Phenolics in Chestnut (*Cas-
  tanea*), and Their Relationships with Resistance to *Endothia parasitica.*
  Doctoral diss., Univ. of Tennessee, Knoxville, 1972.
Biggs, Riley O. The Development of Railroad Transportation in East Tennessee
  During the Reconstruction Period. Master's thesis, Univ. of Tennessee, Knox-
  ville, 1934.
Bruhn, Mary Ellen. Vegetational Succession on Three Grassy Balds of the Great
  Smoky Mountains. Master's thesis, Univ. of Tennessee, Knoxville, 1964.
Bryan, Charles Faulkner. The Civil War in East Tennessee: A Social, Political
  and Economic Study. Doctoral diss., Univ. of Tennessee, Knoxville, 1978.
Burchfiel, William W., Jr. The Unaka Mountains of Tennessee and North Caro-
  lina. Master's thesis, Univ. of Tennessee, Knoxville, 1941.
Edwards, Lawrence. History of the Baptists of Tennessee with Particular Atten-
  tion to the Primitive Baptists of East Tennessee. Master's thesis, Univ. of
  Tennessee, Knoxville, 1941.
Eubanks, David Lawson. Dr. J.G.M. Ramsey of East Tennessee: A Career of
  Public Service. Doctoral diss., Univ. of Tennessee, Knoxville, 1965.
Gamble, Margaret Elisabeth. The Heritage and Folk Music of Cades Cove, Ten-
  nessee. Master's thesis, Univ. of Southern California, 1947.
Garrett, Beatrice L. Confederate Government and the Unionists of East Ten-
  nessee. Master's thesis, Univ. of Tennessee, Knoxville, 1932.
Gauding, Harry H. A History of Water Transportation in East Tennessee Prior
  to the Civil War. Master's thesis, Univ. of Tennessee, Knoxville, 1933.
Gilbert, V.C., Jr. Vegetation of the Grassy Balds of the Great Smoky Mountains
  National Park. Master's thesis, Univ. of Tennessee, Knoxville, 1954.
Glassie, Henry H. Southern Mountain Houses: A Study in American Folk
  Culture. Master's thesis, State Univ. of New York at Oneonta, 1965.
Jones, M. Jean. The Regional English of the Former Inhabitants of Cades Cove
  in the Great Smoky Mountains. Doctoral diss., Univ. of Tennessee, Knox-
  ville, 1973.
Lanham, Ben T., Jr. Type-Of-Farming Regions, and Factors Influencing Type-
  Of-Farming Regions in Tennessee. Master's thesis, Univ. of Tennessee, Knox-
  ville, 1938.
Leab, Grace. The Temperance Movement in Tennessee, 1860–1907. Master's
  thesis, Univ. of Tennessee, Knoxville, 1938.

Ledford, Allen James. Methodism in Tennessee, 1783–1866. Master's thesis, Univ. of Tennessee, Knoxville, 1941.

Mark, A.F. An Ecological Study of the Grass Balds of the Southern Appalachian Mountains. Doctoral diss., Duke Univ., Durham, N.C., 1958.

Martin, George C., Jr. The Effect of Physiography on the Trade Route of East Tennessee. Master's thesis, Univ. of Tennessee, Knoxville, 1932.

Merritt, Frank. Selected Aspects of Early Carter County History, 1760–1861. Master's thesis, Univ. of Tennessee, Knoxville, 1950.

Orr, Horace Eugene. The Tennessee Churches and Slavery. Master's thesis, Univ. of Tennessee, Knoxville, 1924.

Ritt, Arnold. The Escape of Federal Prisoners Through East Tennessee, 1861–1865. Master's thesis, Univ. of Tennessee, Knoxville, 1965.

Rittgers, Fred H. A Geographical Survey of Blount County, Tennessee. Master's thesis, Univ. of Tennessee, Knoxville, 1941.

Roblyer, Leslie F. The Road to State-Wide Prohibition in Tennessee, 1899–1909. Master's thesis, Univ. of Tennessee, Knoxville, 1949.

Scott, Thomas Allan. National Impact of Tennessee Through her Migrating Sons, 1830–1900. Master's thesis, Univ. of Tennessee, Knoxville, 1966.

Smith, Frank P. Military History of East Tennessee, 1861–1865. Master's thesis, Univ. of Tennessee, Knoxville, 1936.

Taylor, Robert Love, Jr. Mainstreams of Mountain Thought: Attitudes of Selected Figures in the Heart of the Appalachian South, 1877–1903. Doctoral diss., Univ. of Tennessee, Knoxville, 1971.

Whaley, John Thomas. A Timely Idea At An Ideal Time: Knoxville's Role in Establishing The Great Smoky Mountains National Park. Master's thesis, Univ. of Tennessee, Knoxville, 1984.

Whelan, Paul A. Unconventional Warfare in East Tennessee, 1861–1865. Master's thesis, Univ. of Tennessee, Knoxville, 1963.

Woods, Frank W. Natural Replacement of Chestnut by Other Species in the Great Smoky Mountains. Doctoral diss., Univ. of Tennessee, Knoxville, 1957.

Index

Cades Cove / A Southern Appalachian Community
was designed by Dariel Mayer, composed by Lithocraft, Inc.,
and printed and bound by Thomson-Shore, Inc. The book is set
in Palatino and printed on 60–lb. Glatfelter Smooth Antique.